Fama

Fama

The Politics of Talk and Reputation in Medieval Europe

Edited by

THELMA FENSTER AND
DANIEL LORD SMAIL

CORNELL UNIVERSITY PRESS

Ithaca and London

First published 2003 by Cornell University Press
First printing, Cornell Paperbacks, 2003

Printed in the United States of America

Library of Congress Cataloging-in-Publication Data
Fama : the politics of talk and reputation in medieval Europe / Edited by Thelma Fenster and Daniel Lord Smail.
    p.   cm.
   Includes bibliographical references and index.
   ISBN 0-8014-3939-6 (cloth : alk. paper) — ISBN 0-8014-8857-5 (pbk. : alk. paper)
   1. Reputation (Law)—Europe—History—To 1500.   2. Law, Medieval—Social aspects.   I. Fenster, Thelma S.   II. Smail, Daniel Lord.
KJ810.F36   2003
340'.115—dc21   2002154830

Cornell University Press strives to use environmentally responsible suppliers and materials to the fullest extent possible in the publishing of its books. Such materials include vegetable-based, low-VOC inks and acid-free papers that are recycled, totally chlorine-free, or partly composed of nonwood fibers. For further information, visit our website at www.cornellpress.cornell.edu.

Cloth printing   10   9   8   7   6   5   4   3   2   1

Paperback printing   10   9   8   7   6   5   4   3   2   1

Contents

Contents

Acknowledgments

This volume emerged from a conference in September 2000 that was made possible by the generous support of the Graduate School of Arts and Sciences at Fordham University and its former dean, Robert F. Himmelberg; we are grateful to both. We would also like to thank Maryanne Kowaleski, Janine Peterson, and the staff of the Center for Medieval Studies at Fordham University for an expertly organized conference. The discussants—Lara Farina, Paul Freedman, Thomas Head, Maryanne Kowaleski, Donald Maddox, David Myers, Pamela Sheingorn, and Jan Ziolkowski—contributed in many ways to the success of the conference and kindly made their comments and criticisms available to the contributors. Finally, it has been a great pleasure to work with the contributors to this volume; we appreciate their conscientiousness, patience, and valuable scholarship.

THELMA FENSTER
DANIEL LORD SMAIL

New York

Fama

Introduction

THELMA FENSTER AND DANIEL LORD SMAIL

Why *Fama*?

This volume took shape from the converging interests of its editors, one a historian of law and society in late medieval southern France, the other a specialist in French medieval literature.[1] Working more or less independently, each had grown curious about the unusual attention given to talk in both literary texts and legal documents. The subject of such talk was often personal reputation. As we shared notes and ideas, we realized that to dismiss what we saw as gossip and idle rumor was to leave unanswered the question of why talk was of such great moment to writers and their audiences, to lawyers, jurists, moralists, and artists. Simply put, there is a lot of talk about talk in the extant texts and documents from medieval Europe, and images from the same period silently convey a similar focus. Sometimes, it is true, talk was seen as sinful gossip, and it was condemned accordingly; at other times, however, talk was appreciated as something to be deployed for good and honest ends. Writers, commentators, and artists of all stripes have left a record of what talk could do: how clothing, demeanor, speech, and other forms of public performance created talk; how talk could fly with astonishing rapidity from mouth to ear; how images could be fixed, information conveyed, and reputations made—or lost—thereby. As medieval people well understood, skill was required to deal with talk and one's *fama*.

Fama with its cognates and derivatives therefore acquired an impres-

---

1. We thank Madeline Caviness, Charles Nelson, and Lori Walters for reading and commenting upon an earlier version of this introduction.

sively wide semantic range. It is "rumor" and "idle talk," "the things people say." It is "reputation" and "memory" or "memories," "the things people know." It is "fame," or perhaps "glory," as well as their opposites, "infamy" and "defamation." Across its semantic range *fama* intersected with a number of other terms, such as honor, shame, status, and witnessing, and it glossed the essential nexus of performance, talk, reputation, and speech regulation that is the subject of this volume. It retained and incorporated meanings that had been active in Latin-speaking cultures: to paraphrase Hans-Joachim Neubauer, it meant public opinion, idle talk, rumor, and reputation as well as fame; both a good name and a bad one were called *fama;* and while *fama* denoted information or news, at the same time it meant the image formed of a person by that information.[2]

The word *fama,* which we have borrowed largely from its repeated use in the recorded proceedings of medieval Roman-canon law courts, figured as an element in medieval jurisprudence, as shown by one question that judges and notaries routinely asked witnesses. Just to be sure that witnesses understood the concept of *fama,* they were asked: *Quid est fama?* (What is *fama?*). "It's the things people say," one witness will say. "It's the public voice and fame," another will observe, perhaps adding, "It's what people say that is good about someone, and never have I heard the contrary"; or, "*Fama* is that which is commonly said among people about any business or fact, and also when good or ill is commonly said among people about any person." The judge's inquiry continues: "Where is the public voice and *fama?*" "It's in the street Bertran lives on," a witness replies, "among his neighbors." And judges wanted to know who made the *fama:* "Does it proceed from his enemies or ill-wishers?" "I didn't know he had enemies," says the circumspect witness. "How many people make the *fama?*" the interrogating notary might ask. "Oh, five or six people," comes the answer, revealing that *fama* can be made by some people, then remembered by others. "Three, four, even more than four make the *fama,*" another specifies, and then, reflecting perhaps that this is not very many, he adds, "as befits the size of the population of the place where the *fama* is." Sometimes *fama* is made by a great number of people: "Ten, twenty, thirty, forty people say these things," reports a witness. *Fama* could be measured, as in a *magna fama* (great deal of talking). "These things are said among both Jews and Christians," asserts yet another, showing that this particular bit of news was very well known, because Jews ordinarily were thought of as constituting a different speech community.[3]

2. Hans-Joachim Neubauer, *The Rumour: A Cultural History,* trans. Christian Braun (London: Free Association Books, 1999), 37.

3. These examples of *fama* talk are ubiquitous in records from the courts of law of late medieval Marseille. Many are discussed, and references given, in Daniel Lord Smail, "Los archivos de conocimiento y la cultura legal de la publicidad en la Marsella medieval," *Hispania: Revista española de historia* 57 (1997): 1049–77.

Though there was *fama* about debts, quittances, and the ownership of goods and property, the *fama* or renown of people—plaintiffs, defendants, and witnesses—was probably of greatest interest to jurists and users of the courts alike. Modern legal systems rigorously try to exclude hearsay evidence, although both it and common prejudice often creep in through the back door of the courtroom. It is startling for the nonspecialist, therefore, to realize that medieval legal systems readily acknowledged the force of common opinion and even devised ground rules for its use. Indeed, the work of thirteenth-century jurists gave *fama* and its equivalents in customary law a precise set of meanings (and thus the practical application of such *fama* can readily be explored through the extant proceedings of law courts). This was so even where vernacular equivalents replaced the word *fama,* as in the customary legal system of northern France in the thirteenth and fourteenth centuries, for example, which featured words such as *renommée* (renown) or *notoire* (notorious). What became a veritable jurisprudence of *fama,* expressed both in statute law and juristic treatises, is elaborated on by several contributors to this volume.[4]

Public talk is, or creates, the *fama* that is useful in courts. Although not all scholars would agree, in the legal context a distinction may be made between *fama* and eyewitness testimony. For example, a man may have seen something like a transfer of property ownership and recorded the event in memory; later, as an eyewitness, as he testifies in court, he recalls the event, saved as a passive memory. But the *fama* about the transfer would be reported not by the eyewitness but by those who, not having seen it, had heard talk about it, either from the eyewitness or from others. On that view, *fama* is necessarily "live" because it is made by talk, embedded in it, and simultaneous with it; in this case, it also validates the memory or memories that had led to the eyewitness testimony.[5] This formulation recalls Neubauer's definition of the rumor as "that about which it is said that everyone is saying it."[6]

Given that personal reputation and the talk about it were probably the most conspicuous sorts of *fama,* medieval *fama* can be conceived of as a general impression that is inseparable from its embodiment in talk. Regarding a person, therefore, *fama* is the public talk that continually adjusts honor and assigns rank or standing as the individual grows up, engages in such publicly performed acts as marriage, takes up offices or other public

4. See the essays in this volume by Akehurst, Bowman, Kuehn, and Wickham. See also Francesco Migliorino, *Fama e infamia: Problemi della società medievale nel pensiero giuridico nei secoli XII e XIII* (Catania: Giannotta, 1985).

5. Unarticulated, and therefore private, memories were susceptible to being thought secret, and they were weakened by the suspicion that invariably hovered over things kept private in medieval Europe. As a result, people talked a great deal about selected facts, the ones they wanted known, and those facts, having been exposed to a validating procedure by talk, were then clearly more worthy of credence at law.

6. Neubauer, *Rumour,* 3.

duties, wins or loses legal or physical contests, and begins to decline. *Fama*, in this sense, can be political, for it serves to define and rank competitors for public honors and functions.

As for honor, *fama* most closely parallels the kind of honor that could be bestowed only by other people, one that had to be plainly visible. It could be made so through material signs (clothing and other possessions) and through the performance of acts agreed on as honorable. This honor therefore required witnesses, who carried reports of *fama* to others. As a visible cluster of acts, appearances, and possessions, then, this predominant kind of medieval honor constituted and was constituted by both a material and a discursive semiotics. (That understanding of honor bears traces of the word's earlier meaning as land, that is, as a visible thing that could be possessed. Over time, honor came to describe the possessor rather than the possession, and it also became less and less tangible; even so, it remained something to be owned, guarded, and sometimes lost or stolen.)

A second conception of honor, applicable to the classical and medieval periods and not entirely out of fashion today, construed it as an internalized system of values that a person held, sometimes in opposition to what others may have asked of her.[7] In that sense, one could *be* honorable without being seen by others as having honor[8]—that is, if the private and public notions did not happen to coincide, there may have been little or no *fama* about such honor.

To work as a vehicle for one's good reputation, of course, *fama* as talk had to be fed. Medieval people, much like people in any society, were intensely aware of public scrutiny, and geared their public appearances accordingly. Good reputation required careful attention to speech, behavior, demeanor, and action, a process that might usefully be called managing one's *fama*—managing one's own behavior with nearly exclusive attention to its mirroring in the public perception of it. By contrast, private acts were seen as occult and furtive; they were regarded with suspicion, if not with outright disapproval.[9] In all cases, it was understood that one's acts would be discussed and evaluated, and that some sort of *fama* would eventually emerge. If a person performed well, the result could be a *fama* useful in the future, a *bona fama* or even a glory, although there were never any guarantees. Such conscious manipulation of *fama* recalls the sense of self implicit in agent-centered sociologies, where people remain ever aware of "the rules"—that is, of "rules" that, unlike explicit juridical formulations,

7. These two definitions can be said to correspond to the "shame" and "guilt" cultures, respectively, as these were defined some time ago by Ruth Benedict and E. R. Dodds. See the essay by Akehurst in this volume, which serves as a helpful introduction to these topics.
8. Frank Henderson Stewart, *Honor* (Chicago: University of Chicago Press, 1994).
9. Wickham, "*Fama* and Memory, " in this volume; Smail, "Archivos."

are rarely spelled out. The resulting necessary alertness to clues about how to behave, and one's responses to the clues, constitute a *habitus,* to borrow a term from Pierre Bourdieu, a set of largely unwritten rules that everyone "just knows" in order to function adequately as social beings.[10]

Explorations of talk and reputation entered many vernacular literary works, as essays in this volume demonstrate.[11] The Latinate *fama* is seen less frequently in literature than its vernacular approximations, although there are instances of its use as early as the twelfth century. In Wace's *Roman de Brut,* for example, a lady is described as follows: "Lettree fu e sage dame, / De buen pris e de bone fame" (lines 3337–38) [She was an educated and wise lady, / Worthy and of good fame].[12] Poetic taste for doublets featuring near synonyms supplies *fame* conjoined with *pris* (worth, value); nor is the rhyme *dame/fame* to be overlooked, for in medieval French a not infrequent spelling of *femme* (woman) was, precisely, *fame.*

Talk about and cultivation of reputation play a prominent role in some important literature from the Old French period.[13] Romances by Chrétien de Troyes, for example, bear witness to the influence of reputation. Joseph Duggan has observed that Enide's father, in *Erec et Enide,* gives his daughter in marriage to Erec merely on learning his name, for Erec is well known as "prouz and hardiz."[14] And where would the story of the newlyweds have been without the barons' talk of Erec's *recreantise* (cowardice) and declining reputation? Far from criticizing the barons for talking about Erec, the text incorporates their talk into the narrative trajectory, making the talk essential to launching Erec's recuperative efforts and thus to the romance itself. Further, the crucial role of public witness is given to Enide, who accompanies Erec to observe and report on his brave acts, which she does when she sends a messenger maiden to Arthur's court after the "Joy of the Court" episode. In *Lancelot,* the demand that the hero step into the cart of shame in order to rescue Queen Guenevere, and the consequent talk about his act by others, takes on greater resonance when seen against the medieval foregrounding of *fama.* In *Yvain ou le chevalier au lion,* Laudine, Yvain's wife, speaks for an entire society when she accuses Yvain of having broken his word. The part played in Chrétien's romances by talk and the

---

10. E.g., Erving Goffman, *The Presentation of Self in Everyday Life* (Garden City, N.Y.: Doubleday, 1959); Pierre Bourdieu, *Outline of a Theory of Practice,* trans. Richard Nice (Cambridge: Cambridge University Press, 1977); idem, *The Logic of Practice,* trans. Richard Nice (Stanford: Stanford University Press, 1990).

11. See the essays by Craun, Horvath, and Walters in this volume.

12. *Wace's* Roman de Brut: *A History of the British,* text and translation ed. and trans. Judith Weiss, Exeter Medieval English Texts and Studies (Exeter: University of Exeter Press, 1999), 84–85.

13. See the essays in this volume by Bardsley, Caviness and Nelson, Craun, and Horvath.

14. Duggan, *The Romances of Chrétien de Troyes* (New Haven: Yale University Press, 2001), 93–106, at 95.

shame it brings (that is, by the disapproval of others, especially of those "whom one respects and whose approval one would like to obtain")[15] is transmitted to the reader as thoroughly acceptable and even useful because it serves to regulate, promote, and comment upon the aristocratic behavior that is the subject of the romances.

Later, in the Middle French period, however, Christine de Pizan, the prolific author of both learned and courtly works in poetry and prose, was less sanguine about talk's regulatory function, especially, but not only, for the aristocracy. Through repeated recommendations and caveats, she emphasized that talk about a person could do great damage, a cautionary note with distant antecedents in, for example, the depictions of *fama* by Virgil and Ovid. Yet, some modern readers have expressed dismay at her pronouncements, occasionally misreading them as self-centered, pusillanimous, and far too dependent on the approval of others, absent a sturdy, morally correct inner self. This aspect of Christine's thought, therefore, has generally been passed over in silence; or, it has contributed to the view that she was a prude. At the same time, however, modern scholarship on Christine has frequently brought to light how she addressed "real world" matters in her writing to an extent largely unsurpassed by writers who were her contemporaries. (Indeed, some of Christine's most distinguished male contemporaries may have trivialized their own advice about personal honor and reputation by failing to consider real social circumstances.)

As Christine well knew, too, *fama*, as talk, was fleeting, aspectual, and notoriously protean; it was a *process*, rather than the fixed, unchanging memory that written records necessarily convey to us. Carried on through conversations, the process of *fama* constructed, deconstructed, and reconstructed the things remembered. As a corollary, there could be more than one *fama*,[16] because different groups might have constructed facts or memories in ways that suited their own political or social interests. That kind of *fama*, as distinct from the historical *fama* of important personages that may be fixed in writing,[17] can exist only in talk. But both kinds could be deeply deceiving, for although *fama* as reputation appears to "belong" to the person being spoken about, it is often presented as if it "belongs" to the voices who make it—and in a very real way, of course, it does. The risks of a self defined as reputation, along with the alienation of ownership of

15. Discussing *Erec et Enide*, Duggan says: "At issue are public qualities: the reward for doing good or for fighting well is not expressed in Chrétien and contemporaneous writers of romance as a feeling of fulfillment or satisfaction, an interior recompense, but rather as approbation by the community. . . . Honor and praise, correspondingly, are acquired by performing well in public view" (94–95).

16. See the essay in this volume by Kuehn.

17. See the essay in this volume by Walters.

the self and its paradoxical location "elsewhere"—this was a repeated theme of Christine de Pizan's writings.[18]

Like Dante, Petrarch, and Chaucer, Christine understood *fama* in another way as well, that is, as worldly glory during and after one's life, associated particularly with the act of writing. The Italian authors were inclined to believe that good and honorable deeds could ensure one's *bona fama*, a view that Christine certainly supported when she wrote the biography of King Charles V of France. On the other hand, Chaucer, in his *House of Fame*, was less sure that good acts would inevitably lead to good repute. Often, Christine seemed to share that pessimism, and the emphasis she placed on restraint, or behavior designed to discourage slanderous talk, could have been but a partial solution. While Christine promoted everywhere the value of possessing a good name, she recognized that neither one's high station nor one's exemplary conduct could assure it.

Finally, another take on *fama* emerges in the *Songe véritable* (True dream), a political pamphlet in allegory, probably dating from 1406, in which an opinion shared by all the people—as the pamphlet implies—aspires to the status of a political force. In French, the term *commune renommée* described one crucial aspect of *fama:* the verbal portrait of a person or situation as others might give it ("common knowledge"). In the *Songe,* Commune Renommée, cast as a character along with others such as Chascun (Everyperson), Souffrance (Suffering), and Povreté (Poverty), is presented as the political voice of the people acting as witness against the government. The anonymous tract pities the ailing King Charles VI, criticizes those who take advantage of his weakness and who are seen as ruining the kingdom—principally, the queen, Isabeau of Bavaria; the king's younger brother, Louis, Duke of Orleans; the king's uncle, Jean, Duke of Berry; and Jean de Montagu, the king's butler. At one point in the poem, Povreté and Chascun, wishing to know why they have been deprived of their worldly goods, are led to Commune Renommée by Souffrance, who says that Commune Renommée will explain everything to them, telling them who has caused their deprivation, "because people say that her voice must be believed, no matter what" (lines 314–20). Commune Renommée is later said to "see more clearly than one can in moonlight" (line 1300). The *Songe véritable* undoubtedly played a role in creating the negative *fama* of

18. See Thelma Fenster, *"Fama,* la femme, et la Dame de la Tour: Christine de Pizan et la médisance," in *Au champ des escriptures: IIIe colloque international sur Christine de Pizan,* ed. Eric Hicks (Paris: Honoré Champion, 2000), 461–77. See also Fenster, "Christine at Carnant: Reading Christine de Pizan Reading Chrétien de Troyes' *Erec et Enide,*" in *Christine 2000: Essays in Honor of Angus J. Kennedy,* ed. John Campbell and Nadia Margolis (Amsterdam: Rodopi, 2000), 135–51.

those surrounding the king, including Isabeau, whose poor reputation persists to the present.

Just Talk?

As we reflected on such legal and literary texts, we noted that few pieces of modern scholarship on the Middle Ages had examined *gossip*, let alone considered that gossip, or simply talk, might have had its good side. Similarly, few scholars had ever reconstructed the political mechanisms that made the nexus of talk and reputation so elemental a force in medieval society. Even the regulation of speech, a marked feature of late medieval moralizing texts, and with it the growing tide of defamation prosecutions, acknowledged the power of talk in a backhanded way.

Outside medieval scholarship, the reevaluation of gossip had been under way for four decades. In a penetrating and groundbreaking 1963 article, Max Gluckman pointed out that gossip was not all bad.[19] Gossip, he explained, plays a crucial role in making and defining social relationships. His reflections led to the creation of gossip as a field of study, which began to mature in the 1980s. Seminal work by Chris Wickham and other medieval historians, inspired by that scholarship, drew attention to the important legal and social roles played by gossip and rumor.[20] Their work, however, was deliberately and self-consciously legal-historical in nature, and did not aspire to connect the legal-historical sources of *fama* to literary texts, commentaries, and art historical images, a task that the present volume undertakes.

At the same time, we propose a reevaluation of the term *gossip*, or perhaps, given gossip's fundamentally pejorative nature, a shunting aside of the term in favor of a larger appreciation of *talk*. The field of "talk studies" has become both dense and pluridisciplinary, with contributions from historians, literary scholars, anthropologists, sociologists, political scientists, social psychologists, evolutionary psychologists, and primatologists, and

19. Max Gluckman, "Gossip and Scandal," *Current Anthropology* 4 (1963): 307–16; see also Sally Engle Merry, "Rethinking Gossip and Scandal," in *Toward a General Theory of Social Control,* ed. Donald J. Black, 2 vols. (New York: Academic Press, 1984), 1:271–302.
20. Chris Wickham, "Gossip and Resistance among the Medieval Peasantry," *Past and Present* 160 (1998): 3–24. See also Andrée Courtemanche, "La rumeur de Manosque: femmes et honneur au XIVe siècle," in *Normes et pouvoir à la fin du Moyen Âge. Actes du colloque "La recherche en études médiévales au Québec et en Ontario," 16–17 mai 1989,* ed. Marie-Claude Déprez-Masson (Montreal: Édition CERES, 1989); *La renommée,* a special number of *Médiévales: Langue, textes, histoire* 24 (1993); Claude Gauvard, "Rumeur et stéréotypes à la fin du Moyen Âge," in *La circulation des nouvelles au Moyen Âge: XXIVe Congrès de la Société des historiens médiévistes de l'enseignement supérieur public* (Rome: École française de Rome, 1994); Phillip R. Schofield, "Peasants and the Manor Court: Gossip and Litigation in a Suffolk Village at the Close of the Thirteenth Century," *Past and Present* 159 (1998): 3–42.

even a mathematician.[21] As their investigations illustrate, talk as something more than mere gossip transmits all kinds of information and opinion about reputation and credit-worthiness, as well as providing the legal facts of personal status. Talk allows individuals to form groups and societies, and it is through talk that we monitor and record reputations, distribute rewards, and create status hierarchies. It has become clear to us that in medieval societies, talk did many of those things that in modern society are handled, officially, by bankers, credit bureaus, lawyers, state archives, and so on. The ways people conceptualized talk in the European Middle Ages therefore emerge as but one instance (or cluster) of the larger, overarching fact that talk is beneficial to human groups, an argument proposed recently, and most forcefully, by the psychologist Robin Dunbar.[22]

But our acknowledgment that talk serves an essential function common to all societies is in no way meant to ignore the historical process whereby talk, in western European societies, has been progressively denigrated and compressed into the single dismissive term *gossip*. Indeed, the "pejorativization" of talk to which the very label "gossip" bears witness is one of the fascinating cultural changes revealed by the study of talk. Melanie Tebbutt, in an important study of gossip among working-class women in late-nineteenth and early twentieth-century Britain, has fully described gossip's "deterioration in meaning." She explains that Old English *godsibb* (relative in God) was associated in the medieval period with good friends and neighbors, with events following the birth of a baby, and with drinking (which accompanied the celebratory feasting that occurred in some places). Gossip's semantic narrowing to denote the idle talk of women did not appear in a dictionary until the eighteenth century.[23]

Why this deterioration in standing? Only if one accepts a priori that gossip is wicked or antisocial can one argue that the historical reduction of talk to gossip was the product of a civilizing trend in European society. We propose a different argument. On some level, the importance of talk as a device for social regulation in Western societies has never been lost. It remains a social constant, even if its social role is commonly disparaged in modern societies. What *has* changed is the capacity of talk to serve as a legitimate and widely acknowledged legal, social, and moral agent. Twelfth- and thirteenth-century secular commentaries on the moral and social role of *fama* are largely positive. Talk and reputation were worked deeply into

21. For some key texts in the social sciences that lend themselves to a positive evaluation of gossip and talk, see Goodman and Ben-Ze'ev, Tebbutt, and Dunbar in the bibliography to this volume.

22. Robin Dunbar, *Grooming, Gossip, and the Evolution of Language* (Cambridge: Harvard University Press, 1996).

23. Melanie Tebbutt, *Women's Talk? A Social History of "Gossip" in Working-Class Neighbourhoods, 1880–1960* (Aldershot, England: Scolar, 1995), 19–22.

the law and legal practice. Yet over time, from the later Middle Ages onward, the positive social and legal functions of talk were progressively handed over to the largely male professional classes, consisting of bureaucrats, state officials, bankers, lawyers, and notaries. Talk, as a way of knowing things, acts as something of a competitor to these professional classes and to the states that sponsor and promote them. Reduced to being called gossip, talk disappeared as an art and a science.

By continuing to use the word *gossip,* scholarship unwittingly lends its stamp to a largely morally determined conviction that obscures, and implicitly condemns, the larger field of talk. Moreover, in creating such a field of inquiry, scholars have found it necessary to try to define gossip, rumor, and the like in ways that bracket them off from each other and from something envisaged as "good talk." For the most part, sure definitions have proved difficult to formulate. Talk, not gossip, is therefore the true subject of this collection, which, as a whole, considers that talk, a human constant and a human cultural construct, is a subject deserving of intellectual inquiry. It is our hope that this collection of essays will go some way toward restoring an appreciation of the work done by talk and reputation in medieval Europe, and that it will encourage others to write, and talk, on the subject.

A Note on the Term *Fama*

As a rule of thumb, words or roots of words that have wide semantic fields are usually doing important things within a culture. *Fama* is no exception, for it had a remarkably diverse array of medieval meanings and uses. The word itself is found predominantly in Latin or Latinized writing, but the vernacular literatures had their own vocabulary for *fama.* Records that derive from the Roman legal tradition, especially from Italy, southern France, and Spain, are the most consistent in using the word *fama.* In other regions of medieval Europe, such as northern France, England, and Germany, the word *fama* and its cognates are found, but rarely.

French equivalents for *fama* may include *los, renoun, renommée, nom,* and *bon nom* (some of which were borrowed into Middle English), as well as the condemnatory *lozengiers* (or *lauzengiers*), those who did harm by revealing secret love affairs; and in English, *name, worship,* and so on. In Italian an equivalent to the French *renommée* is *rinomanza,* but it is rare. *Riputazione* and *notorieta* are common cognates to the English words, and *famigerato,* meaning ill-famed, is occasionally used. The most common terms, not wholly equivalent to *fama,* are *onore, onesta,* and the like. To say that he is a man of honor (*uomo d'onore*) is saying that he has good *fama.* In German too, *ere* (honor) was frequent. When part of legal discourse, *ere* often appeared with the suffix -*los, erelos,* signifying legal incapacity; as punishment for a crime, the convicted party could be stripped of her or his *ere*. In general use, *ere* could mean "respect" or "reputation": when a woman seen as immoral loses her *wipliche ere*, she loses the womanly respect or reputation otherwise due to her. *Ere* can also refer to the sum of all qualities and attributes that define a category of person (as whcn Wolfram von Eschenbach, in *Parzival*, uses the phrase *nach ritters ere*, "as befits a knight"). In that view, loss of *wiplich ere* carries with it the loss of one's standing in the world as a woman.[24]

The etymology of Latin *fama* has classical forebears and deep Indo-European roots. According to historical linguists, *fama* is a suffixed form of the Indo-European root word *bhā* (Latin, *fari*; Greek, *phanai*), meaning "to speak," especially in a public sense. Its medieval European derivatives are many and range from the Germanic *bannan* (to speak publicly), the Old English *gebann* (proclamation), and the Old Norse *banna* (to prohibit, curse), to various other Greek and Latin roots that ended up in modern English as *-phone, -fess, pha-* (phatic, aphasia), *blasphemous,* and the like. To *profess,* for example, is to say something meant to be heard by many people. The *banns* formed part of a system for making public an intent to marry. The term *ban* described a jurisdiction whose inhabitants could be summoned or who could hear a given proclamation. These words do not denote private, regular, or repeated exchanges by two or three people in a conversational tone of voice; rather, all deal with public speech, words uttered so as to be heard by many, words that gain some as yet undefined force by being shared with a larger public.[25] A *band,* by contrast, is a group of people who have been privately summoned. *Bandits,* from the past participle of Latin *bandire* (to band), are those who have banded together in a similar way. They can be defined in part by their affiliation with a kind of speech in-group from which most others are necessarily excluded. The *ban* has an element of coercive or seigneurial authority but its relative, *fama,* does not.

24. We thank Thomas Kuehn for the Italian vocabulary and Charles Nelson for the German.

25. J. L. Austin, *How to Do Things with Words* (Oxford: Clarendon, 1962).

Part 1

FAMA AND THE LAW

CHAPTER ONE

Fama *and the Law in Twelfth-Century Tuscany*

CHRIS WICKHAM

In 1137, a high-ranking dependent of the archbishop of Pisa (we do not know his name) wrote a frank letter to his lord relating the results of an investigation he had made into the running of the archiepiscopal estates, which were huge, and largely leased or enfeoffed out to aristocrats and city notables. The text is a rare shaft of light on the potential difficulties and confusions of large-scale estate management in the period. The tenants regularly lied to the investigator about back rents, or made false promises of amendment. For the archbishop's future reference, however, the investigator listed his most trustworthy informants: "Lanfranco the fat will tell you [the archbishop] about it more fully and faithfully. If you hear his counsels trustingly, you will not repent of it." He cited documents sometimes, but often they were absent (concessions in fief, in particular, were rarely written down), or else not of much use—they would say how much rent should be paid, not whether it had been. About lands held as pledges for loans to previous archbishops, "Your associates know more about them than I. Here are those that I know, however . . . I have discovered more about them by the teaching of *fama* than by the inspection of documents." The investigator then went on to list a set of pledges, with, once again, citations of trustworthy men whom the archbishop could consult for more information. The archbishop would have to do quite a bit of work on his own behalf, his investigator clearly thought. At least one court case in 1138 indicates that, for some of his estates, he actually did.[1]

1. Natale Caturegli, ed., *Regesto della chiesa di Pisa,* Regesta chartarum Italiae, vol. 24 (Rome: Istituto Storico Italiano, 1938), no. 654; cf. no. 366 (anno 1138), a consequential

The *fama* invoked in this document is not quite the same as the concept of *fama* inherited from the ancient world. The word implied talking, in all its meanings; but its traditional meanings tended to cluster around, on the one hand, "rumor," and, on the other, "reputation." These are the meanings that one finds in Cicero, and they recur throughout antiquity, up to the *Corpus Iuris Civilis,* by which time "reputation" has become, I believe, the primary legal meaning. This is its meaning in Gratian (as we know with certainty, thanks to Reuter and Silagi's *Wortkonkordanz*), and in many of the narrative texts of the Middle Ages.[2] But the Pisan investigator meant something slightly different, though obviously related: common knowledge about a set of events or a legal situation, which was more stable than rumor, and often more depersonalized than reputation. He was, indeed, one of the first people I know to do so; it is distinctly harder to trace this precise meaning in earlier sources. From here on, however, its use was pretty consistent for a century and more. Twelfth-century Tuscans used *fama* to mean "common knowledge" very frequently, as a quasi-technical legal term, in numerous court cases and arbitrations, starting in the 1130s and continuing for the rest of the century—and well beyond, for it is one of the primary meanings of *fama* in fifteenth-century Florence, as Thomas Kuehn shows in his article in this volume. Indeed, after 1250 it had become part of legal theory from daily practice, via the late thirteenth-century treatises on proofs.[3]

Fama, most often *publica fama* (public fame), sometimes *vulgaris et frequens fama* (common and frequent fame), *communis fama* (common fame), or *consentiens fama* (accepted fame), was one form of knowledge in twelfth-century Tuscany. It was contrasted with knowledge *per visum* (eyewitness knowledge), which was more reliable; it was also, however, distinct from *per auditum* (hearsay), which was not reliable at all. (In surviving records of

court case. I discuss this text, and some of the others cited later, at greater length in *Legge, pratiche, e conflitti* (Rome: Viella, 2000), a book-length analysis of the sorts of issues characterized in this chapter.

2. Timothy Reuter and Gabriel Silagi, *Wortkonkordanz zum Decretum Gratiani,* 5 vols., Monumenta Germaniae Historica Hilfsmittel 10 (Munich: MGH, 1990), 2:1844. For civil law (not much discussed yet in 1137), see Francesco Migliorino, *Fama e infamia: Problemi della società medievale nel pensiero giuridico nei secoli XII e XIII* (Catania: Giannotta, 1985), esp. 73–83.

3. *Fama* does not appear in Cesare Manaresi, ed., *I placiti del Regnum Italiae,* 3 vols. (Rome: Tip. Del Senato, 1955–60), the basic edition of pre-twelfth-century court cases. For Florence, see Kuehn, "*Fama* as a Legal Status," in this volume, and idem, "Reading Microhistory," *Journal of Modern History* 61 (1989): 512–34; for late thirteenth-century theory, see Migliorino, *Fama e infamia,* 57–70. The theorists in question, notably Guglielmo Durante, Alberto Gandino, and Tommaso di Piperata, were the first not to be hostile to *publica fama,* which by then they separated out from *rumor:* rumor was spoken in private, by a few, but *fama* was *communis viciniae proclamatio/ acclamatio.* Earlier theorists, in the canon law tradition, had stressed the opposite: that *fama* was weaker than *notorium,* self-evident knowledge (Migliorino, *Fama e infamia,* 49–58). But both groups took their assumptions about *fama* from everyday practice, not from the basic civil or canonist texts, which are silent on the subject.

the interrogation of witnesses, "he knows nothing more except hearsay" is a common closing formula: hearsay was not worth recording.) *Publica fama* might seem much like hearsay to us, but it was given more weight by its collective nature. It was what everybody knew, so it was socially accepted as reliable.[4] It is this collective aspect that is clearly stressed in the sources that define it, normally in our period thanks to the questioning in court cases of witnesses by interrogators, who wanted to know whether the witnesses properly understood the meaning of words. In 1203, in a court case to decide whether the Guidi counts were the patrons of the Florentine rural nunnery of Rosano, several witnesses said that it was *publica fama* that the Guidi were its patrons. "Interrogated what *publica fama* might be, he replied 'what all say publicly [*id quod omnes publice dicunt*]'; he said he had been taught this by Ubertino, *iudex* of Faenza." "All" might be a bit risky, even in a united community, of course; in 1192 in Pisa a witness preferred "what the majority of men say" (*id quod a maiori parte hominum dicitur*). How many made a majority, though? In 1257 in Pisa a particularly dogged interrogator managed to extract a strikingly wide range of answers: twenty men, forty, a hundred, a majority "of the locality," and even some don't-knows (including from a notary).[5] The fact that people could not give consistent definitions, but all the same generally stressed the same sort of criteria—the views of a lot of people—confirms the solid place that *publica fama* had in the conceptual vocabulary of ordinary Tuscans: they knew what it meant "really"; they knew it when they saw it; and they believed it when they heard it. And so it was right from the start: the Pisan investigator, a cynical man to be sure, put trust in *fama*.

There are problems in this easy collectivist characterization, of course. These derive partly from our contemporary distrust of common knowledge as reliable, at least in court (it goes without saying that in our daily lives we believe it all the time), but there were also practical questions: how to deal with opposing common knowledges, how to establish majorities, and, perhaps above all, how such knowledge was constructed in the first place, and who had the right to do so.

4. Chris Wickham, "Gossip and Resistance among the Medieval Peasantry," *Past and Present* 160 (1998): 3–24, at 4.

5. Respectively, Claudia Strà, ed., *I più antichi documenti del monastero di S. Maria di Rosano (secoli XI–XIII)* (Rome: Monumenta Italiae Ecclesiastica, 1982), 243; Archivio Capitolare di Pisa, fondo diplomatico, no. 691, 16 aprile 1193 (mod. dating 1192); Archivio di Stato di Lucca, fondo S. Frediano, 2 agosto 1258 (mod. dating 1257), cited in Raffaele Savigni, *Episcopato e società cittadina a Lucca da Anselmo II (†1086) a Roberto (†1225)*, Studi e Testi, Accademia Lucchese di Scienze, Lettere ed Arti, 43 (Lucca: Edizioni S. Marco, 1996). For uncertainties similar to the last of these texts in late thirteenth-century Florence, see William M. Bowsky, *Piety and Property in Medieval Florence* (Milan: A. Giuffrè, 1990), 61–62. For the same issue in Marseille, and for an argument with close parallels to this paper, see Daniel Lord Smail, "Archivos de conocimiento y la cultura legal de la publicidad en la Marsella medieval," *Hispania* 57 (1997): 1049–77.

Not everyone was as unthinkingly complacent about common knowledge as were some of the witnesses just cited. Anyone who attended a court and heard opposing versions of *fama* invoked might have doubted it, of course; one example is an 1188 dispute from Lucca over the personal status of a certain Betto, who maintained that *publica fama* said he was a peasant proprietor and free tenant, whereas the cathedral canons stated (persuasively, as it turned out), that *publica fama* said he was a semi-servile *manens*. In Pisa in 1178, indeed, a party denied in court that *publica fama* could be used as a proof if the opposing party had another group of people saying the opposite. And in a church dispute from Arezzo in 1216, the monks of Camaldoli lost their temper about the issue, as a petition to the pope makes clear: "The bishop [of Arezzo] insists, however, with all his force, on *fama.* We reply that those witnesses testifying about *fama* say something is *fama* because they heard it from certain *fideles* of the bishop and in certain *castra* of the bishop. Once the sayings of these witnesses are inspected, it appears that this *fama* is not proved, or if it is proved it is not of so much moment that it creates proof [*fidem*]. . . . The bishop will vainly base proofs or corroborative evidence on *fama,* for it is never found in written law [*ius*] that *fama* sufficiently creates proof."[6] *Fama* got into city statutes and into legal handbooks because of its currency in the world at large, not because of its legal antecedents. That is doubtless why the Pisan city statutes, highly influenced by Roman law as they were, soon substantially limited the remit of *fama.* The first text we have, from ca. 1186, allowed its use, but later in the century it was limited to cases about inheritance and shipwreck, or to cases occurring over twenty years earlier where there were no charters and witnesses (by 1232 cases about contracts, dowry, and fiefs had been added, and later, piracy).[7] But, it has to be stressed, neither the doubts of parties about the force of *fama* (mainly, one presumes, when their opponents used it) nor the influence of the learned laws had much effect on ordinary Tuscans, witnesses, litigants, and judges alike: even in Pisa, public courts accepted it more freely than these laws ought to have allowed. An instance of this lack of doubt can be found in a text from Prato from the second half of the century that lists the questions an interrogator should ask about a disputed inheritance: "also, inquire if Campiscana married inside thirty days of [her first husband] Panfollia's death; also, in-

6. Respectively, Archivio di Stato di Lucca, fondo S. Maria forisportam, 27 agosto 1188; Caturegli, *Regesto,* no. 529; Archivio di Stato di Firenze, fondo Camaldoli, "1216," no. 6 on the tab ("no. 2" on the text).

7. Compare Yale, Beinecke Library, MS 415, fols. 4v, 27v (the 1186 text with later marginalia) with Francesco Bonaini, ed., *Statuti inediti della città di Pisa dal XI al XIV secolo,* 3 vols. (Florence, 1854–70), 2:696–97, 866 (the 1233 text with later additions). The late thirteenth-century theorists also proposed limits on *fama:* to cases about marriage, or status, or where the witnesses were all dead; cf. Migliorino, *Fama e infamia,* 58–70.

quire if it was *vulgaris fama* that she had done so." The common opinion about the marriage was as important as the fact itself.[8]

Why was this so? Essentially, it seems to me, because of the importance of the public arena as a place where "truth" was created. Twelfth-century Tuscans lived their lives in public—at least those parts of their lives that had relevance for the establishment of their rights. What the public environment accepted as true was, indeed, to an extent valid in law as well. The aspect of *fama* concerned with personal reputation must have had a huge effect on the capacity of people to survive—or fail to survive—criminal accusations (this we cannot check, for we do not have the relevant documentation for this period, but we can safely assume it). In the cases we do have, property disputes above all, someone with more personal *fama* would also presumably have often won out over someone with less. But this latter element, though again likely (it is still true today, after all), is not explicit in our sources; instead, these overwhelmingly stress public opinion about rights, not reputation. Men may have developed complex strategies to establish reputation, as they usually do, but they certainly developed complex strategies to establish rights as well.

One way to establish rights publicly was simply to exercise them in public, repeatedly. Witnesses regularly stress that a party had, for example, "always" cultivated a contested field, or "often" taken rent from tenants who now claimed they owned the land. These public actions were often highly formalized, indeed ritualized: you brought the rent, you put it in a specific, significant place (on the altar of the church, for example, if the church was the landlord); you got a meal in return, called *commestio;* any of these moments could be seen by others and had sufficiently clear meanings that those others could conclude that you were not only a tenant but you accepted your position. If in addition you did certain sorts of labor-service, stone- or wood-cutting or ditch digging or cart service, those observers would conclude that you were a semi-servile *manens,* and that, once again, you knew it. Betto in the 1188 Lucca case cited previously said, yes, he cut stone and wood, but only *pro amore:* that is, as a favor, not as a mark of status. Maybe this was true, but it was an unwise action if so, given the prima facie meaning of such actions. Betto lost the case.

A second way of establishing rights was to talk about them. In another Lucchese case, from 1166, between the cathedral chapter and a rural church—a dispute over who owned a garden that Pietro Argento, the archpriest of the chapter, had bought for the church—the archpriest had made out a charter, which one of the witnesses had read. Most of his and other witnessing for the case, however, concerned what Pietro *said* the charter

8. Renzo Fantappiè, ed., *Le carte della propositura di S. Stefano di Prato,* vol. 1 (Florence: L. S. Olschki, 1977), appendix 2.

contained and meant: this was the element of the transaction that he wanted to put into the public domain. Speech was hugely important. Had the Lucchese urban patrician Antelminello di Antelmino in ca. 1190 said to the cathedral canons, about the church of S. Alessandro minore— whose patronage they each claimed in 1192—"I ask you as patrons and lords of the church . . . ," or "You *claim* to be patrons . . ."? That became a crux of the subsequent case.[9]

These were standard procedures, probably uncontroversial in most cases, even though we hear about them only in later legal disputes. They were aimed at creating a generalized public recognition of rights, and they usually succeeded. It is important to underline that these procedures were used even when people possessed written documentation of rights. Charters were the best evidence in all types of court proceedings, but the public domain that backed up the rights they conferred responded best to the spoken word and the visible action. Also, then as now, writing could never cover everything—where exactly the boundary lay, or whether an element of the rent had been let off that year because of a service rendered, and so on. Such details were most effectively established by talking to third parties, who would, it was hoped and assumed, then talk to others about it.

Contesting the rights of others was an equally public process. This tended to be done by direct actions with more than a minor element of ritual about them as well: turning up and cultivating the contested land in front of witnesses, or forcing one's opponent's men off the land, or blocking or breaking one's opponent's millrace, or, at the upper end of the scale, committing bodily violence or arson. Such direct actions had to be performed in public, or they were not only invalid but, being secret, counted as theft (*clam*, "secretly," and *furtim*, "by theft," are in effect synonyms in the documents). Were the mill canals of Bernardo of Mucciana broken in 1217 by the dependents of his rival, the *pievano* of S. Pancrazio in Chianti, at night, that is to say, *furtim*, or at sunset, that is to say, in public? Witnesses disagreed, but it mattered for the outcome of the case.[10] Direct actions were challenges: if the other party did not respond, with counteractions or with a formal plea to a court or to arbitrators, then he (more rarely she) risked being considered by the public arena to have conceded the case. Common knowledge would recognize the rights of the party who defied the other most effectively, and the carriers of that knowledge could bear witness to this in court. In 1194 the monastery of Cantignano south of Lucca sent its men to a piece of woodland that was contested with the neighboring monastery of Casale, and cleared it, creating a chestnut plan-

9. Pietro Guidi and O. Parenti, eds., *Regesto del capitolo di Lucca*, 4 vols., Regesta Chartarum Italiae (Rome: Instituto Storico per il Medioevo, 1910–39), vol. 2, nos. 1252, 1652.

10. Pietro Santini, ed., *Documenti dell'antica costituzione del comune di Firenze*, Documenti di storia italiana, vol. 10 (Florence: G. P. Vieusseux 1895; Olschki, 1952), no. 2.21.

tation. Casale regarded this clearance as secret (*furtim et clam*)—though of course woodcutting is notoriously widely audible—and sent its own men to expel those of Cantignano. Here, one direct action sparked another, more violent one. In 1200 Casale began to build a mill in the same area, and Cantignano formally prohibited it from doing so (this *interdictum,* another public direct act, was a common recourse in the twelfth-century Tuscan countryside). This time Casale took Cantignano to court. The case hung on whether Casale's earlier expulsion of Cantignano was legitimate or not. Here, it seems that Cantignano had waited too long, six years, to respond; it had to agree that the trees in the area, which by now included fruit trees, largely belonged to Casale, and Cantignano duly lost in court. We may conclude that, if direct action was not countered soon enough, much sooner than the thirty-year period required by law, it created a presumption of right, including in the eyes of judges.[11]

These cases show that one had to be strategic in one's establishment of rights. Some people undoubtedly found it easier than others to do this. I have discussed elsewhere Compagno of Mucciana, a peasant who in 1137 challenged the right of the monastery of Passignano, Florence's largest rural monastery, to build a mill on what he said was his land, taking the monastery as far as a formal arbitration. Compagno had previously tried direct action, in this case public cultivation, against both Passignano and the land's former owner, Arlotto, but had been run off the land by Arlotto. This physical failure contributed to Compagno's eventual failure in the arbitration, because Arlotto's successful response was common knowledge in Mucciana. But Compagno had an uphill battle even before, because it had been *fama* in the locality that his branch of his family had never owned the land. (Nor would his relatively low status have helped, though, as usual in the period, this is not stressed by witnesses.)[12] The more established a piece of common knowledge was, the harder it would be for any direct action to dislodge it. Conversely, it may be that no one cared much who owned a piece of woodland in the mountains south of Lucca before Cantignano planted chestnuts there, so local observers were happier to accept the greater rights of a material victor.

Here, we must make some distinctions. Witnesses in Tuscan court cases clearly respected the force of direct action; they cited it frequently as the basis of their knowledge about who had rights in the event of a dispute. Courts, too, respected such arguments, even in Pisa, which was enough of a consciously Romanist city for people to know and indeed use the Roman

11. Archivio di Stato di Lucca, fondo S. Nicolao, 26 maggio 1200. For the importance of timing, see Pierre Bourdieu, *Outline of a Theory of Practice,* trans. Richard Nice (Cambridge: Cambridge University Press, 1977), 5–9.
12. Archivio di Stato di Firenze, fondo Passignano, "sec. XII, no. 6," discussed in Wickham, "Gossip," 3–5.

legal actions against violent dispossession at the same time as they engaged in violence to establish their rights.[13] The public arena, then, incorporated public direct action into its knowledge about rights or wrongs. This knowledge was what constituted *publica fama,* and it is often called so in texts. This is not quite the same thing as saying that *fama* was a legally acceptable mode of proof; still, all types of judges or adjudicators in the records of disputes that survive for the twelfth century—consular magistrates, papal judges-delegate, agreed arbiters—recognized the force of this sort of witnessing when they made decisions. A papal legate heard a dispute in 1200 in the Pisan community at Constantinople over whether a priest called Pietro, who was now dead, had had the right to baptize children. The legate heard ten witnesses who described Pietro baptizing people in the 1170s, apparently without any contestation. He then refused to hear any more, even though others were ready, "since it was *communis et publica atque consentiens fama* [common, public and accepted fame] with respect to the issue under dispute": so many witnesses saying the same thing created *fama,* and that was enough.[14] Given the presuppositions witnesses held, any reliance on witnessing would involve the incorporation of *fama* into legal decisions, for even when witnesses merely described what they saw, it was common knowledge that gave what they saw meaning, as in the Compagno case. Judges would have had specifically to exclude that common knowledge in their interrogations if they had wanted not to accept it ("just stick to the facts"), and they never even tried to do so. Indeed, as we saw in the case of Campiscana and Panfollia of Prato, judges often specifically asked for information about *fama.* The presuppositions of the public arena extended into the courtroom, seamlessly.

The trouble, of course, is that communities do not always agree. Indeed, they very seldom do. The belief that small-town gossip is a consistent and univocal community judgment—whether of a person's reputation, the commission of a given set of illegal acts, or who has the greater right to a given property—is certainly something that the terminology of *publica fama* presupposes; but it is fantasy all the same. Anyone who has ever gossiped, which is nearly all of us, will know that these are just the kinds of things that people disagree strongly about, and, where there are two or more distinct interest groups in a community (different families, or clienteles, or factions), there will be two or more distinct agreed truths to match. Hence the criticisms of *fama* mentioned above: such discordances were normal, and known to be normal. Even if one whole community had

13. Cf. Chris Wickham, "Derecho y práctica legal en las comunas urbanas italianas del siglo XII: el caso de Pisa," *Hispania* 57 (1997): 981–1007.
14. Archivio di Stato di Pisa, fondo Roncione, 9 luglio 1201 (mod. dating 1200), ed. in Maria Pia De Paola, "Le pergamene dell'Archivio di Stato di Pisa dal 1198 al 1201" (Università di Pisa, Facoltà di lettere, tesi di laurea, a.a., 1966–67, relatore Cinzio Violante), no. 38.

an agreed version of the facts, the next-door community might not, and they could well dispute this too. The 1216 Camaldoli complaint is explicit on the subject: the bishop of Arezzo's *fama* is based only on the talk of his own *fideles* and the inhabitants of his own *castra*, not on that of Camaldoli or indeed neutral parties. In 1185, in a communal boundary dispute between the villages of Rosignano and Castiglioncello in the south of the diocese of Pisa, the Rosignanesi gave a series of detailed accounts of the common rights they held in the disputed area. They periodically reinforced these rights by systematic violence against the Castiglioncellesi, and by a local ritual in which children were shown the bounds, told about a mass boundary-marking by the Rosignanesi in ca. 1168, and beaten to make them remember it. Not surprisingly, those rights were *publica et apertissima fama* (public and well-known fame) in Rosignano. Not in Castiglioncello, however: the case was reopened five times between 1133 and 1202.[15]

What could one do, then? An experienced interrogator might try to undermine these confident assertions of *fama* by finding malcontents, or idiots,[16] or people who could be forced to admit that there was something wrong with the self-confidence of their own side, or people who had at least to admit under oath that they had witnessed some act that contradicted the common knowledge they also possessed; or else by going to neutral, neighboring villages to see what they thought. Not in this case, for on this issue, at least inside the village, Rosignano had it fairly well sewn up. Elsewhere, however, it was possible. In light of this, what contesting parties really needed to do was to manipulate rival versions of *fama*, to win over neutral observers and to reinforce the collective opinion of their own side with significant acts that could be both talked about and remembered.

The best example we have of these sorts of strategies is a large-scale one, nearly in the realm of high politics: the boundary dispute between the dioceses of Siena and Arezzo in 1124–25. This consisted of two reopenings of the longest-running dispute in Tuscan history, which lasted from the early eighth century to the early thirteenth. The dispute involved twenty-one *pievi* (the large proto-parish territories of the early Middle Ages) that lay in the county of Siena but in the diocese of Arezzo, which the bishop of Siena sought, dozens of times, to claim in the papal courts. In 1124, he managed, very unusually, to gain control of them, in a hearing in Rome.

15. Caturegli, *Regesto*, no. 571.
16. In a case over the status of a tenant of the cathedral canons of Siena from 1183, one Giovanni Guduccini, when "asked if it was *frequens fama* in that *terra* that it was true [that the tenant's father Gianni had been a dependent], first replied 'no,' and then at once said 'yes,' and then spoke in a confused/wandering manner [*vagipalanter*], and afterwards added that he did not remember if Gianni had offered [dependency], but did remember the *vulgaris fama* about it": Antonella Ghignoli, ed., *Carte dell'Archivio di Stato di Siena. Opera metropolitana (1000–1200)*, Fonti di storia senese (Siena: Accademia Senese degli Intronati, 1994), no. 85.

That decision was reversed a year later, however, and Arezzo got them back. In 1177, in the next round of the dispute, 106 aged witnesses recalled for a papal legate what had happened in 1124–25 inside the two dioceses. What had happened was largely ritual: the bishop of Siena in 1124 and then the bishop of Arezzo in 1125 traveled from pieval church to pieval church, performing a formal act of claiming possession. In the Aretine case, the papal *nuntius* closed and reopened the church doors of each *pieve*, put them into the hands of the bishop while the church bell was rung, and gave the bishop the altar cloths; then they ate a meal. (There were twenty-one churches, and witnesses recalled that the *nuntius*, perhaps a veteran of such rituals, was very fat.) These were highly public acts. The church bells made that clear; witnesses remembered bells ringing a lot. Witnesses also remembered the bishop and the *nuntius* riding by, with an armed entourage that could fight off resistance, which they had to do in at least one instance; when they came through a village they spoke about their intentions, and the villagers repeated it when they had left. In 1124 the bishop of Siena preached in each *pieve* too; in 1125, for his part, the bishop of Arezzo recounted the story of his successful hearing in public, maybe several times since the speech was so widely remembered. It is not surprising that the news of the dispute was called a *famosus rumor* by one witness: it was not only news, but managed news. The bishops wanted their successes remembered, above all by people in the disputed territories, who might be called on to witness to who rightly controlled the pievi in the future. This is precisely what the papal legate did in 1177, for a high proportion of his witnesses were from the twenty-one pievi. The *fama vulgaris* or *communis vox* about who possessed local ecclesiastical rights was as important to the legate as were more technical legal arguments about ultimate proprietary rights. In both fields, the bishop of Arezzo had a better case, but he also put more work into creating a local memory of his rights. For whichever reason, in 1177 he won again; but he had already won the battle for *fama*, probably much earlier, in 1125.[17]

The public space employed by the bishop of Arezzo was almost always the open air: the street, the piazza, the area in front of the church. These were characteristic spaces for *publica fama* in this period. Fields were more

17. Ubaldo Pasqui, ed., *Documenti per la storia della città di Arezzo nel medio evo*, 3 vols., Documenti di storia italiana (Florence: Presso G. P. Vieusseux, 1899–1937), vol. 2, no. 389; the best discussions of the text are Jean-Pierre Delumeau, "La mémoire des gens d'Arezzo et de Sienne à travers des dépositions de témoins (VIIIe–XIIe s.)," in *Temps, mémoire, tradition au Moyen Âge: Actes du XIIIe Congrès de la Société des historiens médiévistes de l'enseignement supérieur public, Aix-en-Provence, 4–5 juin 1982* (Aix: Université de Provence, 1983), 45–67; Guy P. Marchal, "Memoria, fama, mos maiorum," in *Vergangenheit in mündlicher Überlieferung*, ed. Jürgen von Ungern-Sternberg and Hansjörg Reinau, Colloquium Rauricum, vol. 1 (Stuttgart: B. G. Teubner, 1988), 289–320.

problematic, for one might not be seen; there was space for argument about whether acts were *furtim* or not, even in daylight. Inside buildings was problematic too: the church was public, and so, probably, was the tavern, but private houses were not, unless one was a guest and had a significant conversation with one's host.

This is the context for one striking absence from nearly all twelfth-century witnessing: women. In the Siena-Arezzo case, there are no women at all, not only as witnesses but even in the events recalled by witnesses. This is normal in twelfth-century Tuscany; the exceptions are few and far between. In Pisa, where Roman law allowed women public status as actors, one at least finds female witnesses, but the content of witnessing does not change. The 1203 Rosano case mentioned earlier features women, because it concerns the patronage of a nunnery. Nuns, at least, were autonomous actors, as were leading female aristocrats, but there were not many of either. Even when we know of previous female actions in land transactions or church building, they seem to have dropped out of male memory of the same events.[18] And this is a feature that unifies city and country in this period. There is a sharp distinction between this period and the cities of the late Middle Ages, as in Daniel Smail's fourteenth-century Marseille or Thomas Kuehn's and Gene Brucker's fifteenth-century Florence, where female witnessing, and memories involving the actions of women, had considerable importance.[19] In part, this may be the result of the restricted range of disputes attested in the documentation for twelfth-century Tuscany: land and ecclesiastical disputes may have privileged a specifically male public space. But they nonetheless show that this male space existed, and that the *publica fama* about these issues was a male-dominated gossip: maybe even a male-only gossip, but at least a gossip whose legitimating group was made up of males. It may well be that *privata fama,* the "rumor" of the jurists, which might include female talkers, was differently constructed—less formal, less hierarchical, more interesting—but it did not constitute the kind of common knowledge that was legally acceptable, at least in these sorts of disputes, at least in this period. But the memories we do hear about were capable of being dense and fluid, for all that: they mattered to people.

Fama was not, for these reasons, exactly the same as gossip. It was more formalized, more "legal," than most gossip; it was spoken by people who knew that public words could matter, and for a long time (over fifty years, in the Siena-Arezzo case). But of course it was a subtype of the gossip

18. As in Guidi and Parenti, *Regesto,* vol. 2, no. 1384 (anno 1177).

19. Smail, "Archivos," 1071–75; Kuehn, "*Fama* as a Legal Status," in this volume; Gene Brucker, *Giovanni and Lusanna: Love and Marriage in Renaissance Florence* (London: Wiedenfeld and Nicolson, 1986); compare Wickham, "Gossip," 15–16, on gossip and gender.

process, and it had many of the same functions if looked at from a Gluck-manesque, functionalist anthropological perspective.[20] Gossip—and *fama* —establishes common versions of the relevant past inside the talking group (which can be as small as two, and as many as a whole community), and common versions of a set of moral attitudes to that past. It creates and polices group identity. But it is also transactional: one can contest it, di-rectly, by another version of the past, or strategically, with another framing or interpretation of the past. We can see people doing this with *fama*, in the direct actions that I analyzed earlier, which, if uncontested, would be accepted as modifications of the perceived status quo. Finally, the ability of individual actors to affect *fama*—or any other form of gossip—largely de-pended on their own status (their *fama* as reputation), simply because in all social groups there are some people, or some social categories, who are taken seriously and some who are not. In fact, it is a function of gossip (as of any legal system, for that matter) to police internal social status as much as to look out for danger and moral infraction. Medieval societies delegit-imated large swaths of their members: the peasantry in cities or in land-owning circles, women and the poor everywhere. *Fama* was one of the means they used, all the more effectively and insidiously because it was done in-explicitly and maybe only semiconsciously. Nor is this true just for medieval societies. All societies are structured not only by rules, which people can be taught, and which can be policed, but also by a much less clear body of knowledge about how these rules can be negotiated and bent, about how far one can go before people think one has gone too far, and about which people can get away with more and which with less. *Fama* is the best guide we have in this period to these quasi-rules, what Pierre Bourdieu has called *habitus*.[21] Only if we track *fama* in operation can we find out how those quasi-rules worked then, and how they work now.

20. Classically, Max Gluckman, "Gossip and Scandal," *Current Anthropology* 4 (1963): 307–16; Sally Engle Merry, "Rethinking Gossip and Scandal," in *Toward a General Theory of Social Control*, ed. Donald J. Black, 2 vols. (New York: Academic Press, 1984), 1:271–302, sums up the anthropological debate.

21. Pierre Bourdieu, *The Logic of Practice*, trans. Richard Nice (Cambridge: Polity, 1990), 52–65.

Chapter Two

Fama *as a Legal Status in Renaissance Florence*

Thomas Kuehn

In the late medieval *ius commune* and the statutes of Italian city-states, *fama* was more than gossip, reputation, or common knowledge. *Fama* could also refer to the legal condition or status of a person or even a group (one thinks of the magnate clans of Florence, for example). It qualified people as witnesses, notaries, family members, or citizens—all positions of trust in some manner. At least in late medieval Florence, with its multiple and over-lapping courts and sources of law (including the academic civil and canon law, civic statutes, guild and other mercantile regulations), *fama* operated at times as an element of personal status. That is, just as freedom, legiti-macy, or adulthood (being *sui iuris*) permitted certain rights and actions, so did *fama*. Moreover, though *fama* was palpable on the streets and even began there, it became something else when it filtered into law courts. On the street, *fama* was gossip, reputation, or common knowledge, but in the court *fama* was what the law and judges said it was, and they treated it as a status with consequences for the legal capacities of persons.

It is the contention of this essay that (at least for a city-state like Flor-ence) there was no simple, direct, or automatic connection between social *fama* and legal *fama*. The linkage between the two was mediated by au-thoritative legal texts and by the interpretive devices and traditions of learned jurists and other officials. Those texts and traditions reshaped *fama* and added dimensions of enabling status (or disabling, in the form of the contrary *infamia*) to it. At least within courts of law—and it is the resonance of *fama* in law that largely makes it interesting historically—what they determined gave *fama* legal weight. The predominant scholarly attention to *fama* as a mode of proof has both neglected the status dimen-

sion of *fama* and downplayed the distance it had to travel and the transformations it underwent from the streets to the courts.

Fama as personal status and public trust was thus distinguishable from
fama as a matter of general knowledge regarding events or relationships,
even when the two were present at one and the same time. An example of
their coincidence hails from a relatively famous Florentine case, that of
Giovanni and Lusanna. Witnesses called before the court of the archbishop of Florence were asked to affirm the *fama* in their neighborhood
regarding certain events and also to substantiate the *fama* of the litigants,
particularly Lusanna's.[1] Questions posed to the witnesses from Giovanni's
attorney were designed to prove that Lusanna was of lesser *fama* or even
infamis, such that Giovanni would be shamed to marry her.[2] Also posed was
a question designed to show that Lusanna was reputed "publicly and notoriously" and by "public voice and *fama*" to be sterile and unable therefore to contract a valid marriage.[3] For her part, Lusanna was intent on
proving by means of *fama* that a marriage between her and Giovanni had
been celebrated and consummated. Her legal problem was that proof of
marriage by *fama* was very difficult, if not impossible.[4] In the end it may
well have been her lesser personal *fama* that cost her the case; it certainly
cost her the man she would claim as her husband.

Fama in Law

To use language favored by lawyers, *fama* was a point at which facts met
law. Gossip about people and events was accepted as fact upon which the
rules of law played so that a judgment could be reached. What elevated
fama above mere gossip and into the realm of law was the fact that *fama,* as
Chris Wickham succinctly puts it, was "what everybody knew, common
knowledge," and thus "socially accepted as reliable."[5] What made *fama* legal was its acceptance, within disciplined limits, by communal legislators
and by academically trained jurists and attorneys.

1. As per Archivio di Stato, Florence (hereafter ASF), Notarile M 342 (1439–82, old designation), fols. 121v and 122r. This case was given renewed *fama* by Gene Brucker in his *Giovanni and Lusanna: Love and Marriage in Renaissance Florence* (Berkeley: University of California
Press, 1986). See my "Reading Microhistory: The Example of *Giovanni and Lusanna,*" *Journal of Modern History* 61 (1989): 512–34.

2. ASF, Notarile M 343 (1445–50, old designation), fols. 202r–5r, including item eight
(of nineteen): "Item quod attempta qualitate dicte Susanne et eius vita et fama, et attenta
qualitate dicti Johannis fuisset dicto Johanni et toti eius familie maxima verecundia et maxi-
mum dedecus accipere illam in uxorem et resultasset ipsi maxima infamia."

3. Ibid., question 16.

4. See the illuminating discussion of this case in Chiara Valsecchi, "'Causa matrimonialis
est gravis et ardua': *Consiliatores* e matrimonio fino al Concilio di Trento," *Studi di storia del
diritto* 2 (1999): 407–580, at 490–94.

5. Chris Wickham, "Gossip and Resistance among the Medieval Peasantry," *Past and Present* 160 (1998): 3–24, at 4.

Wickham's point is to urge historical attention to gossip because "groups construct themselves by talking."[6] In his essay in this volume Wickham makes a useful distinction between rumor and reputation (different poles of the realm of talk) on the one hand, and common knowledge, on the other. It is the latter, as he demonstrates, that carried probative value in arbitrations and litigations. I would add only that when one moves into law courts, at least those of northern and central Italy in the late Middle Ages, one enters a different arena; what is common knowledge in the streets becomes something else, in part.[7] The amorphous, fluid, and supposedly nonhierarchical talk of the streets and *piazze* becomes the stilted, arcane, and hierarchical (not to mention Latinized) talk of the courtroom or other legal arena or office. In this setting, some of what was common knowledge on the streets would count, but some would not. We are reminded of Clifford Geertz's important point that "legal facts are made not born, are socially constructed, as an anthropologist would put it, by everything from evidence rules, courtroom etiquette, and law reporting traditions, to advocacy techniques, the rhetoric of judges, and the scholasticism of law school education."[8] Geertz does not address the differences in power and knowledge between laymen and legal professionals (in our case, the notaries and jurists of city-states such as Florence, but also members of the social elite who served as judges and legislators).[9] Yet he is assuredly correct that law is "constructive," "constitutive," and "formational."[10] In some courts, at least, it is also professional.[11] The professional quality of the courts produced paradoxical results as far as *fama* is concerned. On the one hand, courts and jurists treated reputation and gossip as nonprofessional and resisted or limited their scope accordingly. On the other, common talk, properly disciplined, was one basis of proof and status.

The most thorough study of *fama* in civil and canon law is Francesco

6. Ibid., 11.

7. Chris Wickham, *"Fama* and the Law" in this volume, claims that the passage of knowledge from the streets to the courts was "seamless," a point I am questioning here.

8. Clifford Geertz, "Local Knowledge: Fact and Law in Comparative Perspective," in *Local Knowledge: Further Essays in Interpretive Anthropology* (New York: Basic Books, 1983), 167–234, at 173.

9. Perhaps from this perspective some insight can be gained into the fact that "energies that, in the Western tradition, have gone into distinguishing law from fact and into developing procedures to keep them from contaminating one another have, in the Islamic, gone into connecting them, and into developing procedures to deepen the connection" (ibid., 195). Otherwise we are left with incommensurable cultural orders despite Geertz's call for "something rather more than local knowledge" (ibid., 233).

10. Ibid., 218.

11. Paul Hyams sees the law courts as having recourse to *fama* as a mode of proof after Lateran IV removed the possibility of ordeals; see "Due Process versus the Maintenance of Order in European Law: The Contribution of the *Ius Commune*," in *The Moral World of the Law*, ed. Peter Coss (Cambridge: Cambridge University Press, 2000), 62–90, at 82. *Fama* as status, however, would be a different matter. On the professional quality of law, see Wickham, "Conclusion," in *Moral World*, ed. Coss, 240–49.

Migliorino's *Fama e infamia*. Migliorino sees these as opposite poles in a continuum of behavior judged in accordance with norms and shared values. As such, they had an impact on legal capacities as well as on social, economic, and political relations.[12] Migliorino utilizes a distinction found in juristic texts between *fama* or *infamia facti* (of procedural and probative value) and *fama* or *infamia legalis* (status). It is the first, however, that has most caught the attention of legal historians, including Migliorino himself, because it concerns matters of procedure and proof, especially in criminal cases. Less than self-evident *notorium*, which was an irrefutable standard based on evidence, sentence, and confession, *fama* as public opinion about events or personal reputations was not sufficient to condemn a person, but it could create a presumption of guilt.[13] As a matter of local knowledge or reputation, *fama* regarding facts or persons was real, and thus potentially usable, though indistinct. As defined by Thomas de Piperata, a late thirteenth-century jurist of very little *fama* himself, "*Fama* is said to be what the people of a city, village, castle, or hamlet, or any district commonly express and think or feel, asserting it by words or brief exposition, yet they do not have it as certain and true or manifest."[14] *Fama* might confirm eyewitness testimony, but it could not replace it. In civil matters it might create presumptions regarding acts whose validity was under challenge or it might add to other evidence or presumptions, but in itself it could never constitute proof.[15]

It is of course in relation to personal reputation that *fama* acquired a legal status or condition. As F. R. P. Akehurst's essay in this volume usefully reminds us, *fama* was not something one gained. It was assumed, but it could be lost. Thus, although *fama* was at times qualified as *bona*, it was the unpresumed negative side that was conceptually richer, encompassing, as Jeffrey Bowman shows in his essay in this volume, both *mala fama* as reputation and *infamia* as status. As a legal category, *infamia facti*, which was strongly linked to social infamy, brought a degree of direction and definition that enlarged a vague social infamy into "a formidable instrument of social control and of pressure to conform."[16] Most learned jurists rejected or limited the injection of *fama* into proceedings for fear that judges, who

12. Francesco Migliorino, *Fama e infamia: Problemi della società medievale nel pensiero giuridico nei secoli XII e XIII* (Catania: Giannotta, 1985), 9.

13. Migliorino, *Fama e infamia*, 54; Mike MacNair, "Vicinage and the Antecedents of the Jury," *Law and History Review* 17 (1999): 537–90, at 576; on *notorium*, see Jean-Philippe Lévy, "Le problème de la preuve dans les droits savants du Moyen Âge," in *La preuve*, 2 vols., Recueils de la Société Jean Bodin pour l'histoire comparative des institutions 17 (Brussels: Editions de la Librairie encyclopédique, 1965), 2:137–67.

14. Richard M. Fraher, "Conviction according to Conscience: The Medieval Jurists' Debate concerning Judicial Discretion and the Law of Proof," *Law and History Review* 7 (1989): 23–88, quotation 69 n. 69.

15. Cf. ibid., 36–37; also MacNair, "Vicinage," 574–75.

16. Migliorino, *Fama e infamia*, 177. See also Edward Peters, "Wounded Names: The Medieval Doctrine of Infamy," in *Law in Medieval Life and Thought*, ed. Edward B. King and Susan J. Ridyard (Sewanee, Tenn.: Press of the University of the South, 1990), 43–89.

were generally uneducated in the law, would abuse their discretion.[17] But they accepted the notion of *infamia* and its resulting legal effects.

As a quality set in law, *fama legalis* was contained in legal statements and sentences. Alberto Gandino, one of the first academic jurists to attempt a systematic explication of civic statutes (and a judge in Florence in 1288 and 1310), declared that *fama* "is a status of unquestioned dignity, approved by customs and laws, and in no way diminished."[18] As a status it had to do with trustworthiness, good name, and honor. The famed trecento jurist Baldo degli Ubaldi (1323–1400) included the court sentence issued regarding one's fama (*sententia lata super fama*) among examples of judgments that had general effect everywhere, such as those regarding paternity, filiation, marriage, age of majority, inheritance, and more.[19] As something so legally concrete, *fama* also could be taken away, whether by legal judgment or by the process of defamation, which one could contest for damages and recovery.[20]

As a legal status, arising first in Roman law,[21] *fama* gave a person the ability to do things in law. A man of *bona fama* could hold certain offices; his testimony would be taken in court, whereas the *infamis* would have to be tortured first.[22] And loss of *fama* was a threat whose effects could be measured in some fashion, even in the recognition that loss of *fama* was not much of a loss to someone with little of value to lose.[23] Application of *infamia* or relief from it rested mainly in judicial hands.[24] Hence, beyond the provisions and norms regarding *fama* in civil and canon law, what made it operative in Italian cities was its acceptance into local statutes and procedures.

Fama and Honor in Florence

I do not want to deny or downplay the connection between *fama* in the streets and *fama* in law. *Fama* was legally effective in good part because it was always more than legal. To Samuel Edgerton, who has studied pictor-

---

17. On discretion, see Massimo Meccarelli, *Arbitrium: Un aspetto sistematico degli ordinamenti giuridici in età di diritto comune* (Milan: Giuffrè, 1998).

18. Cf. Hermann Kantorowicz, ed., *Albertus Gandinus und das Strafrecht der Scholastik*, 2 vols. (Berlin: 1926), 2:51: "est inlese dignitatis status, moribus ac legibus comprobatus, et in nullo diminutus."

19. Baldo to l. ingenuum, ff. De statu hominis (D.1.5.25), *In corpus iuris civilis commentaria*, 10 vols. (Venice, 1577), vol. 1, *In primam digesti veteris*, fols. 33va–34rb.

20. Cf. Martin Ingram, *Church Courts, Sex, and Marriage in England, 1570–1640* (Cambridge: Cambridge University Press, 1987), 292–319; idem, "'Scolding Women Cucked or Washed': A Crisis in Gender Relations in Early Modern England?" in *Women, Crime and the Courts in Early Modern England*, ed. Jenny Kermode and Garthine Walker (Chapel Hill: University of North Carolina Press, 1994), 48–80; and idem, "Law, Litigants, and the Construction of 'Honour': Slander Suits in Early Modern England," in *Moral World*, ed. Coss, 134–60.

21. Fraher, "Conviction," 33.

22. Migliorino, *Fama e infamia*, 144.

23. Ibid., 140.

24. Ibid., 162.

ial renderings of infamy, the *infamia de facto* of local reputation and gossip was more "insidious" than *infamia* as a legal status, which could be removed.[25] For both men and women *fama* could become a harsh reality on the streets.[26] That is why it served Florentines to be *furbo*—clever, cryptic, vague, evasive, secretive.[27] Florentines have left us rich testimony of their concerns about *fama*. The merchant and moralist Paolo da Certaldo in the fourteenth century opined that one did not want the *fama* of being a traitor, counterfeiter, murderer, blasphemer, sodomite, or usurer.[28] Above all, he advised: "It is better for a man to have good *fama* in this world than to have great wealth; and if you succeed in living in this world rightly, then you gain good *fama* because he who dies with good *fama* is ever alive in this world. You can gain good *fama* in this world by using the virtues and by leaving and driving away from you the vices."[29]

Another Florentine merchant, Giovanni di Pagolo Morelli, celebrated the *fama* won by his ancestors.[30] *Fama* also figured in an exchange between the two figures of Adovardo and Lionardo in Leon Battista Alberti's *Della famiglia* in which Adovardo stressed that wealth did not preserve *fama* and that *infamia* could be avoided by fleeing all vices. Earlier he had asserted that the good were known by many signs, including their name and reputation ("el nome e fama vulgata"). Earlier still, at the end of book 2 of the dialogue, Lionardo had declared that poverty hurt one less than dishonor, and that *fama* and favor were more useful than wealth.[31] Further, Alessandra Strozzi, in a letter of March 1464 to her son Filippo, who had been accused of shady financial dealings, declared "I am content with your good

25. Samuel Y. Edgerton Jr., *Pictures and Punishment: Art and Criminal Prosecution during the Florentine Renaissance* (Ithaca: Cornell University Press, 1985), 64.

26. Cf. Guido Ruggiero, "'Più che la vita caro': Onore, matrimonio e reputazione femminile nel tardo Rinascimento," *Quaderni storici* 66 (Dec. 1987): 753–75, at 766, 770–71.

27. Cf. Ronald F. E. Weissman, "The Importance of Being Ambiguous: Social Relations, Individualism, and Identity in Renaissance Florence," in *Urban Life in the Renaissance,* ed. Susan Zimmerman and Ronald F. E. Weissman (Newark: University of Delaware Press, 1989), 269–80; for an anthropological perspective, see Juliet du Boulay, "Lies, Mockery, and Family Integrity," in *Mediterranean Family Structures,* ed. J. G. Peristiany (Cambridge: Cambridge University Press, 1976), 389–406; and Thomas Belmonte, *The Broken Fountain* (New York: Columbia University Press, 1979), who exaggerates those features of family exclusivity captured in the term *amoral familism.*

28. Paolo da Certaldo, *Il libro di buoni costumi,* ed. Alfredo Schiaffini (Florence: LeMonnier, 1945), reprinted in *Mercanti scrittori,* ed. Vittore Branca (Milan: Rusconi, 1986), 10, 14, 26–27, 66.

29. Ibid., 13: "Meglio è l'uomo avere buona fama in questo mondo che avere un gran tesoro: e però procacciati di vivere in questo mondo dirittamente, acciò ch'acquisti buona fama, però che chi con buona fama muore, in questo mondo sempre vive. Puoi acquistare in questo mondo buona fama usendo le virtù e partendo e scacciando da te i vizi."

30. Giovanni Morelli, *Ricordi,* ed. Vittore Branca (Florence: LeMonnier, 1956), reprinted in *Mercanti scrittori,* ed. Branca, 124, 135.

31. Leon Battista Alberti, *I libri della famiglia,* ed. Ruggiero Romano and Alberto Tenenti (Turin: Einaudi, 1969), 390, 361, 182.

fama and life" ("sono molto contenta della buona fama e dell'esser tuo").[32]
Finally, in the sixteenth century the renowned jurist, statesman, and historian Francesco Guicciardini arrived at the same sense of the matter as Paolo da Certaldo, although he did not use the word *fama:* "Do not put more account in having favor [*grazia*] than in having reputation, because once reputation is lost one loses others' good will and in its place comes being held in contempt; but for him who maintains his reputation there is no lack of friends and their good will."[33]

Guicciardini denounced those who went through life intent only on their own interests, those "who do not know well what is in their own interest, that is, that they consider that it always consists of some monetary convenience rather than in honor, in knowing how to maintain one's reputation, and in good name."[34]

Guicciardini's recourse to the parallel terms of reputation and honor point to one particular anthropological understanding of the problem. Honor too is both a reputation and a state or condition. Although I do not think it possible to maintain the anthropological conceit that honor is and was a peculiar feature of Mediterranean societies,[35] honor certainly was an important cultural concept and social quality in a society like that of Renaissance Florence. *Fama* can be taken as a portion of the entire complex of honor, as honor's outer dimension, that is, reputation and standing in the eyes of others.[36]

Honor surfaced in the law under various guises. Honor gave rise to a sense of right, and, connected to notions like *fama* as a legal status, those rights figured in law.[37] Frank Henderson Stewart has argued that *fama* in the Roman world was a general term given some legal relevance, but he sees the distinctions employed by Roman lawyers as indicating a gulf between the lack of an opening for personal honor in Roman law and the presumptions of the general populace.[38] Although a similar gulf between

32. Alessandra Strozzi, *Selected Letters of Alessandra Strozzi, Bilingual Edition,* trans. Heather Gregory (Berkeley: University of California Press, 1997), 104.

33. Francesco Guicciardini, *Ricordi, diari, memorie,* ed. Mario Spinelli (Rome: Riuniti, 1981), 153: "Non fare più conto d'avere grazia che d'avere riputazione, perché, perduta la riputazione, si perde la benivolenza, e in luogo di quella succede lo essere disprezzato; ma a chi mantiene la riputazione non mancano amici, grazia e benivolenza."

34. Ibid., 193: "la fallacia è in quegli che non conoscono bene quale sia lo interesse suo, cioè che reputano che sempre consista in qualche commodo pecuniario più che nell'onore, nel sapere mantenersi la riputazione e el buono nome."

35. Cf. Michael Herzfeld, "Honour and Shame: Problems in the Comparative Analysis of Moral Systems," *Man,* n.s., 15 (1980): 339–51.

36. Cf. Pierre Bourdieu, *Outline of a Theory of Practice,* trans. Richard Nice (Cambridge: Cambridge University Press, 1977), 14–15.

37. Frank Henderson Stewart, *Honor* (Chicago: University of Chicago Press, 1994), 38–39, 146.

38. Mainly because not a single right was lost to *infamia* in Roman law. Cf. Stewart, *Honor,* 56–57, and on the difference between inner and outer honor, 25, 41–42.

law and fact undoubtedly was at work in later civil law, the influence of canon law and the incorporation of *fama* into local statutes and customs ensured that any such gulf would be different and rather narrower. Within the law *fama* bore the marks of substance (perhaps best seen in the plural, honors), not the mere evanescent reputation of the streets.

There was also a gendered dimension to *honor* and *fama* as reputation and as status. Much of reputation rested, in fact, on webs of gossip, which could be taken as a largely female occupation: "Neighbourhoods are gossip centres, run by women, deserted for the most of the day by men: it is in neighbourhoods that reputations are made."[39] The emergence of female witnesses in the case of Giovanni and Lusanna is just one example, even if the streets of Florence were not as empty of a masculine presence as the streets of villages that anthropologists have investigated. When *fama* got into law, however, it entered a male and citywide realm, if it had not done so before. A reputation-maintaining group of neighbors, most of whom were women, was replaced by male functionaries. Here *fama* acquired weight. In a sort of legal transubstantiation, the noun's gender remained feminine but its substance became masculine.[40] As a form of legal truth, *fama* became something more and other than gossip.

If we can follow a distinction employed by William Miller, *fama* is a form of "disposition talk" that stands in contrast to talk about more particular, less durable emotions. Disposition talk is about reputation rather than state of mind. *Fama,* as the subject of this sort of talk, is a social mask along with its attendant states and behaviors, rather than an inner and self-conscious feeling.[41] Such *fama* had moral and legal implications. We can capture some sense of this in a novella by Franco Sacchetti in which Gherardo Elisei marries a widow of bad reputation. His kin and friends demand of him, "Gherardo, what have you done? You are a wise man and yet have

39. John Davis, *People of the Mediterranean: An Essay in Comparative Social Anthropology* (London: Routledge and Kegan Paul, 1977), 178.

40. Tommaso Astarita, *Village Justice: Community, Family, and Popular Culture in Early Modern Italy* (Baltimore: Johns Hopkins University Press, 1999), 186, sees gender-specific gossip as a way women reduced male control. The degree to which that was the case when such gossip entered court, however, had to be limited.

41. William Ian Miller, *Humiliation: And Other Essays on Honor, Social Discomfort, and Violence* (Ithaca: Cornell University Press, 1993), 109–10. Without going as far as Miller, it is worth repeating here his distinction:

One could hazard the claim that as late as the seventeenth century the self did not feel emotions at all; instead the emotions were borne almost as a quasi-juridical status or as allegorical personae that the subject put on masklike. When one *was* sad, one became the character of Sadness in a moral and social drama, with its behavior thus constrained by the role. But when one could at last feel sad, sadness became a feeling, a perturbation of the nerves coupled with the effects of the thoughts one might have about that perturbation. The new self could thus be something more than its feelings; it could be more detached from them, more ironical, perhaps more restrained, and definitely more self-conscious. (177)

taken whom you have. What *fama* can this woman give you?"[42] Gherardo ended up having to beat her as, Sacchetti claims, her first husband should have. The moral implications of *fama* pushed Gherardo into assuming the mask of good husband (in fourteenth-century male terms, to be sure).

Women could also experience the moral and legal implications of *fama*, as we can see in an incident recorded by a Florentine notary in 1461. With the aid of an attorney, Francesca di ser Giovanni Arnoldi of Florence, citizen and resident of Venice, formally proclaimed in Florence the termination of her betrothal to Jacopo di Piero Tedaldi of Florence, formerly resident in Venice. She gave as her reason that Jacopo, while living with her family following the engagement, had deflowered Francesca's illegitimate sister and then fled from Venice in fear. Assured of this deed by the sister's confession and the testimony of others "by public voice and *fama*" ("ex publica voce et fama"), and in light of Jacopo's flight, Francesca freed herself from the betrothal obligation in order to marry someone else.[43] Although the only allusion to *fama* in the notarial text was to a public awareness, it is not hard to imagine that Francesca would have wondered what kind of *fama* she would have after marrying such a man. One is reminded of the shame that allegedly would have fallen on Giovanni della Casa were he to have married the *infamis* Lusanna—a shame that recalled him to a social and familial status that he had seemed quite willing to ignore in his earlier relationship with her.

Fama in Florentine Law

Fama, Migliorino concludes, had its deepest and most lasting effects when it received the imprint of a judicial sentence ("il suggello della sentenza").[44] In a manner typical of many other cities, Florence's statutes liberally allowed *publica fama* as both a sufficient basis for initiating judicial proceedings on a number of matters and as evidence in them.[45] Thus, in Florence *fama* functioned in all its guises, as *fama legalis* (status) and *fama facti* (of procedural and probative value). As an example of the latter, we

42. Franco Sacchetti, *Il trecento novelle,* ed. Vincenzo Pernicone (Florence: Sansoni, 1946), novella 85, 192–94.

43. ASF, Notarile D 88 (1458–61, old designation), fols. 354r–56v (11 December 1461). It is likely that this bastard sister was older and that age played a role in the sexual incident, because Francesca was said merely to be over seven years of age and the engagement had been established back in 1456. Jacopo appears to have been living with Francesca's family while waiting for his future bride to come of age ("antequam ipsa Franceschina venisset ad etatem legiptimam contrahendi matrimonium"). See also my *Illegitimacy in Renaissance Florence* (Ann Arbor: University of Michigan Press, 2002).

44. Migliorino, *Fama e infamia,* 196.

45. Laura Ikins Stern, *The Criminal Law System of Medieval and Renaissance Florence* (Baltimore: Johns Hopkins University Press, 1994), 24.

may note the case of a Florentine woman named Bartolomea who had given to her nephews or grandchildren (the uncertainty arising from the term *nepotes*) property acquired by her during marriage, despite a statute forbidding married women from alienating their property to the detriment of their husbands' rights to usufruct on it. Her husband contested her actions in court. According to neighbors ("secundum publicam opinionem vicinorum"), however, Bartolomea had been mistreated by her husband to the point of having left his house long before to live with the children of her first marriage, earning her living as a servant.[46] The Florentine jurist Antonio Strozzi (1455–1523) defended her gift (to the extent that *legitim* was reserved for all her children) on the grounds that the husband, following separation, did not have any rights of usufruct that were adversely affected.[47] The term *fama* did not arise in the jurist's *consilium,* but the opinion of neighbors clearly affirmed that the wife departed from her husband's home as an injured and aggrieved party, and that in turn enervated his rights. This particular bit of *fama* was judicially relevant.

Surely one of the better known forms of judicial expression of *infamia* in Florence was the so-called defaming pictures (*pitture infamanti*) exhaustively studied by Samuel Edgerton. The penalty of portraits of shame was largely applied to those guilty of commercial fraud, many of whom fled from Florence and from their creditors (and thus were legally known as *cessantes et fugitivi* [bankrupts and fugitives]). As men of some wealth and social standing, such fugitive bankrupts had something to lose from judicially and artistically applied *infamia.*[48] The pictures had to take the place of the monetary and corporal penalties that could have been inflicted on someone in custody. They were on view to fellow Florentines and to all travelers, who might then reveal the infamy to others in whatever places the bankrupt Florentines had found refuge. Their failure to make good their debts was a form of taking others' property, and in that sense it could be equated with criminal theft. Their flight, leaving them in contumacy of judicial proceedings, was tantamount to confession, although it could not affect others in the way that a judicial sentence of guilt could (which gave them an incentive to flee and avoid judgment for the sake of sons and others).[49] Yet, although Florence's statutes had provided for such portraits since 1283–84, from time to time it was necessary to remind judges of the

46. ASF, Carte strozziane, 3rd ser., 41/9, fols. 156r–57r, at 156r.

47. Ibid., fol. 156v: "Unde cum simus in casu in quo maritus non habebat usumfructum in dictis bonis ex eo quia male tractabat uxorem ut dicitur in dicto statuto, non debet habere locum dispositio dicti statuti."

48. Edgerton, *Pictures and Punishment,* esp. 73–75.

49. On these matters, see my "*Multorum Fraudibus Occurrere:* Legislation and Jurisprudential Interpretation concerning Fraud and Liability in Quattrocento Florence," *Studi senesi* 93 (1981): 309–50; and Umberto Santarelli, *Per la storia del fallimento nelle legislazioni italiane dell'età intermedia* (Padua: Antonio Milani, 1964).

penalty and to reenact the statute. In February 1465, at a time when commercial collapse faced a number of prominent Florentines, legislation reaffirmed that depiction of a bankrupt was designed for his never-ending shame ("ad perpetuam eius infamiam"). That threat more than anything else had kept many from bankruptcy. The city fathers were upset to find that such pictures either had never been painted or had been placed in obscure locations where they did not have the desired effect. So judges were ordered to have pictures painted, with full written particulars regarding name and guild affiliation, on the exterior of the bankrupt's house within one month of passing sentence, or the judges themselves would face a 100-florin fine.[50]

In its way, the failure to render these depictions may be the most eloquent testimony to their damaging effect on the reputations of otherwise well-to-do Florentines: judicially inscribed *infamia* may well have been very hard to overcome (as long as the paint adhered to the wall). But the failure to commission these paintings may also show that *infamia* did not move so easily from the courtroom to the streets. Bankruptcies need not have been, or have been perceived as, the result of moral failings or poor management such that the bankrupt deserved to be shamed. Downward turns of Fortune's wheel could strike anyone, even the mighty Medici. And deceptive practices were widely enough employed to leave others reluctant to tar the reputation of one unlucky enough to be exposed.

Still, the *fama* of the entire city and its merchants was threatened by deceptive business practices. It was to rectify various frauds that "are still of such great infamy and sometimes cause of great scandals" ("sono anchora d'infamia grande et qualche volta cagione di grandi schandoli") that a 1477 law sought to control a number of legal acts that were frequently misused and exploited.[51] On a different statutory level, *fama* lies behind the regulations of the Florentine Arte della Lana (Wool Guild). There, anyone who knew of a *sensale* (broker) committing fraud was enjoined to reveal under oath the names of those he wanted to accuse of fraud or other deceitful dealings, and thus tar with infamy. A *sensale* "infamatus" by six "voices" was to be removed from office.[52] In this way the guild erected its own form of *infamia* operative within its ranks.[53]

Fama was clearly a commodity in business and social relations, and its

50. ASF, Archivio della Repubblica, Statuti del comune 29, fol. 406r. This legislation has been transcribed by Edgerton, *Pictures and Punishment,* 228–30.

51. ASF, Provvisioni registri 168, fols. 4v–6r (20 March 1477, n.s.).

52. *Statuto dell'Arte della Lana di Firenze (1317–1319),* ed. Anna Maria E. Agnoletti (Florence: LeMonnier, 1917–18), 48–50.

53. The same body's statutes also dealt with problems raised by new practitioners and attempted to discipline them through the *fama* of six witnesses. And only two witnesses "fide dignos" were needed "probantes de publica fama" regarding anyone involved in renting a fulling mill (*gualcheria*) (ibid., 102–3, 109–11).

loss was not to be taken lightly. *Fama* also gives us proof of William Miller's admonition that "there is a great risk in talking about a culture's sense of personhood, or sense of self or individuation. The risk is to assume that all people within a culture are governed by the same view."[54] Certainly, whatever the sense of self that may be involved, we have to recognize that views of one's *fama* could be different in different social circles and different within and outside the law. The ability of Florentines to be *furbo* depended on these differences. The 1477 law that sought to control a number of legal acts was merely the culmination of legislative steps taken in that area over the previous century and more.

Legal devices that changed status sometimes belied or undercut social expectations and knowledge. Emancipations freed sons from paternal legal control and dissolved mutual liabilities between fathers and sons. Repudiations of inheritance absolved people from being heirs, whether by testament or intestacy. Consignation of dowry returned dotal property to a woman's control, although she remained married, on the grounds that her husband was mismanaging his affairs and verging on insolvency. In all these cases, however, *publica fama* might well be that so-and-so was someone's son, or his heir, or manager of dotal property. Here, where legal fact and *publica fama* could diverge and in that divergence present opportunities for defrauding the unwary, the solution hit upon in each case was a registration of legal acts, an alternative source of knowledge and one more powerful than *fama*. The registration was not only enrollment in a book, however; it was also a matter of sending a herald into the appropriate streets and neighborhoods to proclaim the legal deed to the same ears that heard and knew the prevailing *fama*. Only if one failed to register the emancipation, for example, and thus did not offer the corrective to *fama*, was *fama* to prevail and the legal act to be deemed fraudulent and fictitious.[55] Interestingly, registration was not required for an act such as legitimation, which (re)created a relationship and liabilities, although that may have been because such acts were so few (as were dotal adjustments for bankruptcy) and not because they were otherwise so well known or liable to be publicized.

Legal Capacities

As a more or less personal substance, *fama* figured in legal acts in one of two ways—either as the *fama* of witnesses, notaries, or others who estab-

54. Miller, *Humiliation*, 226 n. 28.
55. On these, see my *Emancipation in Late Medieval Florence* (New Brunswick, N.J.: Rutgers University Press, 1982) and "Law, Death, and Heirs in the Renaissance: Repudiation of Inheritance in Florence," *Renaissance Quarterly* 45 (1992): 484–516; Julius Kirshner, "Wives' Claims against Insolvent Husbands in Late Medieval Italy," in *Women of the Medieval World: Essays in Honor of John H. Mundy* (Oxford: Blackwell, 1985), 256–303.

lished the facticity of matters, or as an attribute of one of the principals to a transaction. In the first instance, there were serious problems in accepting the testimony of a witness who was himself *infamis*. When faced with a case in which the *fama* of an accusatory witness was impugned by some witnesses but not by others, the jurist Angelo degli Ubaldi (1327–1400) drove a distinction between the time at which the impugned witness gave testimony and the later time at which his *fama* was said to be *mala*. Disqualification required that he be of *mala fama* at the time of his testimony. In the case at hand, Angelo decided that neither set of witnesses provided sufficient proof of the man's *fama* and that when "in doubt one is to presume good condition and *fama*, because it is the presumption in conformity with nature."[56]

The *fama* of officials also affected legal acts. The jurist Paolo di Castro (ca. 1360–1441) claimed that acts of a count palatine were invalidated "propter infamiam notoriam." Such infamy might not remove him from office but it disqualified him from exercising the office.[57] Notaries too had to be of good *fama* as public recorders and certifiers of legal acts. If a notary's *fama* was denigrated (except by casting doubt on legitimacy of birth, which is discussed below), then, said Angelo degli Ubaldi, no *fides* was to be shown to his legal instruments if their truth were plausibly placed in doubt. The notariate was a "vile and abject" profession, so *bona fama* was required for instruments to be accepted.[58]

One of the more interesting areas of law in which *fama* played a role was that of illegitimacy of birth. Here a *fama facti* of the conditions of procreation issued directly in a *fama legalis* of disability and deprecation of the illegitimate person. To call someone illegitimate was to defame him. The rule in canon law was that the person defending his legitimacy should be more easily admitted to court than his adversary because legitimacy was positive or favorable (*favorabilis*), while its opposite was clearly negative or harmful (*odiosa*). But whether the defendant should be given a proclamation of legitimacy (a legal status) or simply a cease-and-desist order against

56. Angelo degli Ubaldi, *Consilia* (Frankfurt, 1575), *cons.* 309, fols. 216vb–17vb, at 217rb: "in dubio ergo praesumendum est bonae conditionis et famae, quia est praesumptio conformis naturae."

57. Paolo di Castro, *Consilia*, 2 vols. (n.p., 1522), vol. 1, *cons.* 190, fols. 87ra–88ra, at 87vb. This was only one argument among several aimed at striking down this legitimation, which was at the heart of the case.

58. Angelo, *Consilia*, *cons.* 284, fol. 198rb:

Et si virtutibus pollet et fama, suis instrumentis fides adhiberi debet plenarie. . . . Si autem fama denigrata est, aliter quam per nativitatem ortum, tunc licet instrumenta ab eo confecta subsistant, non tamen est fides in dubio adhibenda: sed veritas instrumentorum eius in dubium revocatur. . . . Nam cum notarius vilis et abiectus reputetur, vacillat fides instrumentorum ipsius rei in dubium revocata.

In this regard the medieval notariate resembles the situation Geertz finds in Islamic law (see *Local Knowledge*, 191–93).

his defamers was not a settled matter.[59] What was certain was that legitimation restored the *fama* of an illegitimate, requalifying him for civil and ecclesiastical offices and honors.[60] But an illegitimate's poor *fama* did not disqualify him or her completely from all social and legal roles. Angelo degli Ubaldi's assertion that the office of scribe (*tabellio*) was "vile" (*vilis*), as a scribe issued mere "public proofs" (*provi publici*) that were not in themselves true legal proofs, allowed that even *spurii* (those marked by a lower form of illegitimacy) could serve in that office and draw up instruments.[61]

What lay behind the *infamia* of illegitimate birth was the *fama* of the facts of filiation. For the paradox of illegitimacy was that a relationship to a father, or lack thereof, as well as the relationship of the father to the mother, had to be public knowledge. But the relationship to the father was not subject to definitive proof. As Paolo di Castro put it when he began to consider a case circulating about revocation of a gift, "correct filiation is not proven, as direct proof of filiation is impossible . . . and not even indirect proof, which is made by conjecture."[62] He was looking at a person whose mother was married, so he had to raise doubt as to whether this child was by the mother's husband or her lover. And he had to assert that it did not matter that the lover had taken the child and treated her as his own.[63] He left the final determination of filiation in this instance to the *advocatus* on the scene.

The relation between *publica fama* in the streets and personal *fama* is perhaps nowhere more apparent than in cases concerning illegitimacy and filiation, in which practicing attorneys were called on to provide expert guidance to courts and litigants. In 1515 Antonio Strozzi took part in a case between Vincenzo di Benedetto di Simone Rustichelli and Sulpizia di Francesco di Simone Rustichelli, his cousin. The issue was whether Vincenzo was indeed kin to Sulpizia such that he could by statute force her to arbitrate certain matters with him. Strozzi, acting on behalf of Vincenzo, noted that Benedetto in his testament had called Vincenzo his son and named him as heir, so at the least there was a semblance of filiation (*quasi possessio filiationis*) because Vincenzo had been treated as a son. This shifted the burden of proof to the other party in the suit. It constituted a proba-

59. As Innocent IV to c. Causam que, Qui filii sint legitimi (X.4.17.7), *Commentaria in v libros decretalium* (Frankfurt, 1570; reprint, Frankfurt am Main: Minerva, 1968), fol. 479vb. Also Antonio Roselli, *Tractatus legitimationum*, in *Tractatus universi iuris*, 29 vols. (Venice, 1584), vol. 8, part 2, fols. 75ra–90va, at 80ra.

60. Innocent IV to c. Per venerabilem (X.4.17.13), *Commentaria*, fol. 481ra–va.

61. Angelo, *cons.* 284 above, and Angelo's *consilium* (using some of the same language) in Biblioteca Apostolica Vaticana, Vat. Lat. 8068, fol. 73r–v.

62. Paolo di Castro, *Consilia*, vol. 2, *cons.* 434, fols. 225rb–va, at 225rb: "recta filiatio probata non est cum directa probatio filiationis sit impossibilis . . . item nec etiam indirecta que fit ex coniecturis."

63. Ibid.: "et tamen ipsam esse legitime natam videlicet ex matre sua et ex eius marito . . . non ergo sequitur habita et tractata fuit ut filia ab isto d. Francisco: igitur eius erat filia."

ble proof (which was stronger than a presumptive proof established by extrinsic acts, such as the father calling Vincenzo his son in front of others, though less than the "necessary" proof that could apply to maternity). In fact, although the testament had been drafted forty-five years earlier, testimony "by all who know him" asserted that Vincenzo was Benedetto's son.[64] Strozzi thus established a presumptive filiation that rested on *fama* (though he did not use the term).

In another case Strozzi dealt with a gift to a father from his illegitimate son that the son attempted to revoke after the father's death. Seeking to remove the gift from the estate he would now have to share with his siblings, the son raised doubts about the proof of all the good things the father had done for him (the father's *benemerita*). As these were presumably the very acts for which the gift had been given, Strozzi, in arguing against the son, characterized the gift as a remunerative act motivated by the father's generosity toward the son. Strozzi brought to bear no less than nine substantiations of the *benemerita*, the eighth of which turned to *fama*. Witnesses had declared that the father had treated this illegitimate child just as he had his twelve legitimate children, whereas at Pisa "others who have legitimate and natural sons usually treat their spurious sons like servants and slaves."[65] This son, however, had been sent to school and apprenticed in the wool trade. He had been legitimated and named as an heir along with the other sons, despite the fact that a *spurius* was *infamis infamia facti*. Legitimation had restored his *fama,* and "it is clear that *fama* is to be preferred to all monetary convenience."[66] In the context of the witnesses' statements about the lad's treatment at the hands of this father, it was a multivalent *fama* that the son had gained. The judgment was that the gift should remain valid.[67] In this case *fama* was an established matter of status, thanks to the legitimation, and that in turn established *benemerita* and the subsequent judgment. As a professional acting for clients where witnesses were known and deposable, Strozzi did not hesitate to invoke *fama* to strengthen his case.

In the Rustichelli case Strozzi looked at a matter of "common knowledge" and turned it into a presumptive status (filiation). In the second case he faced *fama* as status (by means of legitimation) and the general knowledge, which it confirmed, of *benemerita*. In both instances he had no reason to question the *fama*, and thus credibility, of the witnesses. We can

64. ASF, Carte strozziane, 3rd ser., 41/9, fols. 306r–7v. The date of February 1514/15 appears at the top of the first page.
65. ASF, Carte strozziane, 3rd ser., 41/3, fols. 410r–18r, at 414v–15r: "alii qui habent filios legittimos et naturales soleant tractare filios spurios tanquam famulos et sclavos."
66. Ibid., fol. 415v: "clarum est autem quod fama omni commodo pecuniario prefertur." Strozzi went so far as to assert "causa fame et causa vite equiparantur."
67. And Strozzi returned to the theme of *fama* to demolish a counterargument that legitimation was not a paternal *benemeritum*, ibid., fol. 417r.

consider a third case, however, in which witness evidence and the crucial deathbed confession of the wife and mother presented contradictory versions of *publica fama*. Here the problem of the character and situation of a female—wife of one man and mother to their child, adulterous lover with another man—was at least part of the problem.[68]

This case arose in December 1533 and involved the Panciatichi of Pistoia. The consulting attorneys (*consultores*), bound by longstanding ties of patronage and marital relationships (*parentado*) to them, were Niccolò di Luigi Guicciardini (1500–1557) and his famous cousin, the statesman, historian, and attorney Francesco di Piero (1483–1540).[69] Bartolomeo Panciatichi's brother Piero, who had the advantage of being in possession of the estate, contested the claims of one Giovanni to be the legitimated son of Bartolomeo. The argument against Giovanni was that, because his mother had been married to the notary Claude de Vegio of Lyon, he was Claude's son. That his mother, Jana Gagliarda, could be proved to have had adulterous relations with Bartolomeo Panciatichi did not vitiate the presumption of legitimate birth (unless it could be shown that Claude had been impotent or otherwise did not have intercourse with his wife), as "by favor of marriage, by favor of legitimacy, one presumes rather the honest possibility than the dishonorable."[70] It would have been too easy to throw all filiation into doubt unless such rules were followed. In the case at hand the legal presumption was bolstered by the fact of Claude's cohabitation with Jana at the time of conception in the same house in which Giovanni was later born.[71] That fact began the second line of argument, that Claude had treated this child as his own—"for he suffered him to be born in his house, and it is not plausible that he would have permitted it so evidently and with kin and neighbors knowing it if he knew he was another's son."[72]

---

68. Anne Lefebvre-Teillard shows that the word of a wife counted for more than that of a concubine, which was in turn worth more than that of a servant; see "Mulieri asserenti se ex operibus alicuius praegnantem, an credi debeat, etiamsi hoc medio affirmet iuramento? Les origines d'une célèbre 'decisio' de N. Boerius," in *Proceedings of the Ninth International Congress of Medieval Canon Law*, Munich, 13–18 July 1992, ed. Peter Landau and Joers Mueller, Monumenta Iuris Canonici, Series C: Subsidia, vol. 10 (Vatican City: Biblioteca Apostolica Vaticana, 1997), 575–93.

69. In an illuminating study, Osvaldo Cavallar has examined the elder Francesco's corrections of Niccolò's preliminary draft of this *consilium* to see how the corrections accord with Francesco's views of the rule of law; see *Francesco Guicciardini giurista: I ricordi degli onorari*, Per la storia del pensiero giuridico moderno 36 (Milan: Giuffrè, 1991), 179–80, 295–96. I owe Osvaldo thanks not merely for drawing my attention to this case but also for an elegant typed transcription with annotation.

70. Biblioteca Nazionale Centrale, Firenze, Fondo principale II, ii, 378, fols. 59r–77v, at 59v: "favore matrimonii, favore legittimitatis, et ut potius praesumatur possibile honestum quam possibile inhonestum."

71. Ibid., fol. 61v.

72. Ibid., fol. 62r: "nam passus est nasci in domo sua, quod non est verisimile eum permisisse si scivisset filium alienum saltem palam et consanguineis et vicinis scientibus."

Claude saw to the boy's baptism, education, food, and clothing, as witnesses confirmed. Giovanni had been sent to study in Paris and Toulouse at his father's expense, as appeared in the books of the del Bene firm in Florence. A notarial instrument affirming Giovanni's clerical status as a university student termed him the legitimate and natural son of Claude. Witnesses also testified that Claude treated Giovanni as a son—walking arm-in-arm with him through Lyon's streets.[73] They testified that Giovanni called himself Claude's son and was generally known as Giovanni de Vegio.[74] The most convincing ("fundamento inconvincibili") demonstration was that Claude named him his heir along with his other son, Antonio, whose parentage was not in doubt.[75]

Indeed, according to the *consilium,* all this witness testimony added up to a seemingly undeniable *fama:*

> This amounts to public voice and *fama* lodged by many witnesses, who prove it conclusively at least as far as kin and neighbors whose knowledge and opinion is principally attended to in this matter . . . and although *fama* alone may not prove filiation . . . still joined with the linked evidence it proves it . . . and especially thus in our case in which it cannot be said that it is an empty rumor or voice, as it arose among honest persons and is what they truly know, namely about the father and mother, about neighboring kin, about education, about support offered by Claude, about his testament, about a sentence issued against the fisc: so from causes leading to a legal presumption, namely from birth in Claude's house, from Claude's and Jana's marriage, from their cohabitation at the time of conception, by which causes there is no doubt that *fama* yields a full proof.[76]

But within this complicated case there was also a contrary *fama* to be weighed: the treatment shown Giovanni by Bartolomeo Panciatichi. Here

73. Ibid., fols. 64v–65r: "Item probatum est, quod ostendebat signa dilectionis deferendo eum saepissime et quandoque ducendo ad bracchia per civitatem Lugduni."
74. Ibid., fols. 66v–67v.
75. Ibid., fol. 65r.
76. Ibid., fols. 67v–68r:

Accedit vox et fama publica deposita per multos testes, qui probant eam concludenter saltem quo ad consanguineos et vicinos, quorum scientia et opinio principaliter in hac materia attenditur . . . et licet fama sola non probet filiationem . . . tamen iuncta cum adminiculis probat . . . et praesertim ita dicendum in casu nostro in quo non potest dici quod sit vanus rumor seu vana vox, cum habeat hortum ab honestis personis et quae id verisimiliter sciebant, scilicet a patre et matre, a consanguineis vicinis, ab educatione, ab alimentis praestitis a Cl., a testamento eius, a sententia lata contra fiscum: item a causis inducentibus praesumptionem iuris, scilicet a nativitate in domo Cl., a matrimonio Cl. et Janae, a cohabitatione eorum tempore conceptionis, quibus causis non est dubium quod fama inducat plenam probationem.

After "fama inducat" Niccolò Guicciardini had first written "vehementem praesumptionem et forte," but Francesco, more aware of ambiguity in law, had scratched those words out. Similar revocation of "famam publicam praesertim inter vicinos et consanguineos" comes later (fol. 69r).

the authors of the *consilium*, the Guicciardini, had to be every bit as clever. To Giovanni's claim that Panciatichi's parenthood lay behind his role as godparent, they responded that if he was Giovanni's natural father he could not be godparent without committing a crime. To claims that he had expended sums for the boy, they replied that there was no proof of the authenticity of the account books produced to substantiate the payments. To testimony by Raffaele Corsini that at Panciatichi's request he had delivered money to Jana for Giovanni, the Guicciardini reminded the court of other motives: "So the witness does not depose from knowledge as to why said moneys were given to Jana, and it could be due to love because, as they assert, Bartolomeo was her lover."[77] Other witnesses similarly did not present specific knowledge of Panciatichi's deeds or intentions. Then there was Giovanni's argument that Panciatichi suffered his son to be raised by Claude so as to protect Jana's honor, or that Claude likewise played out a fiction for her sake. But the Guicciardini found it hard to believe that Claude would persist so long in "this artifice." Having borne all the work to make the boy appear to be his son, any assertion to the contrary would prove nothing.[78] It was no more credible that Jana would be able to maintain such a fiction. The Guicciardini took the opportunity to rail against the audacity of such witnesses who testified against all reality ("contra omnem verisimilitudinem") and every honest sense of prudent men ("sensum honestum prudentum"). The veracity of several witnesses was questioned in some detail.

That the son received filial treatment from Panciatichi when he was later in Italy (apparently something that could not be denied by questioning the credibility of the witnesses) did not change his birth status, "and it also was not in Claude's power and Jana's to remove their son and give him to another."[79] More weakly, the jurists denied the relevance of the legitimation performed after Claude's death and Jana's deathbed confession, for she was suspected of wanting to give her child claim to an "opulentissimam hereditatem,"[80]

> because the contrary is proven by the plaintiff's witnesses, who are seen to depose conclusively about public voice and *fama*, from which it appears either that the *fama* and common opinion were that Giovanni was Claude's son, or

77. Ibid., fol. 72r–v: "sic testis non deponit de scientia, quare darentur Janae dictae pecuniae, et potuit esse propter amorem, ex quo ut ipsi asserunt B. erat eius amasius."

78. Ibid., fol. 73r–v. For a sense of the ridicule one might face for raising another's bastard as one's own (hence the power of the presumption the Guicciardini exploited), see Jane Fishburne Collier, *From Duty to Desire: Remaking Families in a Spanish Village* (Princeton: Princeton University Press, 1997), 71–72.

79. Biblioteca Nazionale Centrale, Firenze, Fondo principale II, ii, 378, fol. 75v: "nec etiam fuisset in potestate Cl. et Janae simul subripere sibi filium et dare alteri."

80. Ibid., fols. 75v–76r.

that men have various opinions, some respecting the marriage and birth and education in Claude's house, some the rumor of love and suspicion of adultery between Bartolomeo and Jana; and so, at least *fama* and common opinion do not overturn [the filiation between Giovanni and Claude].[81]

There was at least a countervailing *fama* that accorded well with legal presumptions of paternity in a cohabiting husband. In the eyes of the Guicciardini, that countervailing *fama* was decisive.

Conclusion

In fact, the sham to which Giovanni's witnesses testified was possible—hence the presumed credibility of their testimony. Once in a great while one finds evidence that men of elevated social standing were able to enjoy sexual congress with women of lesser standing, especially in foreign locations, and pass the child off as the husband's.[82] There was clearly something between Bartolomeo Panciatichi and Jana Gagliarda, and there was some evidence that Giovanni showed filial affection to Bartolomeo while the two were in Italy. Even if Giovanni was able to establish filiation, there was a powerful tendency in law to admit a legitimate brother in preference to him (the Guicciardini family had its own case of that sort).[83] He probably settled for something much less than the entire "opulent" estate Bartolomeo had left. For our purposes, it is instructive how *fama* was here exposed as multiple. While it could operate in law in probative contexts and was treated as probative to some extent, *fama* could never be fully probative, because in the end it was opinion, not knowledge, even when held by many. We also see here *fama* being contested on the basis of what the lawyers saw as plausibility or implausibility. Whether or not their arguments held sway, we are reminded that law defined what *fama* was for its own purposes.

Simona Cerutti has argued forcefully that summary judicial procedure was a device by which social practices were allowed to influence and shape norms or their application.[84] *Fama* can easily be seen as similar. But Cerut-

---

81. Ibid., fol. 76r:

Item quia testes actoris probant contrarium, qui videntur deponere concludentius de publica voce et fama, ex quibus apparet vel quod fama et communis opinio erat quod G. esset filius Cl., vel saltem ostendunt quod homines super hoc varie opinabantur respicientes aliqui ad matrimonium et nativitatem et educationem in domo Cl., aliqui ad rumorem amoris et adulterii suspicioni inter B. et Janam, et sic saltem fama et communis opinio non ostabunt.

82. See my *Illegitimacy in Renaissance Florence,* 137, 145–46, 180.
83. Ibid., 105–6.
84. Simona Cerutti, "Normes et pratiques, ou de la légitimité de leur opposition," in *Les formes de l'expérience: Une autre histoire sociale,* ed. Bernard Lepetit (Paris: Albin Michel, 1995), 127–49.

ti's argument goes farther as she attempts to cast doubt on any opposition between norms and practices, to accord them equal analytical status, and thus to see practices as productive of norms.[85] Certainly the characterizations, imaginings, and narratives of witness testimony complicated the relations of norms and practices or of facts and law. And, as Geertz has noted, the normative and experiential have to seem but versions of the same reality for a legal system to be viable.[86] But in courts of law, especially before the development of state-controlled and -staffed courts, which in Florence began with the Ruota of 1502,[87] what jurists said finally carried the day, or at least could not easily be dismissed. Their authority rested on knowledge of norms taken as preexisting (even eternal in some cases). Norms definitely constrained the space permitted to that bundle of social practices, experiences, and knowledge that is *fama*.

85. Ibid., 133–37. She uses my *Law, Family, and Women: Toward a Legal Anthropology of Renaissance Italy* (Chicago: University of Chicago Press, 1991) as an example of the limitations of posing an opposition between norms and practices.

86. Geertz, *Local Knowledge*, 175.

87. See Mario Ascheri, *Tribunali, giuristi e istituzioni dal medioevo all'età moderna* (Bologna: Il Mulino, 1989), 85–183.

CHAPTER THREE

Silent Witnesses, Absent Women, and the Law Courts in Medieval Germany

MADELINE H. CAVINESS AND CHARLES G. NELSON

Fama is part of an accusatorial process in Saxon territorial law, as seen—literally—in the fourteenth-century illustrated recensions of a customary-law book of major importance in German legal history, the *Sachsenspiegel*, or *Saxon Mirror*.[1] Of particular interest is the way in which *bona fama* and *mala fama* intersect with gender in the illustrations accompanying the text. Among these intersections were proscriptions concerning women's public speech that ensured that men talk to men about women in the courts. To support a charge of rape (a woman talking about a man), the most persuasive evidence a woman could muster lay in her physical appearance, not her word (she had to appear disheveled). Men, on the other hand, could avoid prosecution by taking an oath of innocence (*Reinigungseid, iuramentum purgationis*), or might assemble six (male) witnesses (*gezugen selb sibende*) to speak on their behalf. Each of these situations is elaborated below. Analyses are based largely on the images, with appropriate attention to the text, and especially on the hand gestures of the figures when they stand for various kinds of speech that is often defamatory.

The *Sachsenspiegel* is one of the earliest German law books,[2] a compila-

We are grateful to Pamela Sheingorn for a copy of her response to this paper, which suggested some new departures. Her comments helped clarify our argument.

1. Because of the complicated manuscript tradition of this law book, which evolved through some four hundred and sixty manuscripts from its late thirteenth-century origination until the advent of printing, there is no possibility of a definitive edition. A readily available text-only version is one prepared from a fourteenth-century manuscript by Friedrich Ebel, ed., *Sachsenspiegel Landrecht und Lehnrecht* (Stuttgart: Reclam, 1993).

2. Together with the *Mühlhauser Rechtsbuch*, which is considered to have been made at approximately the same time; see Adalbert Erler et al., ed., *Handwörterbuch zur deutschen Rechtsgeschichte* (Berlin: Erich Schmidt, 1998), 3:col. 722.

tion of orally transmitted Saxon legal customs undertaken by Eike von Rep-gow and completed between 1220 and 1224–27.[3] His patron was Hoyer von Falkenstein, advocate (*Stiftsvogt*) of the prestigious collegiate house for women at Quedlinburg, an Ottonian imperial house founded at that time.[4] Eike, as a freeman and "juror" (*Schöffe*), composed a first version of the *Sachsenspiegel* in Latin, but this is now lost. According to a medieval tex-tual tradition, Eike claimed to have been asked by Hoyer to translate this version into German.[5] Conceived as a law book embracing regional law (*Landrecht*) and feudal or fief law (*Lehnrecht*), it had widespread influence beyond the targeted Elbe-Saale basin. The German text, of which some four hundred and sixty manuscripts are extant, was one of the most fre-quently copied vernacular works of the Middle Ages.[6] In addition to the Middle and Low German versions, it was translated back into Latin, and into Dutch, Polish, Czech, and Russian. It became the basis of two south German law books: the *Schwabenspiegel* (1275) and the *Deutschenspiegel* (1275). Various of its pronouncements found their way into a number of important municipal law books (*Weichbilder*) and collections of jury-court decisions (*Schöffensammlungen*).[7]

The entire production of *Sachsenspiegel* texts has been classified into a number of categories following formal, linguistic, and content-related criteria.[8] Prominent among these categories is one designating a group of richly illustrated texts. Four remarkable large picture books survive, though some scholars believe that at least seven were made before 1400.

3. Ibid., 1:col. 896.

4. John W. Bernhardt, *Itinerant Kingship and Royal Monasteries in Early Medieval Germany, c. 936–1075,* Cambridge Studies in Medieval Life and Thought (Cambridge: Cambridge Uni-versity Press, 1993), 138–49.

5. This assumption originates in lines 261–280 from the rhymed preface to the *Sachsen-spiegel,* whose authorship is also attributed to Eike: "Now everyone thanks the lord of Falken-stein, who is called Count Hoyer, for having this book translated into German; Eike von Repgow did this" (lines 261–66).

6. Ruth Schmidt-Wiegand, "Der Sachsenspiegel: Überlieferungs- und Editionsprob-leme," in *Der Sachsenspiegel als Buch,* ed. Ruth Schmidt-Wiegand and Dagmar Hüpper, Ger-manistische Arbeiten zu Sprache und Kulturgeschichte (Frankfurt am Main: Peter Lang, 1991), 1:24, where the reference is to some four hundred and sixty mss. including fragments. It should not be assumed, however, that these are all supported by a single unified text. They reflect rather a variety of forms and versions as they evolved into the fifteenth century, when further development ceases. See Rolf Lieberwirth, "Die Wirkungsgeschichte des Sachsen-spiegels," in Eike von Repgow, *Sachsenspiegel: Die Wolfenbütteler Bilderhandschrift Cod. Guelf. 3.1 Aug. 2°,* edited by Ruth Schmidt-Wiegand, vol. 3: *Aufsätze und Untersuchungen: Kommentarband zur Faksimile-Ausgabe* (Berlin: Akademie, 1993), 63–64.

7. Ruth Schmidt-Wiegand in the introductions to the text volumes of the Wolfenbüttel and Oldenburg facsimiles: Eike von Repgow, *Sachsenspiegel,* vol. 2: *Textband;* and Ruth Schmidt-Wiegand, ed., *Die Oldenburger Bilderhandschrift des Sachsenspiegel* (Berlin: Niedersächsische Sparkassenstiftung, 1993), 16–17.

8. See Karl Gustav Homeyer, *Die deutschen Rechtsbücher des Mittelalters und ihre Handschriften* (Weimar: H. Böhlaus Nachf., 1931–34), and Ulrich-Dieter Oppitz, *Deutsche Rechtsbücher des Mittelalters,* vol. 1: *Beschreibung der Handschriften* (Cologne: Böhlau, 1990).

They are informally called after their present-day locations in Heidelberg (H, 1295–1304), Oldenburg (O, 1336), Dresden (D, 1295–1363), and Wolfenbüttel (W, 1348–1362/71).[9] These dates, except that for O, which is precisely dated in a colophon, are based on the heraldry represented in each book.[10] Fortunately, a facsimile of each manuscript is available for study, although we were also privileged to be able to examine the originals.[11]

Before arguing the thesis of this article, we must make several points about the pictorial cycles in all four manuscripts.[12] The German scholarship on the text-image relationship in the Middle Ages in general and in the *Sachsenspiegel* picture books in particular is voluminous.[13] It moves from a position regarding the illustrations as subordinate to the text, to one acknowledging interdependence between the two.[14] Eventually, one art historian, Norbert Ott, suggested more autonomy for the pictures. While we recognize that these images were created subsequent to the text, we argue that in the extant manuscripts it is the *pictorial cycle* that establishes the authority of the *text* through dramatic visual strategies. Although pictorial and written record each occupy one of the double columns of the

9. A useful comparison of all four was made in Ruth Schmidt-Wiegand and Wolfgang Milde, eds., *Gott ist selber Recht. Die vier Bilderhandschriften des Sachsenspiegels: Oldenburg, Heidelberg, Wolfenbüttel, Dresden [Ausstellung in der Schatzkammer der Bibliotheca Augusta vom 12. Februar bis 11. März]* (Wolfenbüttel: Herzog August Bibliothek, 1993).

10. See the stemma by Schmidt-Wiegand in Eike von Repgow, *Sachsenspiegel*, vol. 3: *Kommentarband*, based on Klaus Nass, "Die Wappen in den Bilderhandschriften des Sachsenspiegels: Zu Herkunft und Alter der Codices Picturati," in *Text-Bild-Interpretation: Untersuchungen zu den Bilderhandschriften des Sachsenspiegels*, Münstersche Mittelalter-Schriften 55/I: *Textband*, ed. Ruth Schmidt-Wiegand and Dagmar Hüpper (Munich: Fink, 1986). Manuscript numbers and references to facsimiles are supplied below.

11. H: Heidelberg, Universitätsbibliothek, cod.pal.germ. 164. See Walter Koschorreck, *Der Sachsenspiegel. Die Heidelberger Bilderhandschrift Cod.Pal.Germ. 164*, ed. Wilfried Werner (Frankfurt am Main: Insel, 1989); O: Oldenburg, Landesbibliothek, Cim I 410, see Schmidt-Wiegand, ed., *Die Oldenburger Bilderhandschrift des Sachsenspiegel;* D: Dresden, Sächsischen Landesbibliothek, Dr. M 32, see Karl von Amira, *Die Dresdener Bilderhandschrift des Sachsenspiegels I: Facsimile der Handschrift* (Osnabrück: Otto Zeller, 1968); W: Wolfenbüttel, Herzog August Bibliothek, Cod. Guelf. 3.1, see Eike von Repgow, *Sachsenspiegel*, vol. 1: *Faksimile.*

12. These observations apply almost equally to a small group of contemporary German manuscripts, including the Willehalm fragment in Munich, Staatsbibliothek, Cgm 193.III, as noticed also by Norbert Ott, "Vorläufige Bemerkungen zur 'Sachsenspiegel'–Ikonographie," in *Text-Bild-Interpretation*, vol. 1: *Textband*, 36–38. Although more than half of each folio of the Biblia Pauperum in Weimar (Thüringische Landesbibliothek, Fol. Max. 4) is given to pictures, the text is on both sides of them. Edith Rothe, *Medieval Book Illumination in Europe in the Collections of the GDR* (New York: Routledge, 1968), 211, 251 pl. 60.

13. See Dagmar Hüpper, "Die Bildersprache. Zur Funktion der Illustration," in Eike von Repgow, *Sachsenspiegel*, vol. 3: *Kommentarband*, 143–62, and esp. note 23 for basic bibliography. Also Norbert Ott, "Vorläufige Bemerkungen zur Sachsenspiegel Ikonographie," in *Text-Bild-Interpretation*, vol. 1: *Textband*, 33–44; and Norbert Ott, "Rechtsikonographie zwischen Mündlichkeit und Schriftlichkeit: Der Sachsenspiegel im Kontext deutschsprachiger illustrierter Handschriften," in Eike von Repgow, *Sachsenspiegel*, vol. 3: *Kommentarband*, 119–41.

14. See Ott, "Vorläufige Bemerkungen," esp. p. 40.

49

folio, the paintings assert themselves more aggressively in a succession of registers (rows of pictures) that extend the full height of the page and in many cases spill over the vertical ruled frames, whereas the script is neatly confined to a fixed number of lines, leaving ample margins at top and bottom (see fig. 2). Where preserved, the colors are strident. There is a preponderance of bright red and green, sometimes creating parti-colored, striped, or plaid fabrics, combined with duller blues, yellows, and purples, and some gold leaf. Emphatically gesturing, overly large hands and the careless application of color washes add to the impression that here everything bursts from its boundaries. In each case, the figure drawing is very crude for the supposed dates, the figural types are extremely repetitive, and the execution appears cheap and hurried. There is a kind of shrillness and vulgarity about these pictures.

The reader encounters the pictures first, in the left column (in O to the right on the recto), and vari-colored initials among the images serve to index the corresponding section of the text, and to that extent, color invades the dense lines of Gothic *textualis* script (see, for example, figs. 1, 2, 5, 11a, b). Authoritative male figures, such as counts and kings and village headmen administering justice, are repeated in most registers, standing or seated, but always positioned adjacent to the text as if they were needed to lend it weight (see figs. 1, 5–9, 13–14). Michael Camille has written about the doubts and suspicion commonly cast on written documents in newly literate groups in the later Middle Ages.[15] We suppose that skepticism about the authority of the written word, as opposed to its enunciation, might be allayed by pictures that represent themselves as authoritative eyewitness accounts. All these qualities contribute to effective mnemonic functioning and to the impression that the pictorial record takes precedence over the written one. We do not negate textual primacy, but it is a question of how we read these illustrated recensions.

We use examples from the Dresden picture book almost exclusively here, for the reason that it is complete, unlike H and O, and it was the model for W, so it has some value as an original work. Furthermore, it lent itself well to our deciphering hand gestures because modern water damage has made the drawing more visible. Unfortunately, however, the parchment is now so darkened that the old black-and-white photographs, used for the original facsimile edition of 1902, will best serve as illustrations. Within the rather wide span of dates allowed by the heraldry, a time close to mid-fourteenth century is plausible for the style that derives from more elegant court productions.

To identify representations of *fama*, we need to understand the ways in

15. Michael Camille, "Seeing and Reading: Some Implications of Medieval Literacy and Illiteracy," *Art History* 8 (1985): 26–49.

which speech of various kinds is conveyed in these pictorial images, and why verbal communication was of great import to the artists and their audience. Oral exchange dominated the practice of "law" in the Middle Ages, which may explain why written codification of customary law and written court records are a relatively late development. During the thirteenth century, which has been called the century of the law book, a body of oral custom was being textualized in many regions of Europe. As in France, however, as F. R. P. Akehurst notes in this volume, written court records of cases did not yet exist in Germany. The figural representations in the four picture books of the law that we are examining place the viewer in touch with the oral exchanges that were essential to the working of the courts, in a way that the text does not. They therefore serve to overcome the doubts that a scarcely literate audience may have had about the authority of the book: users could see people taking oaths on relics, giving testimony, being charged, presenting cases, and so on, and the judges' responses were also rendered visible.[16] To do this rhetorical work, the figures had to operate as speaking signs, not just as visual records or allusions; the illustrators therefore employed a highly sophisticated and elaborate system of hand gestures to convey speech acts.

The problem of representing the content of speech was not new in the thirteenth century, when a first pictorial version of the *Sachsenspiegel* was probably produced. The author of the ninth-century *Libri Carolini* referred wittily to the difficulty painters have in representing what is said, but by the high Middle Ages various strategies had been developed to make speech visible, such as including scrolls with the spoken words inscribed, as Camille and others have shown.[17] Art historians have also taken pains to decode the various gestures that denote speech acts, and there are a number of useful recent studies. Yet, not surprisingly, one of the pioneering studies was legal historian Karl von Amira's 1905 analysis of the arm and hand positions in the fourteenth-century manuscripts of the *Sachsenspiegel* (see fig. 3).[18] Indeed, gesture is so important in the *Sachsenspiegel* manuscripts that the hands are exaggerated over other features (there are no speech-scrolls). Close scrutiny of the underdrawing in the Dresden manuscript of about 1350 reveals that the hands were often drawn first, sometimes overly large in relation to the figure, as with the woman on folio 16, register 3, and the judge in the next register below (fig. 1). In addition to

16. Ibid.

17. Caecilia Davis-Weyer, *Early Medieval Art 300–1150: Sources and Documents* (Toronto: University of Toronto Press, in association with the Medieval Academy of America, 1986), 100–103.

18. Karl von Amira, *Die Handgebärden in den Bilderhandschriften des Sachsenspiegels*, Abhandlungen der Bayerische Akademie der Wissenschaften, I. Kl., vol. 23/2 (Munich: Königlich Bayerische Akademie der Wissenschaften, 1905).

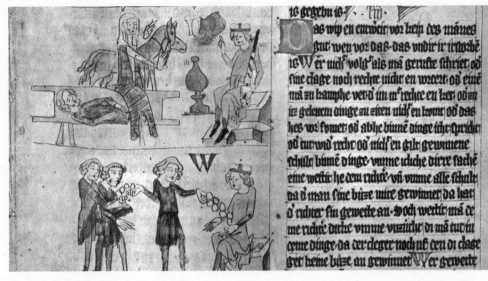

Figure 1. Dresden *Sachsenspiegel*, Mainz ca. 1295–1363. Upper register, a women testifies with respect to her deceased husband's property. Below, a lawbreaker pays a fine to a judge and damages to a plaintiff. Dresden, Sächsische Landesbibliothek, Dr. M 32, fol. 16, detail, registers 3–4, after the 1969 reprint of the facsimile. Reproduced with permission from Biblio Verlag, Bissendorf.

speaking/telling/listening, hand positions indicate feudal relationships, oaths taken, appeals denied, and so on. Later authors have integrated the observations of Amira into broader studies; François Garnier's book of 1982 is one of the most useful syntheses, providing a number of alternative readings to Amira's, though it tacitly claims (or constructs) gesture as a universal "medieval" code, a position we want to avoid (see fig. 4).[19] In codifying these gestures both authors relied on simplified line drawings that divorce the figure—or even the hands—from its context. Ruth Schmidt-Wiegand recognized the "intervisuality" (the ways images resonate with each other) of the gestural signs, and contextualized them to some extent, although she did not explore discrepancies between text and image, nor the ability of pictures to expand upon textual meanings.[20] Other studies of the function of gesture in various genres of art have followed; Moshe Barasch has written of the "speaking hand" in Giotto's paint-

19. François Garnier, *Le langage de l'image au Moyen Âge: Signification et symbolique* (Paris: Léopard d'Or, 1982).
20. Ruth Schmidt-Wiegand, "Gebärdensprache im Mittelalterlichen Recht," *Frühmittelalterliche Studien. Jahrbuch des Instituts für Frühmittelalterforschung der Universität Münster* 16 (1982), esp. 364–66 and 369.

ings.[21] Jean-Claude Schmitt has described the Middle Ages as a "civiliza-
tion of gesture," that is, a period when certain movements signified feudal
relationships as clearly and as incontrovertibly as written documents. Indeed, he sees in gesture a reflection of the hierarchical relationships between God and humans, man and woman, knight and subject.[22] Yet he was
little interested in pictorial representations of speech acts.[23]

To test Amira's method, we have recontextualized the gestures he codified. By way of an example, we first look at the images in the second prologue to the Dresden manuscript of about 1350 (fig. 2).[24] Of the four
books, this one has the most deftly drawn hands, clearly visible even in its
present damaged state. In the upper register, two rulers hold their right
hands aloft in a typical gesture of command, two fingers extended and the
palm held upward as in number 5b in Amira's chart (fig. 3). Eike approaches humbly from the left, inspired by the Holy Spirit and with an
empty scroll to indicate the conception of an as yet unwritten work.[25]
Eike's right hand is held up in the gesture used by witnesses elsewhere (fig.
3, nos. 3a, 3b, 12), two fingers extended and the palm turned forward, and
his left hand, fingers loosely open, rests at his waist, as is often the case with
witnesses.[26] By "testing" these gestures in other contexts, we can argue with
confidence that Eike's gesture here represents a speech act, namely, that
he is ready to testify or be a witness to the law.

In the next register, the Almighty is enthroned with attributes of book
and sword, as we will comment on later with respect to many earthly judges.
This image makes clear not only that the law stems from God or, as the text
says, "Got ist selber Recht" (God himself is law), but also casts the oaths
that will be taken before judges in the light of the "supernatural fear" invoked by Akehurst in this volume as an important ingredient of truth-find-
ing in the French courts. In our picture, a ruler next to the Almighty holds
his left hand up, all fingers extended, in what appears to be a sign of ac-

21. Moshe Barasch, *Giotto and the Language of Gesture* (Cambridge: Cambridge University
Press, 1987); Peter Burke, "The Language of Gesture in Early Modern Italy," in *A Cultural
History of Gesture from Antiquity to the Present Day,* ed. J. Bremmer and H. Roodenburg (Cam-
bridge: Polity, 1991); Jean-Claude Schmitt, *La raison des gestes dans l'occident médiéval* (Paris:
Gallimard, 1990).

22. Schmitt, *La raison des gestes,* 14–16, 357–58.

23. For Schmitt's thoughts on speaking gestures, see ibid., 253–60. It is a useful reminder
that systems of signing that are known to have existed among the deaf and dumb, and especially among monks in Lent, are not represented pictorially, and also that speaking gestures
are only a very small part of the medieval language of gesture.

24. Karl von Amira, ed., *Die Dresdener Bilderhandschrift des Sachsenspiegels,* 1st ed., vol. 1 (Leipzig: Karl W. Hiersemann Verlag, 1902).

25. Pamela Hoyt, "Creating Presence: Two Medieval Bibles and Their Embodiment of
God" (master's thesis, Tufts University, 1996), 36–37.

26. Schmitt, *La raison des gestes,* pl. 24, illustrates the same gestures in the witnesses to a
marriage in a fourteenth-century French manuscript of Gratian's *Decretals,* Paris, Bibliothèque Nationale de France, MS Lat. 3898, fol. 293.

es heilige geistis mmne o ster
ke mine sinne·Das ich rechr
vnre vnrecht o sachse beschei
re·Noch gocis hulden vn noch o
ivde vrimmen·Des en kan ich alleine niche
gerun·Dar vmme bite ich zu helfe alle du
re lute·di rechtis gern ab keine rede begei
ne·Dy min tvnime sin vor mide·vn da
dis buch niche von eu sprichit·das si das
noch rechte bescheire noch irme sinne·so tis
rechte wissen·von rechte en sal niernst wile
liebe noch leire zor'n noch gift·Got re sel
be recht dar vmme is yn recht lip·Dar vm
me sen si sich alle vor di den gerichte von
gocis halbin beuolin si·das sie also richir
alse gocis zorn vn sin gerichte genedi
clich vbir sie irgen muise·Got der da
is beginn vnre ende aller gurr dinge der
machter alrest himel vnre erce vn machir
den menschin merrriche vn satzte en in
das parads·der brach den gehorsam
vns allin zu schaden·Dar vmme ginge wir
irre alse oy herrelosin schaf·wen an dy
zyt das he vns irloste mit siner marter
Dv abir wir bekart sin·vnre vns got
widir geladin hat·so halde wir sine·e·vn
sin gebot·Das vns sine wisheit in gelart
habin·vn gure geistliche lute·vn ouch cri
stne kunige habin gesatzt constantin
vn karle in sachsin lanre nach sines rech
tis mitz

Figure 2. Dresden *Sachsenspiegel*, fol. 3v. Reg. 1, inspired by the Holy Spirit, Eike speaks of the law to Charlemag[ne] and Constantine. Reg. 2, God with a law book offers the sword of justice to a king. Reg. 3, God instructs Ada[m] Reg. 4, Adam and Eve partake of the fruit while the serpent looks on. Reproduced with permission from Bibl[io] Verlag, Bissendorf.

Figure 3. Karl von Amira's drawings of hand gestures after the illustrated *Sachsenspiegel* mss. From Amira, *Die Handgebärden in den Bilderhandschriften des Sachsenspiegels* (Munich: Königliche Bayerische Akademie der Wissenschaften, 1905).

ceptance (fig. 4, J, K), though Amira puts this type in a category of dissent (fig. 3, no. 8b). According to Garnier, this is multivalent.[27] The distinction lies in the angle of the arm and hand, a difficult thing to codify; the higher position of the hand, like an *orans* gesture, resonates with the obedient acceptance of the Virgin annunciate, whereas a lower position with flexed wrist likely indicates resistance.[28] In fact, the humble position of the king's right hand, held low with palm down, supports the interpretation that he is accepting God's command.

In the third register, the Almighty communicates aggressively with Adam, who approaches his throne in *proskenesis:* God holds up his right hand in a sign of refusal (fig. 3, no. 8b), and commands Adam with his left hand, apparently enunciating the command *not to* eat the fruit of the Tree of Life (fig. 3, no. 6a). Adam holds both palms open, in a gesture of acquiescence, according to Garnier rather than Amira (fig. 4).

In the final register, there is no speech. Eve does not tempt Adam to eat the fruit; in fact the serpent very unusually looks *Adam* in the face as he takes it. He and Eve both cover their genitals in shame, a postlapsarian gesture. Adam is fully culpable and therefore must answer to the law, whereas Eve has no direct relation to it. This sets the scene for the law as men's business, which it most decidedly is throughout the *Sachsenspiegel.*

Anxiety about women speaking was not, of course, confined to law courts, but the law provides a rich case study, even though no case law or court records exist for medieval Germany, which might have contained accounts of verbal communication. But if we do not know what actually happened, we have embedded in the regional and municipal law books the traditions, rationales, and attitudes about women and their speech that were institutionalized in legal practices. Women's words held almost no truth value. The *Sachsenspiegel,* which purports to record custom in Saxony, explains at the outset that women are not allowed to represent themselves in court because one once substituted a lewd gesture for speech (*Landrecht* [hereafter Ldr.] II, 63).[29] In each illustrated manuscript, this ill-reputed woman is shown standing before the royal judge (fig. 5, reg. 4). The moment is recorded in the Digest of Justinian (ruled 527–565) under the topic "Applications to the Magistrate":

> On the grounds of sex, he [i.e., Ulpian] forbids women to make applications
> on behalf of others. There is a reason for this prohibition, to prevent them
> from involving themselves in the cases of other people contrary to the modesty in keeping with their sex and to prevent women from performing the ac-

27. Garnier, *Le langage de l'image,* 174–79.
28. *Orans* (Latin "praying") signifies the early Christian way of representing a prayer gesture, with both hands at shoulder level, palms forward.
29. Schmitt, *La raison des gestes;* Koschorreck, *Der Sachsenspiegel.*

Figure 4. François Garnier, hand gestures in medieval art. After François Garnier, *Le langage de l'image au Moyen Âge,* copyright Le Léopard d'Or.

tions of men. Its introduction goes back to a shameless woman called Carfania who by brazenly making applications and annoying the magistrate gave rise to the edict.[30]

As this tradition found its way into the illustrated Saxon Mirrors, generally in the form of an amusing anecdote, Carfania became Calpurnia, and her "brazen behavior" is represented by a woman leaning aggressively forward and pointing upward with her index finger, an authoritative or commanding speaking gesture, according to Garnier and Amira; and she exhibits a brush-like tail appended to her backside (figs. 5, reg. 3; 3, no. 6a).[31] What has apparently happened is that the illustrator was aware of a gossipy embellishment found in a *Schwabenspiegel* manuscript from 1287 (Ldr. 245) in which it is alleged that Carfania scolded the king and bared her backside (*hinderschamme* or "rear pudenda") to the king.[32] As is so often the case in the law books, the possibility of representing women fairly, let alone positively, becomes an opportunity to do just the opposite. Such instances accrue to create for them a gratuitously negative reputation, that part of *fama* that robs their verbal testimony of validity. The mooning of the judge has no basis in fact or record, and its invention may well have

30. Alan Watson, ed., *The Digest of Justinian,* rev. ed., 2 vols. (Philadelphia: University of Pennsylvania Press, 1988). We are grateful to James Brundage for this reference.

31. Garnier, *Le langage de l'image,* 169.

32. F. L. A. von Lassberg, *Der Schwabenspiegel* (Tübingen: Ludwig Friedrich Fues, 1840), Ldr. 245.

Figure 5. Dresden *Sachsenspiegel*, fol. 34v, detail. Reg. 4, left, a cleric agrees to represent an outlawed man not eligible to appear in an ecclesiastical court; at right, an enraged Calefurnia misbehaves before the emperor (mooning him). Reg. 5, instances of cases where the "hue and cry" will initiate a court hearing. Reproduced with permission from Biblio Verlag, Bissendorf.

served to justify and prolong a practice by then going out of date; *mala fama,* in this instance, is part of memory. The silencing of "Calpurnia" evokes an imaginary field occupied by the normal stereotyping of gossiping women, the wagging tongues and fingers that all men feared, even though the *Sachsenspiegel* does not contain specific clauses about defamation as a category of legislated behavior. The image, combining verbal and sexual aggression, also invokes the association of vulva and mouth that was a part of medieval popular lore—or, as Irigaray stated in this century, the female's possession of horizontal and vertical lips.[33] With this powerful im-

33. Luce Irigaray, "This Sex Which Is Not One," trans. Claudia Reeder, in *New French Feminisms: An Anthology,* ed. Elaine Marks and Isabelle de Courtivron (New York: Schocken, 1981), 99–106. Talking cunts commonly figure in the earlier French *fabliaux,* and Ro-

Figure 6. Dresden *Sachsenspiegel*, fol. 8v, detail, register 5. A Swabian (man) takes hold of a stalk of grain (symbolizing his inheritance) while pushing away unqualified (female) non-Swabians. (The text is sex-blind.) Reproduced with permission from Biblio Verlag, Bissendorf.

age, women's speech is discredited in the *Sachsenspiegel* so that they are prevented from making application to magistrates for others or for themselves.

An earlier clause in Ldr. I, 17, to the effect that a Swabian could not inherit from the woman's side can be understood in the context of denying privilege to women because of "the transgressions of their female ancestors." And in folio 8v, 5, we see two women vainly gesturing as witnesses while being pushed to the outer margin of the page by a short-haired Swabian, who lays claim before a judge to his inheritance, represented as cultivated plants (fig. 6).[34] The text, Ldr. I, 18, then states that Saxon law follows Swabian law, rather than that of Charlemagne, "durch der wibe haz" (in "enmity towards women"). This is illustrated at the top of the following folio by a woman directly addressing Charlemagne, whose status, however, is not that of the emperors in the prologue because he lacks the elaborate throne and canopy accorded them (figs. 7; 2, reg. 1).[35] She

manesque and Gothic sculptures of exhibiting women holding their labia open are widespread in western Europe: See several essays in Jan Ziolkowski, ed., *Obscenity: Social Control and Artistic Creation in the European Middle Ages*, vol. 4 (Leiden: Brill, 1998), notably those by Bloch, Caviness, and Ford.

34. Maria Dobozy, ed., *The Saxon Mirror: A* Sachsenspiegel *of the Fourteenth Century*, Middle Ages Series (Philadelphia: University of Pennsylvania Press, 1999), 74.

35. Madeline H. Caviness, "Putting the Judge in His P(a)Lace: Pictorial Authority in the *Sachsenspiegel*," *Österreichische Zeitschrift für Kunst und Denkmalpflege (Festschrift für Ernst Bacher)* 54 (2000): 318.

Figure 7. Dresden *Sachsenspiegel,* fol. 9r, detail, register 1. The figures represent aspects of Car-olingian law rejected by Eike, who records the right to limit women's property rights, to es-tablish (a man's) innocence "with the right hand," and to challenge a judicial decision. Right to left, a women addresses Charlemagne, a man swears with his right hand, a man will seek justice through judicial combat. Reproduced with permission from Biblio Verlag, Bissendorf.

speaks authoritatively while he listens, his status thus doubly reduced, a rare instance in which an image seems to contradict current custom. Yet it is not uncommon for these pictures to place before the eye a woman's in-fringement of custom—a negative example. In fact, the woman speaking to Charlemagne resonates with Calpurnia, who makes her improper solic-itation of a judge later in the book; both women are discredited not only by the accompanying texts but also by intervisuality. The illegitimate pres-ence of the woman who addresses Charlemagne is contrasted in this reg-ister with the authority that a man is given in Saxon law "to clear himself with a cleansing oath," or to dispute a judgment of the king's court by com-bat. To the contemporary reader, there must have been no doubt about these negative and positive images, because it was unthinkable for a woman to approach a king with such aggressive speech. Once more, women's speech is problematized while men's is validated.

We are now in a position to look at the particular legal circumstances in the body of the *Sachsenspiegel* in which applicants, suitors, plaintiffs, de-fendants, oath-takers and witnesses—rarely including women—speak be-fore the judge, and the extent to which he maintains his authority by "speaking gestures" as well as by his clothing and seated position; these are all the outer signs of men of good repute. We will also examine practices regarding advocacy—who may speak for whom, and which kinds of cases are selected as examples.

Swearing on relics "with fingers and with tongue" (*mit fingere unde mit zungen*) was an important part of legal discourse that reinforced the claim that the law originated with God, and it thus vouches for the good stand-ing of the oath-taker. In Ldr. I, 46, W, out of any specific context, Eike pro-nounces that "wo is den vrouwen zu den eiden kumt, di sulen si selbe tun

60

unde nicht ir vormunde" ("when women must swear an oath, they shall do it themselves and not with a guardian").[36] This is seen in the picture where two women approach a reliquary, each with one hand held up in a speech gesture (figs. 8, middle register, left; 3, no. 3b). The woman on the left dangles her other arm in a position that Amira associates with acquisition or appropriation (fig. 3, no. 10b). Her companion holds her other hand cupped as if to receive something, as Eve received the apple. Thus, the picture expands beyond the text to imply that the matter of their oath has to do with acquiring something.[37] Yet in the next clause we learn that the woman's legal guardian must swear surety for her, must accept and execute that responsibility: "Ir rechte vormunde sal och gewer vor [si] geloben unde enphan unde leisten." In the picture he does not take an oath, which would place him on a par with the women, but instead confronts the judge directly and seems to speak as well as listen, while the judge directs (compare the gesture of the kings in the prologue, fig. 2). The two women hover behind their guardian, to the left of him, one of them communicating through him as indicated by her using the same speech gesture as he does. Here, it seems, the draftsman has adhered to the general precept that women may not swear without a guardian. Yet this is clearly far from an indication of their autonomy and trustworthiness; rather, their oaths have to be validated by a guardian. Furthermore, as the random organization of the *Sachsenspiegel* would have it, in the register above, a woman authorized by her husband to sell her own property is closely attended by him with the baton or insignia of authority, while she holds a "male" glove (fig. 8, top).[38] She is thus bracketed by the masculine staff and glove as she stands before the judge as a petitioner. And in the register below the oath-taking women and their guardian, the general category of thief takes on female form, namely a woman with a goose strapped to her back (fig. 8, bottom). A female who is charged with a crime may appear directly before the judge, yet we remember she cannot respond to the charges herself. Her hands are crossed over her lower body in deference, in a reversal of the exhibiting threat of Calpurnia (fig. 5).[39] The deferential posture is adopted in another picture by a male vassal (fig. 9).

Elsewhere, when there is a context for swearing, the text too is careful to delimit the oath-taking practice for women; like the pictures examined above, it gives a negative cast to the general custom we quoted from Ldr.

36. Dobozy, ed., *Saxon Mirror*, 81.

37. All images can be found in Amira, ed., *Die Dresdener Bilderhandschrift des Sachsenspiegels.*

38. Erler, *Handwörterbuch*, 1:col. 1975: "Handschuh." In numerous symbolic representations, the glove is associated with the male. Here it seems to represent the property being sold. See the note to folio 20v, register 2, Eike von Repgow, *Sachsenspiegel*, vol. 2: *Textband*, 137.

39. This gesture, however, is not unknown to men, as represented by Amira (our fig. 3, nos. 9, 14).

Figure 8. Dresden *Sachsenspiegel*, fol. 14v, detail. Reg. 2, a married woman presents a glove (symbolizing a property transfer) while her husband indicates approval (staff also a symbol of property transfer). Reg. 3, women as legal incompetents stand behind their guardian, who addresses the judge on their behalf; at left, two women swear on a reliquary. Reg. 4, examples of persons with diminished legal capacity: an illegitimate child and a convicted thief. Reproduced with permission from Biblio Verlag, Bissendorf.

46. Although the text never specifically notes this, when women are shown swearing, they do so only in instances where no second party is involved, that is, only in matters concerning themselves as oath-takers.[40] A noteworthy example of this limited exercise of competence to swear is the instance of the morning gift (*Morgengabe*, the husband's gift to his bride after the wedding night). Ldr. I, 20, ¶8, states that a widow may substantiate her morning gift by swearing on relics but hastens to add that her claim to other property has to be supported by compurgators (*Eideshelfer*). Such

40. Mariella Rummel, *Die Rechtliche Stellung der Frau im Sachsenspiegel-Landrecht* (Frankfurt am Main: Lang, 1987), comments on this question in the larger context of guardianship of the female. See esp. the section on her right to bear witness and to testify, 106–14.

62

vor den anden des urteil sal man erst vinden
Offenbare en mag der man nicht sprechen
inlentrechte me den rinen thidlichen zu siner v
sprechen vrager all d hir en ab he an sines
vor sprechen wort se he miz wol sprechen of

Figure 9. Dresden *Sachsenspiegel*, fol. 82v, detail, register 1. A vassal enjoined from speaking aloud at a hearing in a feudal (not criminal) court. With a gesture of deference to his over-lord he whispers to his advocate, who listens and speaks for him. The other figures represent other hearings with vassals responding to questions from the overlord. Reproduced with permission from Biblio Verlag, Bissendorf.

persons are more like modern character witnesses than witnesses who testify from knowledge of the "truth" of the matter.[41] Thus even the woman's *sworn* word is suspect. Contrarily, there are numerous circumstances when a man may swear and have his word accepted without the necessity of such "witnesses." In fact, the power of the man's oath extends beyond the assumption of his credibility, for it permits him to deny facts already in the public domain (that is, his *mala fama*). According to Ldr. I, 18, "Even if the act is well known, he may clear himself with a cleansing oath, and no one can press charges against him with compurgators."[42] There is no clearer example of the male appropriation of language or of the devaluation of a woman's speech.

In the case of the morning gift, as in scores of other examples, the illustrator chooses to represent women in a negative light. The text affirms the exercise of her permitted oath-taking, affirming the gift that, after all, only she could know about. On folio 9v, 4, she is shown not swearing on relics but accepting the morning gift (fig. 10). The problem with this anything-but-innocent representation is that the husband is not a knight, as indicated by his clothing, and is presenting her with a gift of land, symbolized by the branch, a practice prohibited to a member of his class. The artist thereby rejected the chance to show a woman with the standing to swear an oath on her own authority. Instead he elected to show her participating in proscribed behavior. The two women on the left of the regis-

41. Henry Campbell Black, *Black's Law Dictionary*, 6th ed. (St. Paul, Minn.: West Publishing, 1990), 1604.
42. Dobozy, *Saxon Mirror*, 74.

Figure 10. Dresden *Sachsenspiegel*, fol. 9v, detail, register 4. For his wife's morning gift, a peasant (legally) offers his best horse and (illegally) land (symbolized by the branch). The two observing women call attention to the illegality. Reproduced with permission from Biblio Verlag, Bissendorf.

ter appear to be protesting the purported gift as members of a higher class, additionally subverting the possibility of crediting another woman's speech. Their gestures indicate refusal and general speech (fig. 3, nos. 8b, 1a). In case we wanted to adhere to the text in seeing a legitimate morning gift, the illustrator has exploited the opportunity to show women as meddlesome and interfering, their hurtful gossip being a kind of defamation or *mala fama*. Or, if the bridegroom is in the wrong, the accusation of the two women negates the bride's rights.

There is one fascinating exception to the custom of not permitting a woman to swear an oath as primary party to an event when second parties, such as other witnesses, are involved. This necessity arises when a woman declares herself pregnant or gives birth after her husband has died (Ldr. I, 33, figs. 11a, b). The issue turns on whether the child is born alive or is stillborn, obviously a critical factor in questions of inheritance. To prove that the deceased father's child was indeed born alive, two women who witnessed the birth (no men would have been present) could testify on the matter from visual evidence. But even then, for the women's statement to be credited, four men had to be within earshot of the newborn's cry and to swear they had heard it. The men's testimony took precedence over the midwives' eyewitness account. (Akehurst points out that Philippe de Beaumanoir appealed to the superior value of the eyewitness account, a typical position in this strongly ocular culture.)[43] In the *Sachsenspiegel* picture (fig. 11a) these male "witnesses" are portrayed as if they were actually eyewitnesses standing behind the reclining mother and her newborn and are shown testifying with the usual authoritative gesture, whereas the women

43. Philippe de Beaumanoir, *The* Etablissements de Saint Louis: *Thirteenth-Century Law Texts from Tours, Orléans, and Paris,* ed. Edward Peters, trans. F. R. P. Akehurst, Middle Ages Series (Philadelphia: University of Pennsylvania Press, 1996). See paragraphs 1157, 1197, 1812, and 1815.

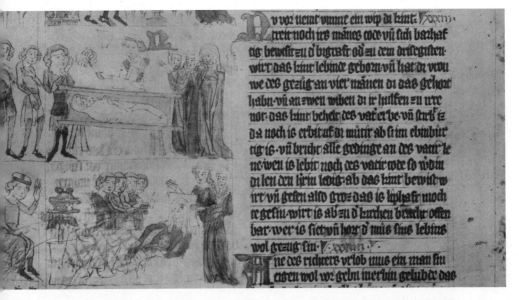

Figure 11a. Dresden *Sachsenspiegel*, fol. 12v, detail. Reg. 3, a widow and other heirs gather at the funeral of her husband. Reg. 4, four men and two women testify to the legitimacy of the widow's child. Reproduced with permission from Biblio Verlag, Bissendorf.

Figure 11b. Oldenburg *Sachsenspiegel*, Landesbibliothek Oldenburg, Cim I 410, fol. 22, detail, register 1. The widow suckles her newborn before the male and female witnesses, and a priest receives their testimony (unfinished picture with baby's face added later). Courtesy of Niedersächsische Sparkassenstiftung.

65

who observed the birth listen from the head of the bed (Amira's "testifying gesture," fig. 3, no. 5a). The positions of the two categories of witness to the live birth are inverted by the artist. Through another inversion the judge is unusually placed at the outer end, to the left, furthest from the text but next to the relics that the men have to swear on, as if he is also a witness to the event that unfolds to the right. The slightly earlier Oldenburg recension leaves out the judge, giving room instead, at the right, to a priest who verifies that the child presented before him at the church is alive (fig. 11b).[44]

The practice by which a number of male witnesses, usually six, may testify to the good reputation of a man accused of certain misdemeanors raises the question of the reputation of the witnesses themselves. It is not stated, as it is by Philippe de Beaumanoir, that such witnesses must themselves be of good repute.[45] When swearing, witnesses in the *Sachsenspiegel* mimic the gestures of Eike at the beginning of the book, an intervisuality that ascribes ultimate legal authority to them (figs. 2, 12). The Saxon law is silent on the subject of the good or poor reputation of the compurgators themselves. In this most class-conscious of texts, distinctions with regard to such witnesses are more likely to be associated with their station in life, as if the value of such testimony was enhanced by a higher social position: the higher up the ladder, the more credible, pointing to an association of *bona fama* with rank, an association that further links rank with good character. Thus, at the top of the legal hierarchy there is one very high office, that of the *schultheiss,* "a count's appointed court officer and judge,"[46] which can be filled only by a man and a landowner of unblemished character. There is a passage, for example, in the edicts (*Sprüche*) of the Ingelheimer Oberhof (superior court) that specifies as much, in a matter involving the nuns of Saint Rupertsberg: "If it is their court, they should appoint a *biderbe* man as *schultheiss* and then discharge him." *Biderbe* covers a number of meanings, most having to do with being upright, honest, decent, and respectable, and also noble.[47] Women could not aspire to such *bona fama.*

Might there be exceptions, such as the rare cases in which a woman is given legitimate speech, as before a judge in Ldr. I, 41?[48] On folio 13v, 5, two women, one unmarried as designated by her loose hair, the other veiled as a wife or widow, approach a seated judge with very deferential gestures

44. Ruth Schmidt-Wiegand, ed., *Der Oldenburger Sachsenspiegel: Vollständige Faksimile-Ausgabe im Originalformat des Codex Picturatus Oldenburgensis Cim I 410 der Landesbibliothek Oldenburg,* 3 vols. (Graz, Austria: Akademische Druck- und Verlagsanstalt, 1993–95).

45. Beaumanoir, *Etablissements,* para. 1170.

46. Dobozy, *Saxon Mirror,* "Glossary," 197.

47. Erler, *Handwörterbuch,* 4:col. 1520. Jeffrey Bowman (this volume) has indicated that one category of judges in Spain was that of *boni homines.*

48. Dobozy, *Saxon Mirror,* 80.

Figure 12. *Dresden Sachsenspiegel,* fol. 64v, detail, register 4. At a hearing on a lord-vassal relationship, of seven witnesses, four were absent who should have testified and three were present who did testify before the overlord. Reproduced with permission from Biblio Verlag, Bissendorf.

(fig. 13; see also fig. 4, K). The first implores him, her hands joined as in prayer; the other seems to listen, as does the judge, who may give a negative response. The text states that if a girl or a widow brings a complaint that her guardian is misappropriating her rights to land, and if the guardian does not appear in court to defend himself, then the judge can become her guardian and her property rights are fully restored. It is thus only in the delinquent absence of the guardian that women can be empowered to address the court. The norm is reestablished on the facing folio (fig. 14, top; cf. fig. 13), where a guardian has to be assigned to women after they have complained of being raped. He is thus shown mediating between them and the judge, even though their complaint had been heard first (Ldr. I, 43).[49] And below, the girl and widow whose guardian had been discredited both reappear, but this time it is made clear that "with this complaint she [i.e., either the girl or the widow] establishes the court as guardian" (Ldr. I, 44), by representing a guardian figure in front of the judge, mirroring his gestures as both hear the testimony of the women. And although gesturing like male witnesses elsewhere, these women are not represented as having the authority to swear on relics (fig. 14, bottom; cf. fig. 12).

As in the case of that private and possibly gentle moment, the bestowing of a woman's morning gift discussed above, so also with that private and cer-

49. Ibid., 81.

Figure 13. Dresden *Sachsenspiegel*, fol. 13v, detail, register 5. An unmarried woman and a widow enter a complaint to a judge about a delinquent guardian who is taking their property (grain). Reproduced with permission from Biblio Verlag, Bissendorf.

tainly brutal moment, the perpetration of her rape, her simple word is not enough. Both text and image are clear on this point. Ldr. II, 64, insists that "a woman or girl bringing charges for rape shall do so with hue and cry [*gerufte*] for the red-handed deed [*hanthafte tat*] and for rape, which she must prove."[50] The "red-handed deed" means that the rape should have just taken place. If she can't report it immediately, she is in trouble. The "hue and cry" is necessary because it is intended to produce pursuers, that is, witnesses, who will corroborate, or not, her claim from common knowledge, which other legal codes find sufficient to establish *fama*. The artist goes even further than the text in devaluing the victim's word (fig. 5, bottom). Women's reputation for irresponsible speech has preceded her appearance before the judge. The artist makes abundantly clear that her report alone would not say enough.[51] She stands before the judge in an obviously disheveled and barefoot state, a condition generally taken as necessary to a convincing charge of rape, according to Jacob Grimm.[52] The artist takes it upon himself to inform the book's users that it is what they must see, not what they might hear, which will persuade them. The point is also brought home by the placement of the rape victim under the image of Calpurnia, so that intervisuality requires us to read her dishevelment as that of another uncontrolled hussy.

50. Ibid., 112.
51. The representation of her ragged dress is even more remarkable in the Heidelberg manuscript of ca. 1300: Koschorreck, *Der Sachsenspiegel*, fol. 10v, register 5.
52. Jacob Grimm, *Deutsche Rechtsaltertümer*, vol. 2 (1922), 191, cited by Koschorreck, *Der Sachsenspiegel*, 156 n. 42.

Figure 14. Dresden *Sachsenspiegel*, fol. 14, detail. Reg. 3, an unmarried woman and a widow complain of rape through the advocacy of a guardian. Reg. 4, an unmarried woman and a widow accept a guardian appointed by a judge. Reproduced with permission from Biblio Verlag, Bissendorf.

Outside the courts, women are occasionally shown taking a more active role in decisions, particularly as widows. For instance, Ldr. I, 11, states that a father who retains guardianship of his children after the death of their mother must turn over her property to them when they leave home and that "a wife should do the same for the father's children" if he dies (fig. 15, top).[53] The two survivors are shown with very similar commanding speech gestures, though slightly more authority may be given to the father here; according to Amira, the angle of the wrist is pertinent: the straighter the hand and forearm, the stronger the authority (fig. 3, nos. 6a–7c). One crucial decision of the artist, however, has clearly put the widow in an inferior position to the widower: the text mentions the widower first (at letter H), and so we might expect him on the left; but instead his privileged position is recognized by placing him at the right, next to the text, where judges often sit. The wife's position immediately below, splendidly enthroned (nor-

53. Dobozy, *Saxon Mirror*, 72.

Figure 15. Dresden *Sachsenspiegel*, fol. 7v, detail. Reg. 2, right, a widower exercises guardianship over the surviving children; at the left the situation is reversed, with the widow in charge of the children. Reg. 3, the eldest brother shares the inheritance with his brothers, but keeps the property his wife brought to the marriage. Reproduced with permission from Biblio Verlag, Bissendorf.

mally only judges are shown seated) and holding the symbol of her property, the stalk of grain, relates to Ldr. I, 12, which states that a husband does not have to share with his brothers any property that he came into through marriage (fig. 15, bottom). She speaks (of his rights?) with a calmer speech gesture than he uses, while he argues his case gesturing "pointedly" to his brothers. This appears at first to be a rare positive image of a woman, until we remember that the law declares elsewhere that in marriage she loses whatever previous control she had of her property. This dispute is about which male relatives after her husband have the right to "her" property, her sons or her brothers-in-law.

In another instance, a widow does preside over the distribution of property, and from a position at the top right of a column of pictures, yet her upheld hand shows some reticence compared with the aggressive command of the heir who approaches from the left (fig. 16, top). The text informs us that he is there "before the thirtieth" to assert his rights of inheritance, and that "the lady must [after the thirtieth] divide among the

he ftarp Dar noch mus dir widwve mit den erbn
muf teilen·alle gehouere thife dir noch eine drite
gude·vbir bleip midudzeine houe irs mannes
oder wo he fi hatte binnen finen gewern So
fal di vrouwe zu hergewere gebn irs manes
fwert·vnde das befte ros oder pherr gefatilt
vn das befte harnafch das he hatte zu eins
mannes libe da he ftarp binnē fine gewern
da noch einen her phil·das is ein beite vnde
ein bulftin·vn ein hlachen·vn ein tiſchlachē zwei
bedzin vn eine twele·dis is ein gemeine herge
were zu gebene vn recht alleine ſetzen di lure
manchirhande dinc darzu das nicht darzu ge
hort Wes das wip nicht en hat dirre dinge
des en darf fi nicht gebin ab fi ir vnfchult
tar da vor tun·Das fis nicht en habe vmme
iclicke fchule fundirlichen·was man abir da

Figure 16. Dresden *Sachsenspiegel,* fol. 10v, detail. Reg. 1, thirty days after the death of her husband, the widow distributes all remaining foodstuffs (fish) among the heirs. The double-lidded vessel symbolizes inheritance. Reg. 2, the widow hands over all her husband's military equipment to eligible male heirs. Reproduced with permission from Biblio Verlag, Bissendorf.

heirs all stored food supplies."[54] Her status is immediately diminished further, in the next register, by a scene in which she complies with the requirement to divest herself of all her husband's military equipment (*hergewete*) after the thirtieth (fig. 16, bottom).[55] Suddenly the text gives her the prerogative to take an oath, but it is not shown in the pictures: "The wife need not supply the articles she does not have as long as she dares to swear that she does not possess them. This is to be done separately for each and every one of them. However, if it can be proven [that she has them], no man or woman can cleanse himself with an oath." In other words, a false oath contravened by contradicting proof obviates the possibility of a

54. "Vor dem drîsigsten": *Drîsigster,* the "thirtieth," refers to the thirtieth day after the burial of the deceased and/or to the mass celebrated on that day. Before that day heirs may not take possession of their inheritance. See Eike von Repgow, *Sachsenspiegel,* vol. 2: *Textband,* 119 n. 4, and for a fuller account, Erler, *Handwörterbuch,* 1:col. 785–87.
55. Dobozy, *Saxon Mirror,* 76.

cleansing oath. Compare this with the oath taken by a man in Ldr. I, 18, cited fully above, "Even if the act is well known, he may clear himself with a cleansing oath." Rumor or gossip, so often associated with women's speech, may be dismissed by the oath-taking man. The widow's oath, however, which she must swear for *each item* she denies having in her possession, seems to carry much less weight. For its administrators, the law worries about her swearing falsely and—almost darkly—links her oath to the possibility of successful challenges.

Fama in its several medieval meanings—reputation, common knowledge, defamation—played a crucial role in the oral culture of the law courts. Our scrutiny of the pictorial and textual representations in the *Sachsenspiegel* has shown the extent to which the construction of *bona fama* and *mala fama* was controlled by men. Women's verbal input was severely curtailed, at best indirectly reported by a guardian, at worst subject to negation by men, whose aural witness was privileged over women's eyewitness to a birth. On the other hand, male witnesses in sufficient numbers could bolster the reputation of a man accused of a crime, or his own oath might exonerate him. They were also in a position, as women were not, to defame men, though women might defame each other. And the pictorial cycle, by imaging the misdemeanors of women, colludes with the male voice of the accusers. Pictures, being mute, cannot distinguish between "this is the crime a woman is accused of" and "this is the crime a woman committed," or even "this is an example of a crime" (fig. 8). We have observed elsewhere that men are less often represented committing misdemeanors or crimes. This bias contributes to their superior reputation, a condition that is energetically proclaimed in the authoritative speech acts discussed here.

Part 2

FAMA AND REPUTATION

CHAPTER FOUR

Good Name, Reputation, and Notoriety
in French Customary Law

F. R. P. AKEHURST

The governance of human society and the restraining of individual ten-
dencies toward anarchy have occupied philosophers, religious leaders, and
lawmakers throughout history. In thirteenth-century France, increased
commercial activity in the growing towns led to a new set of rules for the
maintenance of order and the successful pursuit of wealth. The relations
between men (and to a lesser extent women), often formerly expressed by
comprehensive oral ceremonies such as vassalage, began to be expressed
in limited oral and written contracts on particular matters, and there also
developed a series of customs or laws governing enforcement of these contracts and procedures for settling differences. These rules (among others)
were first written down in France in the thirteenth century in compilations
called customaries. Their existence did not, of course, mean that speaking,
listening, oral contracting, and the like were then or ever would be entirely
replaced.

For modern crimes, modern punishments. In the French epics, which
portray a warrior society, some characters have to live with the results of violence and crime, because their adversary is too strong for them to punish, as for example in *Raoul de Cambrai*.[1] Here, various characters such as
Raoul's squire Bernier must wait to avenge violence against them or their
families, sometimes for many years, and they must even form alliances with
their enemies. But city society found a nonviolent way to exclude those who
broke certain rules. This exclusion or ostracism took many forms, not the

---

1. *Raoul de Cambrai: Chanson de geste du XIIe siècle,* ed. Sarah Kay, trans. William W. Kibler
(Paris: Librairie Générale Française, 1996).

least of which was excommunication. Here, I am concerned particularly with how legal rules, enforceable in courts, excluded people who had behaved in a certain way from participation in legal procedures, with the result that they lost the ability to use the courts for their own advantage. In some regions of Europe, the price of breaking the rules was infamy. Late thirteenth-century commercial society required that people be reliable, truthful, and respectful of the rights of others (including the security of their marriages). To enforce these requirements, it provided legal tribunals. Failure to conform led to exclusion from commercial society and from the opportunity to gain wealth and power.

Three areas of Old French customary law address the problem of behavior and exclusion: good name or reputation, notoriety, and the use of witnesses. Many of my examples come from the *Coutumes de Beauvaisis* (1283) of Philippe de Beaumanoir, a late thirteenth-century jurist from fifty miles north of Paris. Beaumanoir's compilation addresses those who are unfamiliar with the way law works in the Beauvaisis, and thus it is highly useful to the modern reader. Other examples are drawn from the *Etablissements de Saint Louis* (ca. 1257), compiled by an unknown lawyer or judge, and the *Conseil a un ami* (1253) of Pierre de Fontaines, composed by a judge working for Louis IX. These compilations are less complete than the *Coutumes de Beauvaisis,* and they show the growing influence of Roman law. In addition, I have included some remarks based on the *Costuma d'Agen,* an anonymous thirteenth-century customary compilation in Old Occitan, the language of southern France until the Revolution.[2] Finally, evidence from well-known Old French literary works, although not of course probative of ordinary conduct, rounds out the discussion.

The editions of the legal texts are all somewhat dated: The *Etablissements* and the *Conseil* have not been reedited since the nineteenth century, and the Beaumanoir was last edited in 1900 (the 1970 reprinting is identical to the 1900 original). The latest transcription of the *Costuma d'Agen* dates

2. Philippe de Beaumanoir, *Philippe de Beaumanoir: Coutumes de Beauvaisis,* ed. Amédée Salmon, 2 vols. (1899–1900; reprint, Paris: Picard, 1970) (hereafter, Beaumanoir); *Les Etablissements de Saint Louis,* ed. Paul Viollet, 4 vols., Société de l'Histoire de France (Paris, 1881–86) (hereafter, *Etablissements*); *Le conseil de Pierre de Fontaines, ou traité de l'ancienne jurisprudence française,* ed. M. A. J. Marnier (Paris, 1846) (hereafter, *Conseil*); and the *Costuma d'Agen,* my transcription from the *Copie juratoire,* Archives départementales du Tarn et Garonne, Agen (hereafter *Costuma d'Agen*). I have published English translations of the first two of these works (see below). My translations of the *Conseil* and the *Costuma d'Agen* are in the late stages of preparation. The *Costuma d'Agen* exists in several manuscripts, and three of these have been published; see, for example, Henri Tropamer, *La coutume d'Agen* (Bordeaux: Cadoret, 1911). This edition includes a modern French translation, often abridged. When quoting these works and others in Old French I have provided my own translations; see *The* Coutumes de Beauvaisis *of Philippe de Beaumanoir,* trans. and with an introduction by F. R. P. Akehurst (Philadelphia: University of Pennsylvania Press, 1992); *The* Etablissements de Saint Louis: *Thirteenth-Century Law Texts from Tours, Orléans, and Paris,* trans. and with an introduction by F. R. P. Akehurst (Philadelphia: University of Pennsylvania Press, 1996).

from 1911, and it has been little studied in the United States. None of these works has yet been entered into the computer to facilitate word searches, but in any case the issues here require us to deal with more than words. When we are dealing with concepts, we may find that there is a cluster of words that together denote the concept. Thus, if we are interested in *fama,* or its Old French equivalent *fame,* we will seek it in vain in the customary texts.[3] Instead, we may find such words or expressions as *notoire* (well known), *renomee* ("reputation," with or without accompanying adjectives), *a la veüe de tote gent* (in the sight of everyone), and the various antonymic expressions *disfame* (bad reputation), *maldichs* (badly spoken of), *soupeconeus* (suspicious), *malrenomé(s)* (with a bad reputation), and *vilenie* (slander, bad reputation). In addition to the problem of the words, there is also the problem of defining the concepts. And here the examination of literature may be helpful.

The father of Philippe de Beaumanoir the jurist is the probable author of two romances, *Jehan et Blonde* and *La Manekine.*[4] At the beginning of *Jehan et Blonde,* we are told that the hero Jehan, whose father is a ruined nobleman, is setting off for England to seek his fortune. We are told no less than eight times that he is seeking "honeur."[5] His specific goal is to win a greater fief than his father has.[6] This is a rather unusual ambition, since heroes usually go to Bretagne to seek a chivalric education followed by fame, generally designated in Old French romance as *pris et los* (reputation and praise). In literature, reputation is something that must be won before it is lost; it is a chivalric value that epic heroes especially hold very dear. As we have learned from Ruth Benedict and E. R. Dodds,[7] this is a characteristic of a shame culture, in which what matters is a person's reputation, what others think of him. Benedict and Dodds also identify another type of culture, the guilt culture, in which what matters is what a man knows

3. *Fame* does appear in the twelfth-century *Roman d'Eneas,* lines 1539–1566, as a translation of the purple passage in the *Aeneid* book 4, lines 173–88, that uses the word *fama.* I suppose that in the homonymic clash of *fame* as "fame" with *fame* as "woman," the latter survived. In Chrétien's *Lancelot,* where word of the hero's ride in the cart seems to precede him almost everywhere, the word for what flies is *novele:* "Novele qui tost vole et cort" (The news that quickly flies and runs); see Chrétien de Troyes, *Les romans de Chrétien de Troyes, III: Le chevalier de la charrete,* ed. Mario Roques, Les Classiques Français du Moyen Age 86 (Paris: Champion, 1970), line 4140.
4. *Jehan et Blonde de Philippe de Remi,* ed. Sylvie Lécuyer (Paris: Champion, 1984), and *Le roman de la Manekine,* ed. from Bibliothèque Nationale de France fr. 1588 and trans. by Barbara N. Sargent Baur, with contributions by Alison Stones and Roger Middleton, Faux titre 159 (Amsterdam: Rodopi, 1999). There is no Modern English translation of *Jehan et Blonde.*
5. Lines 13, 20, 33, 36, 46, 47 (twice), 70.
6. *Jehan et Blonde,* lines 80–82: "Ne veut pas despendre la tere / que ses peres tient folement, / ains conquerra, s'il peut, plus grant" (He does not want to spend the land his father holds foolishly, instead he will acquire a greater one, if he can).
7. Ruth Benedict, *The Chrysanthemum and the Sword* (Boston: Houghton Mifflin, 1946); and E. R. Dodds, *The Greeks and the Irrational* (Berkeley: University of California Press, 1968).

about himself, his inner or secret worth, no matter what others think of him.

The first and most striking example of a shame-culture character in Old French literature is obviously Roland, eponymous hero of the *Chanson de Roland* (late eleventh, early twelfth century). Roland is in a situation where he can call for help, an action he considers shameful, or run the risk of fighting against overwhelming odds. Rather than lose his renown (*los* and *valor;* antonyms *blasmet* [blamed] and *hontages* [shame]), and create the possibility of having bad songs sung about him, Roland goes to his death and takes with him the entire rearguard of Charlemagne's army. In those famous *laisses similaires* (where the content is repeated over and over in new sets of lines with different assonances), he repeats this point of view several times.[8] The most important thing to Roland, more important than life itself, is thus what is said or sung about him, or about *France dolce* (sweet France), in an oral tradition. National reputation is associated with personal reputation. This renown is often designated by the Old French word *pris* (renown).[9] Old French also has the word *renomee*, but it is something a little different.

Words change their meaning over time and when they are borrowed from one language to another. And concepts may exist in different cultures under different names, and in the same culture by different names at different times. Take the concept of "honor," not entirely foreign to our theme of *fama*.[10] The modern concept grew up during the middle ages, where it was designated by various words, in Old French, for example, in variations of the word *loial* (honest, fair, loyal). The word *honor* or *honeur* was already in use in Old French and Old Occitan, however, to mean a piece of land (see, for example, the *Costuma d'Agen*) and less frequently to mean an honor bestowed on a person. By the end of the sixteenth century, Montaigne could say in the modern sense: "Any honorable person chooses to lose his honor, rather than his conscience" and to remark that *honneur* depends on other people's opinion: "other people's knowledge, on which honor depends."[11]

---

8. Laisses 79, then 83–85.

9. See also Alexander H. Schutz, "The Provençal Expression *Pretz e valor*," *Speculum* 19 (1934): 488–93.

10. On honor, see Frank Henderson Stewart, *Honor* (Chicago: University of Chicago Press, 1994).

11. Michel de Montaigne, *Oeuvres complètes*, 2.16 *in fine*, ed. Albert Thibaudet and Maurice Rat, Bibliothèque de la Pléiade (Paris: Gallimard, 1962), 614: "Toute personne d'honneur choisit de perdre plustost son honneur, que de perdre sa conscience" and "la connaissance d'autruy, d'où l'honneur dépend." In the *Conseil*, 79–80, the word *honeur* is used once in the modern sense: "Vilains . . . ne sont mie si honouré come li gentix homs, ne si ne sevent qu'est honeurs, et por ce ne sont-il mie si tenu de garder le" (Serfs . . . they are not as honorable as gentlemen, and do not know what honor is, and are therefore less expected to observe it).

The fame of an epic hero must not be confused with a legal good name (Old French, *bonne renomee*), nor with the fortune that Jehan de Dammartin goes to seek in England. A man's legal good name is something he possesses until it has been taken away from him.[12] The assumption is that a man is honest, tells the truth, and does not commit fraud, until it is otherwise proved in court. At that point, the loss of good name may be part of the punishment and made public in some quasi ceremony, such as being exhibited on the pillory.[13] The shame attached to public exhibition was also known in northern France. In Chrétien's *Chevalier de la charrete*, the author explains that the *charrete* of the title marks with infamy those who ride in it:

> Qui a forfet estoit repris
> s'estoit sor la charrete mis
> et menez par totes les rues;
> s'avoit totes enors perdues,
> ne puis n'estoit a cort oïz,
> ne enorez ne conjoïz.[14]

[Whoever was convicted of a serious crime was placed on the cart and paraded through all the streets; and he had lost all honors, and was no longer listened to in court, nor honored nor welcomed.]

The loss of *bonne renomee* has serious legal and social consequences, which are to be avoided by any man wishing to play even a modest part in society. Although the effect in the *Chevalier de la charrete* is mixed, some of the people who have heard about Lancelot's ride assume that he is a criminal, and he is certainly mocked and derided because of it.

Philippe de Beaumanoir the jurist, whose book of law from 1283 is written for the guidance of the party and the practitioner, and is thus very firmly grounded in the court practice of his time, speaks several times of *bonne renomee* and how it can be lost.[15] Of course he never mentions how

12. Cf. Latin *existimatio* as defined by Stewart, *Honor*, 57–58: "*Existimatio* is especially interesting. It was evidently thought of as something that could be preserved, lost, diminished, or restored, but not as something that could be increased."

13. For example, a man could not be elected to serve on the Agen city council if he was a heretic, or illegitimate, or, among other things, "uencuz de lachs crim aissi cum es de corre uila [punished for adultery] e de puiar en espillori" (condemned for an evil crime, for example to run [the gauntlet] through the town or to mount the pillory); see *Costuma d'Agen*, fol. 87v.

14. Chrétien de Troyes, *Le chevalier de la charrete*, ed. Roques, lines 333–38.

15. *Renomee* (*bonne renomee, maus renomés, mal renomés, mauvese renomee*, etc.) appears in the following sections of the *Coutumes:* 34, 38, 47, 213, 422, 549, 634, 815, 913, 940, 941, 942, 985, 991, 1046, 1076, 1078, 1113, 1136, 1187, 1189, 1197, 1223, 1258, 1354, 1601, 1634, 1815, 1949, 1955. Other words, such as *vilenie* and *disfame*, appear in these sections (less exhaustive list): 16, 19, 26, 29, 52, 804, 1205, 1721, 1982.

it can be won, because that is not possible. A first notion of the expression *bonne renomee* can be gained by examining it in a list of similar terms: a judge's substitute, says Beaumanoir, must be "a man who is very honest and of good reputation and wise."[16] This good repute can be lost. If an agent is supposed to collect money but denies having received a payment from debtors who then prove payment, the agent pays a fine and *demeure mal renomés* (keeps a bad reputation) (§815).[17] If an heir who is bringing property back into the hotchpot conceals some of it and is found out, then he *demeure mal renomés* (§913).[18] To diminish your reputation is *abesser sa renomee* (§34). These are rather formal instances of the loss of *bonne renomee*, and it is possible that the person thus stigmatized was exhibited on the pillory and thus (re)marked by the local population. There are other instances when persons who are *mal renomés* are thereby prevented from doing something. One example is the person who cannot become a custodian (*bail*). When a minor child inherited property on coming of age, a custodian was sometimes appointed to care for the child and look after the estate. A custodianship could be quite lucrative, since the custodian was entitled in some circumstances to the profits of the land and to the personal property of the decedent (§518). However, a person who was of bad reputation could not be appointed a custodian (§549).[19] It was a moral but also a publicly known flaw, the result of conviction for some serious crime (*vilain cas*), that prevented his appointment. Custodianship was also denied to spendthrifts and to those physically incapable, such as madmen, the blind, the deaf, and the poor (§549).

Having a good reputation might make it easier for a person to prevail in a lawsuit. Thus, Beaumanoir states that when a person is found in possession of property that someone else claims is stolen, the person in possession will have to show how he obtained the property, perhaps by producing the person from whom he claims he obtained it, known as a *garant* (warrantor). Clearly, this might be difficult in many cases. The way to resolve the doubt about the ownership of the property is to investigate the *bonne*

16. Beaumanoir, §38: "homme mout loial et de bonne renomee, et sage."

17. And see also ibid., §1601: "he will be of bad repute."

18. Another expression equivalent to *estre mal renomés* is *vilenie avoir*, as in the statement: "Car qui se parjure il a grans erres de vilenie avoir" (For a person who perjures himself is well on the way to having ill repute); see ibid., §29.

19. Ibid., §549:

A briement parler l'en ne doit lessier la garde des enfants sousaagiés ne des orfelins a nului qui soit mal renomés de vilains cas, ne a nul fol naturel, ne a nul avuegles . . . ne a povre persone s'il ne fet seurté de rendre bon conte. (Briefly, the guardianship of minor children should not be confided to anyone with a bad reputation for a serious offense, nor to imbeciles [*fol naturel*], nor to blind persons . . . nor to poor persons, unless they give a security for giving a good account.)

renomee of the parties. Beaumanoir explains this at some length in §940,[20] and then returns to it in §1815.[21]

One effect of being *mal renomés* was an inability to sue someone for fraud.[22] Once a person had a bad reputation, he would not be heard to accuse of fraud another person of good reputation (§991).[23] An innkeeper with a good reputation could avoid charges of having stolen property from his guests, but if his reputation were not very good he would be the most obvious suspect, even if there were signs of forced entry and broken chests and the like (§1113). In such a case, the reputation of the innkeeper would be determined by a judicial inquiry. The only kind of evidence such an inquiry would turn up would be oral: what people *said* about a person could make or break him. The inquiry also delved into what other people thought of a person, what they remembered about him. *Bonne renomee* was certainly in the collective memory of a person's neighbors. In Agen, the creation of a bad reputation for those whose word could not be trusted was a public ceremony and punishment. A person convicted of false testimony was led through the town, preceded by trumpets, and with a metal skewer thrust through his tongue (fig. 17). After that, he could not be a witness or be believed in any matter.[24]

Bonne renomee, then, is a quality that a person is presumed to possess until the reverse is shown, for example in a suit on fraud. Certain kinds of persons are prevented from testifying, as listed in Beaumanoir §1186: "those who are convicted or condemned for a serious crime they committed previously or for false testimony that they gave, or those who are perjured." A witness who

20. Se cil qui est pris atout le larrecin puet trouver son garant qui li bailla, il est delivres; et s'il ne puet, si comme s'il en est fuis ou s'il est en lieu ou il ne puet estre justiciés, bonne renomee puet bien aidier a celi qui est pris a toute la chose emblee ... se uns hons de mauvese renomee acusoit un homme de bonne renomee de tel cas [where a person named as a *garant* denied having given the disputed item], il ne devroit estre oïs. (If the person who is arrested in possession can find the person [*son garant*] who gave it to him, he is released; and if he cannot, for example if he has fled or he is in a place where he cannot be brought to justice, good reputation can come to the aid of the person arrested in possession ... if a man of bad reputation accused a man of good reputation in such a case, he should not be listened to.)

21. There are nine occurrences of the word *renomee* in this paragraph alone.

22. De Fontaines lists a number of acts for which a man may "perdre respons" in court, meaning that a person whom he wants to sue will not be summoned to the court (*Conseil*, chap. 13, 6–28), but many of these rules are translated from Roman law, and it is not clear how many were in fact "good law" in France in the middle of the thirteenth century.

23. Beaumanoir, §991:

L'en ne doit pas oïr toutes persones en plet de tricherie. Car si li fius veut pledier a son pere ou a sa mere en aus metant sus tricherie ... ou li parjure ... ou cil qui sont disfamé contre ceus qui sont de bonne renomee: toutes teus manieres de gens ne sont pas a oïr en plet de tricherie. (Not everyone should be allowed to make a complaint of fraud. For if a son wanted to make a complaint against his father or mother accusing them of fraud ... or one convicted of perjury ... or people of bad reputation [*disfamé*] against those of good repute: all these kinds of people are not to be allowed to sue for fraud.)

24. Agen, France, Archives départementales de Lot-et-Garonne MS 42, fol. 44v, preceding the chapter on fol. 45r that deals with false testimony and its punishment.

Figure 17. Creation of *mauvaise renommée:* perjury. The convicted perjurer, his tongue stuck through with an iron skewer to mark his crime, is paraded before the townspeople. As a result of his conviction and punishment, he loses some legal rights. Reproduced with permission from Agen, France, Archives Départementales de Lot-et-Garonne, MS 42, fol. 44v, detail.

could not be prevented from testifying for these and other reasons is called by Beaumanoir and others "loial," the etymological origin of which is clearly the Latin *legalis*. There is a modern legal concept that continues this tradition of exclusions of witnesses because of prior acts suggesting their lack of trustworthiness; in the U.S. Federal Rules of Evidence there is a provision that under certain circumstances juries can be informed of a witness's recent earlier conviction for serious crimes but especially for fraud.[25]

Bad reputation is something that attaches to a person, as something commonly known about him or her. But common knowledge may extend to facts, such as criminal acts, and a whole body of doctrine surrounds this notion of well-known or commonly known facts. The Old French adjective that is used to characterize such facts is *notoire* (notorious).

25. U.S. Federal Rules of Evidence, 609:

(a) General rule. For the purpose of attacking the credibility of a witness, evidence that he has been convicted of a crime shall be admitted if elicited from him or established by public record during cross examination but only if the crime (1) . . . or (2) involved dishonesty or false statement, regardless of the punishment. (b) Time limit. Evidence of a conviction under this rule is not admissible if a period of more than ten years has elapsed.

Note that rule 608 of the Federal Rules of Evidence states that "the credibility of a witness may be attacked or supported by evidence in the form of opinion or reputation," subject to rather severe limitations.

As late as the thirteenth century virtually all lawsuits in French secular courts were conducted in oral form, and most of what happened was never committed to writing.[26] The original complaint, the answer, the pleadings, the deliberations of the judges, and the decision were all carried out viva voce. The only exception seems to have been that by the end of the thirteenth century, in some areas at least, the witnesses presented by a party were interrogated outside the court by special auditors, and these men gave the judge their report in a written document under seal (§1225). Written documents could be used in evidence, but their authenticity could be challenged by a party, and small physical imperfections (such as tears in the parchment that reached the text, erasures and corrections, even writing between the lines) could easily invalidate them (§§1082–85).

We are now very familiar with grand jury indictments, but there was no such thing in thirteenth-century France. Another way in which a prosecutor issues an indictment today is on the basis of an "information," and the equivalent of this did exist in Beaumanoir's time—a *denonciacion* (§1157).[27] It is simply a report to the judge that a crime has taken place. It was probably oral, and it caused the judge to commence an investigation. We are so familiar with this procedure, in which someone, probably a policeman, makes a report to a court officer such as a prosecutor, and the latter issues an arrest warrant, that we might lose sight of the fact that it was relatively new in Beaumanoir's day.

Without quite showing how the process worked in detail, Beaumanoir suggests that information might reach the judge as the result of public knowledge, namely that the identity of the perpetrator was known to many people. For this, he uses the word *notoire*. A word of caution must be injected here, for the Old French word *notoire* is applied to events or crimes, not to persons. If a crime is observed by enough people, it becomes "notoire" and little proof is required (§§1157, 1197, 1812, 1815).[28] At one

---

26. Jeffrey Bowman is fortunate in having available some transcripts of trials in Catalonia that illustrate the application of laws available elsewhere. See his "Infamy and Proof" in this volume. Madeline H. Caviness and Charles G. Nelson, on the other hand, are obliged to state that there are no court records available to show how the laws they discuss were applied in practice in medieval Germany; see their "Silent Witnesses" in this volume.

27. In this context *denunciation* and the verb *to denounce* are used in the sense of "report to the authorities," rather than in their usual modern sense of "speak disapprovingly about, stigmatize."

28. Beaumanoir, §1812:

La quinzisme resons des defenses a l'apelé si est quant cil qui apele est atains notoirement du cas pour quoi il apele: si comme se Pierres apeloit Jehan pour une occision d'un sien parent ou pour un larrecin et il seroit aperte chose et bien seue que li dis Pierres meismes avroit fet ou fet fere l'occision ou le larrecin. (The fifteenth defense of the appellee is when the appellant himself is convicted by public knowledge of the matter on which he is appealing: for example, if Pierre appealed against Jehan for the homicide of one of his relatives or for a larceny, and it was a well-known thing that the said Pierre himself had committed or procured the committing of the homicide or the larceny.)

This quotation is helpful because it uses the word *notoirement* as well as the words *aperte chose et bien seue* ("obvious and well-known thing"), which we find elsewhere in the customaries.

point Beaumanoir even attempts a definition of *fet notoire:* "a well-known fact, something done before so many honest men that it is clearly known, for example in the presence of six or more persons of good reputation."[29] But Beaumanoir's definitions often leave something to be desired. On the other hand, it is clear that the modern *concept* of notoriety of a person is also known to Beaumanoir, who advises the judge in certain cases to "round up the usual suspects."[30]

This practical-minded judge lists eight manners of proof that are used in courts, but he does not include among them the idea of notoriety. His seventh manner does sound like it, but only for matters of law, not of facts:

> The seventh manner of proof is when the thing that you have to prove is so clear that no other testimony is needed, such as when I ask one of my men to pay me five sous as a fine for a blow which he gave someone else in my jurisdiction and he admits the justice of the fine but he denies that it is five sous. There is no need for a proof for the custom is so clear that it is proof of itself. . . . But when cases arise where there is a doubt about the custom, then proofs may be required.[31]

Another manner of proof is through a presumption, and his example speaks of the "serement de bonnes gens" ("sworn testimony of honest folk") and explains that a presumption based on this can be enough to convict even though there is no "fet notoire" (§§1156–57). Nevertheless, he does affirm that cases proved "par fet notoire" cannot be contested, "for cases which prove themselves cannot be contested."[32] All this suggests that "common knowledge" of a crime is incontestable proof of guilt. It also makes accusations easier and less perilous to the accuser. In another paragraph, Beaumanoir sums up his thinking on this question:

29. Ibid., §1197: "fet notoire, liqueus fu fes devant tant de preudommes qu'il est apertement seus, si comme devant .VI. de bonne renomee ou plus."

30. Ibid., §942:

Et pour ce, quant tel larrecin sont fet la justice doit prendre tous les soupeçoneus et fere mout de demandes pour savoir s'il pourra fere clere ce qui est orbe; et bien les doit en longue prison et destroite tenir, et tous ceus qu'il avra soupeçoneus par mauvese renomee. (And for this reason, when such larcenies are committed, the judge should arrest all the suspects and ask lots of questions to see if he can make clear that which was obscure; and he should keep them in close confinement for a long time, along with all those whom he suspects because of their bad reputation.)

See also the *Etablissements,* chaps. 1.38 and 2.17.

31. Beaumanoir, §1155:

La setisme maniere de prueve si est quant la chose que l'en a a prouver est si clere de soi meisme qu'il n'i convient autre tesmoing: si comme se je demande d'un mien homme qu'il me pait .V. s. d'une amende qu'il me fist pour une buffe qu'il donna a un autre en ma justice, et il connoist bien l'amende, mais il nie qu'ele n'est pas de .V. s., il n'i convient pas de prueve, car la coustume est si clere qu'ele se prueve de soi meisme. . . . Mes quant aucun cas avient qui sont en doute de coustume, la pueent cheoir prueves.

32. Ibid., §1169: "car les causes qui se pruevent d'eles meismes ne doivent pas estre debatues."

And if someone does me harm so openly that he does not conceal himself from those who could see, and I accuse him of the offense as a well-known fact [*fet notoire*], he must await the trial of the fact without obtaining a wager of battle; for it would be a bad thing if someone set fire to my house in the presence of the neighbors and I had to fight the offender to get vengeance and damages for his offense.[33]

The normal way for a crime to get into court, then, was for the victim or a family member to ask a judge to summon to court a person who was then accused by the victim of some crime. This procedure is today more familiar in tort cases, where an injured plaintiff seeks redress against the person he claims has wronged him. Whereas a modern tort victim is usually seeking money damages, the medieval victim of a crime may be asking the court to punish someone, by a fine paid to the court or even by death or dismemberment. The summons, carried out orally, of course, might not even state why the person was being summoned, or even who had asked the judge to summon him. A plaintiff-accuser who commences an action against someone by alleging that she or he has committed a crime is said to appeal, but in modern law that is not what we would call an appeal.

An example of an appeal that is avoided is given in Beaumanoir in §1710, where the issue is the wager of battle, or challenge to a judicial duel by the accused. The danger to the accuser can be avoided by the use of the *denonciacion,* which gives the judge the power to make inquiries, but does not give the accused a party-accuser to challenge to a duel (§1710). One can see here the modern procedure taking over from the primitive, irrational one in Beaumanoir's time. It is arguable that the newer procedure gave more opportunity for redress of grievances to the weaker plaintiff and to those who could not fight judicial battles.

It is clear that this French customary notion of *notoire* or notoriety differs in some respects from the Roman and canon law concept, where the *notorium facti* (well known in fact) is defined as "That which is exhibited and offered to the eyes of everyone" ("Quod exhibet et offert se oculis omnium," in Johannes Teutonicus's gloss to the *Decretum* C. 2. q. 1. c.15) and the *notorium iuris* (well known in law) is defined as an in-court admission.[34]

33. Ibid., §1353: "Se aucuns me fet aucun damage si apertement qu'il ne se cele pas de ceus qui le vuelent veoir, et je l'acuse de cel fet comme de fet notoire, il convient qu'il atende l'enqueste de ce fet sans venir as gages, car male chose seroit qu'aucuns boutast le feu en ma meson en la presence des voisins, s'il me convenoit combatre au maufeteur pour querre la venjance et le damage du mesfet."

34. For the canon law origin of the proof by notoriety see Jean-Philippe Lévy, "Le problème de la preuve dans les droits savants du Moyen Âge," in *La preuve,* 2 vols., Recueils de la Société Jean Bodin pour l'histoire comparative des institutions 17 (Brussels: Editions de la Librairie Encyclopédique, 1965), 2:137–67, esp. 160–65, from which these citations are taken. The examples given of the *notorium facti* make it sound more like what modern law calls "judicial notice."

F. R. P. AKEHURST

It is also somewhat different from the *publica fama* or "common knowledge" of twelfth-century Tuscany as discussed by Chris Wickham in this volume. Only once in Beaumanoir is there a mention that "what everyone
knows" may have evidentiary weight. This is when a person is claiming
damages consisting of more than his net worth as that is "publicly known."
Beaumanoir steps into the role of the claimant: "For example, if my reputation was that I had a net worth of no more than one hundred pounds,
and I tried to swear that my damages were five hundred or a thousand
pounds, I would not be believed."[35]

While common knowledge of facts removed from the accuser certain requirements of proof, the opposite problem is presented by the use of individual speech to perform certain acts regarded as illegal. Speech can
after all be used for both proper and improper purposes. The making of
an oral contract is a proper use, while slander or defamation is an improper use. Beaumanoir has a whole chapter on contracts (chap. 34), and
another on written contracts, which were evidently becoming more common in his time (chap. 35). Wills had to be oral to be valid, according to
Beaumanoir (§370),[36] but were written by the public notary in Agen, or at
least there was a set tariff for the service, and notaries had to be prepared
to write a will whenever called on to do so, day or night.[37] These are examples of permitted or required speech, and they could be proved in the
usual way.

In thirteenth-century France, bad speech, namely slander, could lead to
very serious consequences. If a man heard himself and his wife defamed,
he might attack the speaker, and even kill him, and the provocation of the
words might excuse him (§932). This situation is called *homicide* in Beaumanoir, and although it is one of the crimes that can be punished by hanging, the sudden and unpremeditated nature of the crime might be a
mitigating factor, as in the "crime of passion" that exists in some law codes
even today. Another modern expression that deals with a lesser manifes-

35. Beaumanoir, §1223: "si comme se commune renomee me tesmoignoit que je n'eusse
pas vaillant .c. lb. en toutes choses et je vouloie jurer mon damage a .v^c. lb ou a mil, je ne
seroie pas creus."
36. Ibid., §370: "Nus lais ne vaut s'il n'est fes de persone qui soit en bon sens et en bon
memoire, et s'il ne le dit de la bouche" (No legacy is valid unless it is made by a person of
sound mind and memory, and unless he says it aloud).
37. *Costuma d'Agen*, fol. 84r: "De carta d'ordre de .M. sous .xij. diners. e de cada .M. sols
entroque .d. libres per razo" (For a written will of 1000 sous, [the charge is] 12 deniers, and
for each will up to five hundred livres [the charge is] in proportion). Ibid., fols. 84v–85r:

E si alcus hom de la uila d'Agen uenia de la meissa uila de nochs o de dias que l'agues obs per negun
home que fos cochadz de malaudia que uolgues far ordre. l'escriuas i deu anar ab aquel que obs l'aura.
e si anar no i uolia el estaria en la merse del cosselh en uoluntat de perdre l'ofici de la notaria. (And
if some man of the town of Agen came from the town by night or day who was in need because of some
man who was laid up with sickness and who wanted to make a will, then the writer should go there
with the person who needed him, and if he would not go he would risk losing his appointment of notary at the discretion of the council.)

86

tation of the same situation is "fighting words." In the thirteenth century, some kinds of speech could justify a physical attack against a speaker, although in times and places less tolerant of physical violence—in modern common law jurisdictions, for example—the rule is that no mere speech can justify a physical attack: "The general rule in common law jurisdictions . . . is that provocative words unaccompanied by an overt act of hostility will not justify an assault regardless of how opprobrious or insulting the words may be."[38] In these jurisdictions, there are no "fighting words." In thirteenth-century France defamation constituted "fighting words." As has been shown by Claude Gauvard, in the fourteenth century and later there were many appeals to the highest level by people who claimed to have been provoked by the words of their victim.[39]

A curious law from a southern French charter states that slander can be punished by a fine. Slander committed by a woman, however, draws only half the fine exacted from men. There is no justification given in the charter for this difference in treatment.[40] The same rule appears in the Orléans section of the *Etablissements de Saint Louis,* where the fine for a man's slander is five sous and for a woman's three sous.[41]

It might be said that slander is an attempt to create a bad reputation for someone. Since reputation is so valuable, it must be guarded with care, and even violence used to protect it is condoned. One way in which speech can properly be used to destroy reputation occurs when it forms part of the evidence given in court, which may lead to the condemnation of a criminal. In thirteenth-century France, when a person lost the privilege of being a witness, it was because he had shown himself to be unreliable. In some codes he was said to be marked with infamy, that is, he was, in Old French, *disfamez.* A discussion of witnesses and testimony can help show what such a person lost.

A full trial, with testimony by witnesses and oral arguments by the parties or their lawyers, is called in Old French an *enqueste,* which is once again confusing because the words *inquest* and *inquisition* have another meaning in ordinary English, bringing up images of dead bodies and Torquemada and the whole yelping pack of Dominicans. In Beaumanoir, a sort of preliminary investigation by the judge is called an *apprise,* and this has no counterpart in Anglo-American law. It must have been a useful procedure at a time when there were no police or detectives whose job preceded indictment. Even today in France it is a judge (called the *juge d'instruction*)

38. David L. Graven, "Recent Cases," *Minnesota Law Review* 37 (1953): 200.
39. Claude Gauvard, *"De grace especial": Crime, état et société en France à la fin du Moyen Âge* (Paris: Publications de la Sorbonne, 1991).
40. Cited by Jean-Marie Carbasse, *Consulats méridionaux et justice criminelle au Moyen Âge* (thesis, Faculté de droit et des sciences économiques de l'université de Montpellier I, 1974), 258 n. 14.
41. *Etablissements,* 145.

who conducts the preliminary interrogation of an accused before making a report to her fellow judges when she is satisfied that she has learned enough.[42] The thirteenth-century *apprise* must have produced quite a bit of common knowledge, if not notorious fact, although it was much less formal than an *enqueste* with its interrogation of witnesses under oath.

There is not much written about witnesses and their testimony in any of the thirteenth-century law books except that of Beaumanoir (although the problem of false witnesses is raised in each). He insists that witnesses must testify to what they have seen, and not at second hand or by hearsay (§1234). Already for Beaumanoir, personal knowledge of some action alone qualified a person to be a witness. Nevertheless, the intricate modern rules for admitting or not admitting out-of-court statements, also called hearsay, had clearly not been formulated when the *Coutumes de Beauvaisis* were composed. Some out-of-court statements were considered to raise a presumption of guilt, however. The best example is threats. If the perpetrator of a crime is not easily identified, then the judge has to seek out people who have made threats against the victim, for this represents a rebuttable presumption of guilt (§1158). Beaumanoir tells the gruesome story of the woman who threatens a man she thinks has swindled her. She tells him that she will send to his barn the *rouges charpentiers* (red carpenters), which is taken to mean flames or fire. Less than six months later his barn burns down. The woman's threat, which might have been merely gossip, is remembered, she is arrested, the threats are proved, and although she denies the crime she is burned to death (§1159).

These examples of legal procedures in which the spoken word plays a large part point up some of the difficulties of a legal system that had relatively few written laws or court records. But speech still plays a part in modern American law, where it is thought important for the jury (or the judge) to see the demeanor of the witnesses as they are testifying. All that surrounds the words themselves—the tone of voice, the hesitations and pauses, the body language—can be weighed against the words as recorded in a transcript, which records only the words used, and not, for example, the intonation that might signal irony.

The problem of proof is of interest in connection with crimes against or by women. Two of the customaries discuss the proof of crimes in which women are involved: rape and adultery. In the case of rape, the woman is at a real disadvantage and her proofs have to conform to a loosely stated standard;[43] in the case of adultery, it is the authorities who have to conform to a standard very carefully delineated and full of possibilities for escape, especially by the man. I will deal with these in turn.

---

42. *Code de procédure civile,* art. 779 al. 1er et 2.
43. See Caviness and Nelson, "Silent Witnesses," in this volume.

In Beaumanoir, a woman who goes off with a man and subsequently accuses him of rape will not be believed without a thorough investigation (§929). Beaumanoir alleges that the woman may be making a false accusation to please some other man, or to hide her shame. The woman must demonstrate that she did not agree to the act, by showing that she cried out, and that her cry was heard (thus making the incident *notoire*), unless she was in fear of her life. Her testimony must be without contradictions and generally satisfactory to the judge, a loose standard allowing the male judge considerable latitude.

An even greater difficulty of proof faced those who wanted to accuse someone of adultery in Agen. For the crime of adultery to be prosecuted, the guilty pair had to be observed in the act by the appointed judge (*bailli*) and two council members. If the man could escape before he was arrested, or even after, then he was free from punishment.[44] The punishment for adultery was a public humiliation: the man and the woman, roped together and naked, preceded by trumpeters, were led through the town for all to see and even to beat with clubs (fig. 18).[45] Evidently the word of an ordinary citizen was not taken seriously enough to convict: only members of the council were appropriate witnesses. Since the *Costuma d'Agen*, unlike Beaumanoir, does not speculate or explain very much, one is left to wonder what series of cases or societal experience led to the formulation of such a hard-to-prove custom. Was it merely the adaptation of the law to what may have been a common "crime"? Was this process of adaptation the foundation of other sections of the code?[46]

A legal system, after all, has to have a foundation. John Austin, the early nineteenth-century English legal scholar, said that laws were orders, backed by a threat of punishment.[47] Justice Oliver Wendell Holmes thought that

---

44. *Costuma d'Agen*, fol. 43r:

E quant seran espiat deu lo balles uenir al cosselh. o cossels al balle quals que primers o sapia. E deu i anar lo balles ab dos proshomes del cosselh o d'aqui en sus. e no senes homes del cosselh que sio duj o plus. E deuo estre pres aquil adoltre si son trobat essemps l'us sobre l'autre. e si son nu e nu en un leghs. e que l'om aia las bragas trachas. e no en autra manera. E si l'om pot escapar auant que sia pres. o apres: es quitis. senes que·l senher no·i a re. ne aquel hom non deu passar neguna pena. (And when they have been detected the *bailli* must come to the council, or the council must go to the *bailli*, whoever hears about it first. And the *bailli* must go there with two good men of the council, or more, and not without two or more men from the council. And the adulterers must be arrested if they are found together, one on top of the other, and if they are naked in a bed, and the man has his trousers down, and in no other manner. And if the man can escape before he is arrested, or after, he is acquitted without the lord getting anything [as a fine], and the man should not be subject to any penalty.)

45. Agen, France, Archives départementales de Lot-et-Garonne, MS 42, fol. 42v. The public humiliation was similar to that created by the punishment for false witnesses.

46. See Jean-Marie Carbasse, "Currant Nudi, La répression de l'adultère dans le Midi médiéval (XIIe-XVe siècles)," in *Droit, histoire et sexualité*, ed. Jacques Poumarède and Jean-Pierre Royer (Paris: Publications de l'Espace juridique, 1987), 83–102.

47. John Austin, *The Province of Jurisprudence Determined*, ed. Wilfrid E. Rumble (1832; reprint, Cambridge: Cambridge University Press, 1995), 18 (my paraphrase).

Figure 18. Creation of *mauvaise renommée:* adultery. The adulterers are exposed to the towns-people, thereby incurring infamy. Reproduced with permission from Agen, France, Archives Départementales de Lot-et-Garonne, MS 42, fol. 42v, detail.

the law at a given time was anything you could get a judge to enforce.[48] In a radio interview, President Richard Nixon's attorney general said that the foundation of justice in the United States is the supposition that a person who has been placed under oath in due form will tell the truth.[49] This is disingenuous: in a great many lawsuits contradictory claims are made by two parties, so one of them must not be telling the truth. These contra-dictory claims rarely result in perjury suits, yet it is clear that people fre-quently lie under oath. Perhaps the attorney general should have said that the ability of judges and juries to tell who is lying under oath is the cor-nerstone of our legal system. When parties tell the truth, it is very often possible for a jury or a judge to arrive at a just and equitable solution to a problem.[50] However, a party, let us say a thirteenth-century French defen-dant, often has a good reason not to tell the truth: if he does, he may be hanged. The wager of battle, still available in some courts in Beaumanoir's time, included an accusation by the appellee that the person who chal-

48. Oliver Wendell Holmes, "The Path of the Law," *Harvard Law Review* 10 (1897): 457 (my paraphrase).

49. *All Things Considered,* 22 September 1998. In a somewhat different context, William Safire wrote, "Without equal compulsion to tell the truth, equal justice becomes a mockery"; see *Minneapolis Tribune,* 25 August 2000, A23.

50. Obviously, if everyone told the truth, there would be no need for proofs. Yet in every case, according to Beaumanoir, a party who makes an allegation must offer to prove it; §§200, 209. Just as modern lawyers spend a lot of time and effort attacking their opponents' evi-dence, and even their right to introduce certain evidence, medieval lawyers must have spent some time trying to exclude certain persons from giving evidence at all. The law provided some help, by categorizing certain persons as excludable because of their "lack of trustwor-thiness" (*mauvese renomee,* or infamy, or *enfamamiento*), or merely being female; see the essays by Wickham, Bowman, and Caviness and Nelson in this volume.

lenged him was not telling the truth. Since this accusation led to a battle, these were the ultimate "fighting words."[51] What could induce a person to tell the truth against his own interest in a thirteenth-century French court? The customaries imply that the most powerful inducement was thought to be the fear of hell, but it is clear that this fear was evolving into that of societal exclusion.

In a period such as the thirteenth century in France when the torture of witnesses was not systematic and may not have been practiced at all, perhaps only a supernatural fear could force witnesses or accused persons to tell the truth when it was to their probable detriment. This statement might be more or less accurate according to the person's social class, with the nobility held to a higher standard, which was not yet called honor. While many witnesses today probably swear on the Bible in all sincerity that they will tell the truth, and then do so, it seems likely that other persons who swear just as believably are prepared to lie through their teeth.[52] The fear of hell, perhaps even hell itself, no longer looms large in modern consciousness. There are indications in Beaumanoir that he knew that some people, even under oath, did not tell the truth (§894). We are familiar with the swearing match, where one party swears something is one way, the other party swears it is another. How can a judge decide who is telling the truth, and which side should win the point or the suit? By Beaumanoir's time, the courts had abandoned the old, irrational proof of the ordeal, and in the royal domain, at least, the wager of battle was also proscribed by Louis IX.[53] The appeal to God's wisdom, as manifested in the result of the ordeal, was thus not available to late thirteenth-century French courts. Beaumanoir was quite skeptical about the wager of battle, permitted in the Beauvais district in some cases. He says he does not permit it in cases in which the stakes are low (§1818).

We see this thoughtful and pragmatic *bailli* wrestle with the problem of justice and truth. In minor matters, he is prepared to let one of the parties swear an oath, and he seems to realize that some parties will not dare to do so, for fear of stating a falsehood under oath, with its consequences to their hopes of eternal life.[54] The establishment of the facts of a case can in some

51. Beaumanoir, §1839.
52. See the remarks of Lévy, *La preuve*, 20–21: "In the most advanced civilizations, the oath plays only a minor role, for belief is limited by scepticism with respect to this self-interested information. Even deeply religious centuries like those of the Christian Middle Ages gave it no greater a place, experience having proved that the fear of God did not often stop people on the road to perjury" (my translation).
53. See *Etablissements*, 1:3, p. 8.
54. See, for example, Beaumanoir, §§60, 122, 127, and esp. 227:

Cil qui ne veut jurer que sa demande est vraie ne doit pas estre receus en sa demande, car il se met en soupeçon qu'il ne demande fausseté. Et se li defenderes ne veut jurer que les resons qu'il met en ses defenses sont vraies, eles ne doivent pas estre receues. Et se les parties se vouloient soufrir de fere serment par acort, ne le doit pas la justice soufrir. Ainçois apartient a son office qu'il prengne le sere-

instances be automatic: if two witnesses agree, then their testimony represents the essential minimum required for a decision (§1149), and perhaps this is the minimum kind of common knowledge. However, the minimum two witnesses might agree on one set of facts, and two more might agree on another set. How to decide then? First, Beaumanoir suggests counting witnesses, so that the side with the most witnesses who agree will win (§1257); the greater the number of witnesses who agree, the more you have a *fet notoire*. Second, look at quality, that is, whether some witnesses have a bad reputation, and which ones made the best proof (§1205). "Best" is not defined very clearly, because there is always a degree of freedom involved in the judge's decision—or, to use another meaning of the word, it is a matter of judgment. In modern French law, the judge is supposed to reach a decision based on his intimate conviction. In Anglo-American law the parties have to convince the judge or the jury to find for their side, so that arguments presenting a more convincing case, by reason of logic or rhetoric, may win the day. In thirteenth-century France, a man's judgment was now called on to replace God's, so that human frailty, inattention, lack of memory—in short, human weakness—had to be overcome if justice was to be served. Beaumanoir's solution, with respect at least to the law (but not the facts), was to write everything down.[55] For the facts, he was still struggling to find a system that would be less dependent on unreliable testimony.

For weakness of memory, which meant that customs were forgotten, writing presented a solution. In the thirteenth century the great work of recording customs began, forever changing customary law, which could no longer be defined as oral law, preserved only in men's memories. It is the danger of forgetting, the weakness of the human memory, that drives Beaumanoir as well as Pierre de Fontaines to write down the law.[56] When memory is relied on, even the best intentioned ad hoc solutions may not turn out well; but when the procedure is set out in advance, a relatively fairer or at least more consistent result can be obtained. This consideration may have driven Louis IX to prescribe certain procedures in court.[57]

---

ment des parties pour encherchier la verité de la querele, car de ce dont il sont a acort par leur serement ples est finés, et seur ce dont il sont en descort doit estre li ples maintenus, et li tesmoing tret. (A plaintiff who will not swear that his complaint is true should not be admitted to complain, for he falls under the suspicion that his complaint is false. And if the defendant will not swear that the defenses he raises are true, they should not be allowed. And if the parties agreed not to swear, the judge should not permit it. His duty is to take the oaths of the parties in order to seek out the truth in the dispute, for the pleadings are at an end concerning what they agree on under oath, and the pleadings must be continued concerning what they disagree on, and the witnesses called.)

55. He hinted, too, that the whole suit could be conducted in writing, as ecclesiastical suits already were; see ibid., §211.

56. Beaumanoir, §7; *Conseil*, 4.

57. *Etablissements*, chaps. 1–9.

In earlier descriptions of legal procedures, as found in literary works such as Marie de France's *Lanval,* where the hero is tried on two counts—soliciting the queen (false) and saying that his own mistress's servant is more beautiful than the queen (true)—and the *Chanson de Roland,* where Ganelon is charged with treason, but has a very powerful champion, the judges' discussion centers around crafting a solution to the knotty problem facing them, a solution that appears somewhat ad hoc or improvised.[58] They are motivated by fear (in the *Chanson de Roland*) or by pity (*Lanval*). In later literary works, the action tends to center on the preliminary parts of the procedure. These include attempts to recuse the judge or the opposing advocate (the *Advocacie Nostre Dame,* where the plaintiff Satan tries to have the opposing advocate, the Virgin, removed on the grounds that she is the judge's mother, and the *Condamnation de banquet,* where the judge is asked to recuse herself because she is a woman); chicanery (as in *La Farce de Maistre Pierre Pathelin,* where the advocate succeeds in persuading the judge that his client is a speechless idiot); and innovation, such as the application of Novel Disseisin (a legal procedure by which a person dispossessed of real property could sue for reinstatement) to people as well as inanimate personal property.[59] These later literary pieces tend to be farces, whereas the earlier ones had been tragedies. Figuring out how to behave is a lofty theme; trying to get away with something is a lowly one.

The problem of discovering the truth, or at least of prying information from those unwilling to give it voluntarily, led in later centuries to the use of judicial torture. The best proof of guilt is a confession, and if a suspect can be tortured and made to confess it resolves many difficulties. An in-court admission that produced a *notorium iuris* had already been recognized by the canon law courts as needing no further proof. Torture was not much used in thirteenth-century France to extract confessions; there is hardly a mention of it in the four customary law books I have consulted. The abandonment of irrational proofs, which coincided with the abandonment of oral tradition and with the writing down of customary law, may seem like progress when looked at from a modern perspective; but it was not a wholly successful transition, as it cleared the way for judicial torture.

The three areas of French customary law that I have discussed concern a person (reputation), a fact (notoriety), or a problem (proof by witnesses).

58. Marie de France, *Le lai de Lanval,* ed. Jean Rychner (Geneva: Droz, 1958); *La Chanson de Roland,* ed. Frederick Whitehead (Oxford: Blackwell, 1946).

59. Guillaume Coquillart, *Le plaidoyé de Coquillart d'entre la Simple et la Rusée,* in idem, *Oeuvres,* ed. Michael J. Freeman (Geneva: Droz, 1975), 3–55; *Maistre Pierre Pathelin,* ed. Richard T. Holbrook, Classiques Français du Moyen Âge 35 (1924; reprint, Paris: Champion, 1963); Nicolas de la Chesnaye, *La condamnation de Banquet, Moralité,* in Edouard Fournier, *Le théâtre français avant la Renaissance 1450–1550: Mystères, moralités et farces* (Paris, 1873), 216–71.

They are closely linked. A person's reputation might make him ineligible to be a witness, and notoriety of a fact might make the use of witnesses unnecessary. Societal needs were changing, and the law was evolving to solve societal problems. People discovered that it is hard to discover the truth when some want it hidden, and that forcing people to tell the truth by non-physical coercion is quite difficult. The expectation that God would reveal the truth about recent human events had been abandoned. As the practitioners and jurists groped their way to a solution for this problem, they at least excluded from testifying those who had shown themselves unworthy of trust. It was not a radical or a complete solution, but it may have acted as a deterrent to some degree. It would be a long time before the courts had lie detectors and DNA analysis. It is fascinating to see medieval people grappling with problems that are even today far from being resolved.

CHAPTER FIVE

Infamy and Proof in Medieval Spain

JEFFREY A. BOWMAN

To say that a person "has a reputation" is not to make a neutral observation. The phrase suggests not only that a large number of people share distinct opinions about the person in question but also that those opinions are predominantly negative. There is, in other words, a dark side to *fama*. Fame, renown, and glory have counterparts in notoriety, infamy, and disgrace. The currents and eddies of bad reputations are every bit as complicated as those of good ones. When we refer to bad reputations, we often think of suspicions or insinuations that circulate informally and privately. Bad reputations are made in whispers, rolled eyeballs, and confidential letters of recommendation that are stinting in praise. In medieval Europe, the creation of bad reputations often involved the delicate interplay of informal gossip, on the one hand, and formal, public representations, on the other. Many communities developed institutional mechanisms for erecting, publicizing, and dismantling bad reputations. They created rules that, at least in theory, instructed people how to evaluate and respond to the *bona fama* or *mala fama* of their neighbors. These mechanisms are especially interesting because they stand at the intersection of social behavior (innuendo, suspicion, and gossip) and legal thought (jurisprudence, justice, and power).

Medieval understandings of legal proof afford a rich opportunity to examine this intersection of social and legal categories related to reputation. Courts administering justice relied on various forms of proof. Someone accused of theft or adultery might prove her innocence by appealing to witnesses or oath-helpers. Litigants embroiled in disputes over property used written proofs, judicial ordeals, and witness testimony to substantiate their claims. Those who administered justice (counts, countesses, bishops, professional judges, informal arbiters, or *boni homines* [lit. "good men"]) had to assess the merits of different proofs, a task made especially difficult by the irrelevance, ambiguity, or technical flaws of some proffered documents. Forgeries were common. The outcomes of judicial ordeals were often difficult to interpret. Judging the probative value of witness testimony was no less complicated, for witnesses might be misinformed or their memory of the events about which they testified might be clouded. Finally, some witnesses tried to deceive judges, their neighbors, and their opponents— some witnesses lied.

For these reasons, legal thinkers strove to develop guidelines for assessing different proofs. They tested documents for authenticity, examining signatures and dating formulae. Some courts tried to achieve greater certainty by relying on multiple forms of proof. Judges called on witnesses to corroborate written proofs, or turned to judicial ordeals when witness testimony was for some reason inadequate. Legislators created tools for sorting good proofs from bad—tools that made some proofs especially valuable and excluded others from consideration. Among these tools was one that related to a person's reputation: the idea of infamy. *Infamia* was a condition the law imposed on certain people that entailed legal and social disabilities. Prominent among these disabilities was the fact that *infames* could not testify. Judges, lawyers, and communities used infamy to exclude possible witnesses whose testimony was likely to be unreliable and/or whose participation in judicial hearings would taint the administration of justice. Some people were thus deemed categorically unfit to participate in legal proceedings because of their behavior and the reputation that their behavior generated. Then, as now, it was hard to quantify reputation or to anatomize the components of a bad name. The legal concept of infamy was especially useful because it allowed legal professionals and communities to bridge gaps between the ephemeral, social quality of the word on the street (or at the mill, at the bath, or in the vineyard) and the steely realities of one's legal status. Through infamy, a nebulous *mala fama* became a concrete, institutionalized legal category.

This chapter is divided into four parts. Parts one and two are devoted to law codes, which in medieval Spain described what made one infamous and legislated the consequences of infamy. First, I describe seventh-century Visigothic legislation related to infamy. Second, I examine legislation related to infamy in the thirteenth-century *Siete Partidas*. These legal traditions tell us a great deal about medieval understandings of proof and reputation, but it is not always easy to see how rules in law codes affected legal practice. The law is one thing; the ways in which people learn to live within the law is something else. In the third part, I turn to the practice of law, exploring connections between law codes and litigation. Charters, especially those related to property disputes, often record witness testimony and provide clues about how judges assessed the reliability of witnesses; I trace links between the reflections of jurists and the experiences of medieval litigants, pointing to the ways in which litigants and judges applied rules related to infamy. Several eleventh-century cases suggest that the question of witnesses' *infamia* regularly played a role in judicial proceedings. In the last part, I offer some concluding observations.

The Visigothic Code

The Visigoths who governed the Iberian Peninsula during the sixth and seventh centuries were avid lawmakers. In 481, within a few years of their arrival in southern Gaul and the Iberian Peninsula, King Euric promulgated his *Code*.[1] In 506, Visigothic legislators issued a set of rules designed to govern King Alaric's Roman subjects called Alaric's *Breviary*, or the *Lex Romana Visigothorum*, which was to exercise a lasting influence throughout western Europe during the Middle Ages.[2] The greatest achievement of Visigothic legal thought, however, was the *Visigothic Code*. Isidore of Seville says that King Leovgild's desire to amend earlier law was the original impulse behind the creation of the *Code*. According to Isidore, Leovgild "corrected those things which seemed to have been set up inadequately, adding very many laws that had been omitted and removing some superfluous ones."[3] The *Code* was the fruit of a century of tinkering by several generations of Visigothic leaders and jurists, as Visigothic kings issued several versions of the *Code* during the seventh century, each of which added to the *Code*'s complexity and to the sheer number of rules in the *Code*'s twelve books.

The Visigoths were eager students of Roman law and energetic legislators. They labeled each of the rules included in the *Code* with its presumed origins, and fully a third of those labeled *antiqua* were derived from Ro-

---

1. Ernst Levy, "Reflections on the First 'Reception' of Roman Law in Germanic States," *American Historical Review* 48 (1942): 20–29. For Euric's *Code* and its debts to Roman legal traditions, see Katherine Fischer Drew, "The Barbarian Kings as Lawgivers and Judges," in *Law and Society in Early Medieval Europe: Studies in Legal History* (London: Variorum Reprints, 1988), 13; Eelco Nicolaas van Kleffens, *Hispanic Law until the End of the Middle Ages* (Edinburgh: Edinburgh University Press, 1968).

2. In the Iberian Peninsula, Alaric's *Breviary* was abrogated in the mid-seventh century by the *Visigothic Code*. In southwest Gaul and in the Rhône Valley, the breviary was used throughout the sixth century and became the main channel by which Franks, Lombards, and Bavarians received Roman legal thought. Drew, "The Barbarian Kings," 17; van Kleffens, *Hispanic Law*, 62. François Ganshof, however, argues that the *Lex Romana Visigothorum* had relatively little influence on later legislative projects; see *Droit romain dans les capitulaires*, Ius Romanum Medi Aevi I, 2, b, cc (Milan: Giuffrè, 1969).

3. Isidore of Seville, *History of the Kings of the Goths, Vandals, and Suevi*, trans. Guido Donini and Gordon B. Ford Jr. (Leiden: Brill, 1966), 24.

man sources. The *Visigothic Code* was thus both more Romanized and more comprehensive than any other code created in early medieval Europe. It included detailed procedural rules governing property, injury, inheritance, the organization of courts, and the assessment of proofs.

Rules in the *Code* related to infamy were the joint legacy of Roman jurisprudence and Visigothic traditions.[4] Roman law had gradually developed a complex set of rules designating certain members of Roman society as *infames*. This designation fell upon those convicted of certain crimes: sexual transgressors, those marked by moral turpitude, and those who pursued certain professions. Prostitutes, pimps (*lenocini*), auctioneers (*praecones*), undertakers, gladiators, professional performers, men who submitted to anal intercourse, guardians who neglected their charges, and those who demanded excessive interest on loans were all *infames*.[5] The legal disabilities that infamy entailed were described in praetorian edicts, municipal regulations, and the *Digest*, a summary of earlier Roman laws produced for the emperor Justinian in the sixth century. *Infames* could not represent others in court, and in certain cases they could not engage others to represent them. They could not serve in the army, nor could they vote in assemblies or hold public office. *Infames* could not serve as witnesses; they could neither offer evidence in criminal trials nor witness many acts of private law related to property. They could not make legal wills.[6] They could not marry freeborn Romans. Finally, Roman law did not accord *infames* the same legal protections afforded other Romans; *infames*, for example, were subject to corporal punishment and torture.[7]

Like the Roman legislation that preceded it, Visigothic law relating to infamy concentrated on two distinct but intertwined anxieties. The first of these concerned truth and reliability in courts. People who had provided

4. See Edward Peters, "Wounded Names: The Medieval Doctrine of Infamy," in *Law in Medieval Life and Thought*, ed. Edward B. King and Susan J. Ridyard (Sewanee, Tenn.: Press of the University of the South, 1990), 43–89, esp. 55.

5. A. H. J. Greenidge, *Infamia: Its Place in Roman Public and Private Law* (Oxford: Oxford University Press, 1894); Jane Gardner, *Being a Roman Citizen* (London: Routledge, 1993); Catharine Edwards, *The Politics of Immorality in Ancient Rome* (Cambridge: Cambridge University Press, 1993), 123–26; and Vincent Tatarczuk, *Infamy of Law: A Historical Synopsis and a Commentary* (Washington, D.C.: Catholic University of America Press, 1954), esp. chap. 1, "The History of Legal Infamy."

6. Gardner, *Being a Roman Citizen*, 118.

7. Edward Peters, *Torture* (Oxford: Oxford University Press, 1985), 31: "The infamous person, like the slave of old, lacks the *dignitas* to offer voluntary testimony merely under questioning; torture must validate his testimony." The Roman law of infamy coalesced only slowly and at most points offered considerable flexibility. The Emperor Hadrian, for example, issued rescripts that encouraged judges to use their own discretion in weighing proofs: "Sometimes the number of witnesses, sometimes dignity and authority, at other times a commonly held rumor confirms the credibility of the matter about which there is a question." Cited in Frank R. Hermann, "The Establishment of a Rule Against Hearsay," *Virginia Journal of International Law* 36 (1995): 14.

false testimony or used deceptive documents were barred from testifying because they were likely to do so again; allowing them to testify, the logic went, was likely to frustrate justice. The second anxiety was more closely related to purity and pollution than to reliability. Someone guilty of incest would not necessarily be more likely to offer false testimony, but his presence would certainly violate the dignity consonant with the administration of justice. In Visigothic law, the depraved kept company with the dishonest under the umbrella of *infamia*.

The *Visigothic Code*'s more than two dozen rules relating directly or indirectly to infamy echo Roman legislation in other ways as well. The largest number of these are in the fourth title, "Concerning Witnesses and Testimony" (*De testibus et testimoniis*) of the *Code*'s second book, "On Judicial Procedures" (*De Negotiis causarum*). One of the primary legal consequences of *infamia* was disqualification as a witness, so it is hardly surprising that much of the *Code*'s guidance on infamy clustered around questions of testimony, forgery, and proof. Many of the same categories of wrongdoer (murderers, thieves, and perjurers) were subject to infamy in Visigothic law, although, unlike their Roman predecessors, Visigothic legislators devoted little attention to the *fama* or *infamia* of pimps, entertainers, usurers, and jugglers—those who, in one scholar's account, constituted the "core of the Roman concept of '*infamia*.'"[8]

The first rule in the title provided an expansive, though not comprehensive, list of people who were not allowed to testify, including murderers, thieves, poisoners, and those who consulted sorcerers (*Leges Visigothorum* 2.4.1). Those who gave false testimony, a crime the *Code* described as especially reprehensible because it violated both human and divine law, were *infames* (2.4.3, 2.4.7).[9] Those who perjured themselves were rendered infamous, flogged, and in some cases subject to fines (2.4.14). Those who committed crimes of omission might also incur infamy; potential witnesses who had relevant information about a case but who refused to testify or claimed to be ignorant of the facts were no longer permitted to testify in any court. Non-nobles were subject to an additional penalty of one hundred lashes (2.4.2). Those who deceived others in business dealings, whether with deceptive language or tampered documents, were "publicly marked with infamy" (7.5.7).

---

8. *Leges Visigothorum*, ed. Karl Zeumer, Monumenta Germaniae Historica Leges (Hannover: MGH, 1902), 2.4.4 (hereafter *Leges Visigothorum*); Thomas McGinn, *Prostitution, Sexuality, and the Law in Ancient Rome* (New York: Oxford University Press, 1998), 68: "Those who stand at the core of the Roman concept of '*infamia*' I identify as prostitutes, pimps, gladiators, trainers, beast-fighters, and actors."

9. See also Juan Antonio García Alejandre, "El delito de falsedad en el derecho histórico español," *Historia, Instituciones, Documentos* 3 (1976): 9–140. For the political and theological background to Visigothic legislation regarding infamy, see Carlos Petit, "De Negotiis Causarum," *Anuario de historia del derecho español* 55 (1985): 173–92.

The *Visigothic Code* included procedural guidelines for labeling false witnesses *infames*. After any hearing involving witness testimony, the *Code* mandated a six-month period during which that testimony might be challenged. If one suspected that a witness was ineligible to testify or had offered false testimony, one had to prove the accusation of infamy using other witnesses or legitimate documents within six months of the original testimony. After the six-month period had expired, courts and judges would not consider any challenges to witness testimony or accusations of infamous behavior.[10]

References to judicial infamy in the *Code* are concentrated in the title devoted to witness testimony, but there are also references scattered elsewhere. Those who tampered with the will of a dead person or tried to conceal a will became infamous (7.5.7). Anyone who killed his own slave maliciously was obliged to "pay a pound of gold to the fisc and afterwards will be forever known as infamous and will not be allowed to testify" (6.5.12: *insuper perenni infamio denotatus testificare ei ultra non liceat*). Those who made contradictory agreements, conveying property to one person in writing and conveying the same property to a different party orally, were infamous and subject to fines (2.5.18). Lords who persuaded freeborn women to marry slaves were rendered infamous (3.2.7). So too were those who incited riot and bloodshed (8.1.3). Members of religious orders who abandoned their habits and tried to resume secular life were to perform perpetual penance in a monastery and were branded with the mark of infamy (3.5.3). Certain sexual relations also inspired the revulsion of Visigothic legislators, and infamy marked those who had sex with consecrated virgins, widows in religious orders, or penitents, and those found guilty of incest (3.5.2). Indeed, Visigothic legislators were so eager to punish what they saw as corrupting sexual practices that they allowed judges and priests to pursue those suspected of these crimes independently, even though Visigothic law generally allowed only injured parties to bring accusations. Finally, the anti-Jewish legislation of the *Code*'s twelfth book stipulated that Christians who helped Jews to oppress or to deceive slaves were to be enslaved, suffer the confiscation of half of their property, and become infamous (12.2.14).[11]

The *Code* offered no definition of *infamia*, but several passages equated infamy with the inability to offer testimony. Although disqualification from

10. *Leges Visigothorum* 2.4.7: "Quod si infra sex menses non potuerit et vitia predictorum testium querere et coram iudice eorum infamiam conprobare, exactis sex mensibus nullum iam ei ultra temporibus spatium dabitur, quod aut prolatum testem infamem esse convincat aut alium testem pro eadem causa in iudicio proferat." See also 2.4.8.

11. A Jew's right to testify was already circumscribed, see *Leges Visigothorum* 12.2.9; and P. D. King, *Law and Society in the Visigothic Kingdom* (Cambridge: Cambridge University Press, 1972), 136.

testimony was but one of the prominent consequences of infamy in Roman law, in the *Visigothic Code* it was the *only* legal disability discussed in any detail. There was very likely a wide range of legal and social disabilities that affected *infames* in Visigothic Spain, but the *Code* says little about these.

In both Roman and Visigothic law, there was a close connection between corporal punishments and infamy. The general principle in Visigothic law seems to have been that physical punishment of any sort marked one as infamous, except in cases in which a wrongdoer submitted to physical punishment in lieu of a financial penalty.[12] Those who schemed to injure others in unlawful ways while claiming that they were not acting contrary to the law would, according to the *Code,* suffer ignominy, torments, and fines; they received one hundred lashes in public and were scalped "as a mark of perpetual infamy" (*Leges Visigothorum* 6.4.5). The connection between physical punishment and infamy is most apparent in those provisions of the *Code* that strove to disconnect the two. In certain cases, the *Code* stipulated that a wrongdoer would *not* be marked with infamy even though he had been subjected to physical punishment. Further, when a wrongdoer ordered to pay compensation to injured parties or fines to the fisc could not do so, in some instances she could undergo a physical punishment— usually a flogging—instead of paying the fine. In such cases, however, the punishment would not have brought about the infamy of the wrongdoer. A noble who scorned a royal command was to pay a fine of three pounds of gold to the royal fisc, but if he could not do so, he would receive one hundred lashes without being rendered infamous (2.1.33).

Flogging and infamy were distinct punishments, but they tended to be so closely linked that Visigothic legislators labored to separate them in certain cases.[13] The *Code* mentions several ambiguous cases in which wrongdoers do *not* incur *infamia.* If a person killed another through strenuous discipline or punishment, the guilty party was not marked with infamy as long as the death was unintentional (6.5.8). Rambunctious Visigoths who killed others recklessly or "in play" did not become infamous since the crime was not committed intentionally (6.5.7). Similarly, judges who rendered unjust decisions because they were coerced by royal commands were not marked with infamy (2.1.29).[14]

12. The connection between certain types of corporal punishment and *infamia* was established in Roman law, and commented upon by canonists from Gratian on. By the early twelfth century, canon law differentiated *infamia ex genere poenae*—infamy incurred because of certain types of punishment. Francesco Migliorino, *Fama e infamia: Problemi della società medievale nel pensiero giuridico nei secoli XII e XIII* (Catania: Giannotta, 1985), 87, 129; Tatarczuk, *Infamy of Law,* 17; Peters, "Wounded Names," 64–65; Rafael Serra Ruiz, *Honor, honra e injuria en el derecho medieval español* (Murcia: Sucesores de Nogués, 1969), 27–28; and John Morgan Livingston, "Infamia in the Decretists from Rufinus to Johannes Teutonicus" (Ph.D. diss., University of Wisconsin, Madison, 1962).

13. King, *Law and Society,* 89.

14. See also *Leges Visigothorum* 2.4.11: "ut ista disciplina non ad infamie notam eis per-

The rules of the *Code* are the most eloquent witness to Visigothic ideas about infamy, but other sources suggest that infamy had broad currency in Visigothic culture. Isidore of Seville, for example, mentioned fame and infamy in his *Etymologies.* The canons of the Fourth Council of Toledo forbade those marked with infamy from entering the priesthood and lamented that some priests did not enjoy *bona fama.*[15] In his *Rule for Monks,* Fructuosus of Braga marked with infamy those monks who reserved things for their own private use.[16] Finally, a canon of the Twelfth Council of Toledo indicated that deserters from the army were no longer able to testify.[17]

For all its concern with *infamia,* the *Visigothic Code* provided no single rule that defined infamy. It is perhaps one of the ironies of the Visigothic rules related to one's social identity and public reputation that one was simply supposed to know what constituted infamy. Similarly, the *Code* provided no exhaustive statement about those who incurred infamy. Some rules positively stated that certain crimes (perjury, forgery, incest, for example) marked the guilty with infamy, but in other cases, the connection was less explicit. The infamy of one who committed homicide, for example, was most clearly expressed in the rule, mentioned above, that explains where infamy *is not* to be found (among those who kill unintentionally) but not where infamy *is* to be found.

The *Siete Partidas*

The *Visigothic Code* remained the most programmatic and widely used law code in Spain for centuries. Muslim armies toppled the Visigothic kingdom in the early eighth century, but Christian communities continued to turn to Visigothic law for guidance. Many surviving records from the fragmented Christian principalities in the north of the peninsula refer to rules related to property, inheritance, proof, and dowry drawn from the *Code.* Only gradually did respect for local *fueros* (charters of laws and rights issued to municipalities) replace a selective adherence to Visigothic law. The *Visigothic Code* had no real rival as a comprehensive law code until the thirteenth century, when the *Siete Partidas* was created under Alfonso X of Castile. Alfonso's seven-part code was the most ambitious and influential

---

tineat." For other rules describing misdeeds that do not incur infamy, see *Leges Visigothorum* 3.4.15; 4.5.1; 12.1.3.

15. Patrologia Latina 84, col. 372B: "Praeteritis omissis, deinceps qui non promoveantur ad sacerdotium ex regulis cannonum necessario credimus inserendum: crimine detecti sunt, qui infamiae nota aspersi sunt, qui scelera aliqua per publicam poenitentiam admisisse confessi sunt, qui in haeresim lapsi sunt."

16. Patrologia latina 87, col. 1104.

17. *Leges Visigothorum,* 476.

of his many legislative projects.[18] The *partidas* are even more sweeping in scale than the twelve books created by Visigothic legislators, covering the nature of the law, kingship, sacraments, contracts, testaments, crimes, ecclesiastical offices, government, property, procedure, marriage, and relations among Jews, Christians, and Muslims.

The seventh *partida,* dealing with criminal law, devotes two titles to disgrace and infamy. These describe the loss of privileges and legal rights that accompanied a devaluation in one's reputation. According to one title, anyone who committed an offence that caused him to suffer disgrace, or *valer menos,* "cannot be considered the equal of others in battle, nor make any accusation, nor offer testimony, nor have part in any honors for which good men should be chosen."[19] Subsequent rules charted the two principal ways in which one could suffer such disgrace. First, a person might fail to discharge an obligation after making an agreement. Alternately, one might incur disgrace by retracting "in court or in a legal court" an earlier statement (*Siete Partidas* 7.5.2).[20]

The next title of the seventh *partida,* "Concerning the Infamous (*De los enfamados*)," provided the most systematic and thorough treatment of legal infamy in medieval Spanish law. The title described how one became the object of public reproaches that injured one's *fama.* Unlike the *Visigothic Code,* the Alfonsine legislation provided careful definitions of key terms: "Reputation (*fama*) is the good state of a man who lives justly according to law and good customs, having no defect or mark. Defamation means an attack made *contra la fama* of a person, called in Latin *infamia*" (7.6.2).[21] *Infames* could no longer obtain the same dignities or honors that those of good reputation could claim. They could no longer serve as councillors to kings or occupy important ecclesiastical posts. They could neither make wills nor offer testimony (4.9.4).

Drawing on Roman legal categories, the *Siete Partidas* distinguished two

18. For an overview, see Jerry R. Craddock, "The Legislative Works of Alfonso el Sabio," in *Emperor of Culture: Alfonso X the Learned of Castile and His Thirteenth-Century Renaissance,* ed. Robert I. Burns (Philadelphia: University of Pennsylvania Press, 1990), 182–97.

19. *Siete Partidas* 7.5.1. *The Text and Concordance of* Las Siete Partidas de Alfonso X, *Based on the Edition of the Real Academia de la Historia, 1807,* ed. Jerry R. Craddock, John J. Nitti, and Juan C. Temprano, microform (Madison, Wis.: Hispanic Seminary of Medieval Studies, 1990) (hereafter *Siete Partidas*). A rough equivalent of the Castilian *valer menos* in contemporary French law might be *abesser sa renomee.* See Akehurst, "Good Name," in this volume.

20. Julio Caro Baroja, "Honour and Shame: A Historical Account of Several Conflicts," in *Honour and Shame: The Values of Mediterranean Society,* ed. J. G. Peristiany (1966; reprint, Chicago: University of Chicago Press, 1974), 79–137; and Serra Ruiz, *Honor,* 238–39.

21. The thirteenth-century canonist Alberto Gandino repeated a definition of *existimatio* formulated by the Roman jurist Callistratus that echoes the *Siete Partidas*'s formulation: "inlesae dignitatis status, moribus ac legibus comprobatus, et in nullo diminutum." Compare also Piacentino's *Summa*: "fama est illesae dignitatis status moribus et legibus comprobatus et in nullo diminutus." See Migliorino, *Fama e infamia,* 61, 80. Peters also mentions Callistratus; see "Wounded Names," 62.

varieties of infamy, each of which incurred the same disabilities: infamy of fact (*enfamamiento de fecho*) and infamy of law (*enfamamiento de derecho*).[22] Infamy of fact branded those who engaged in particular activities. Those born outside lawful marriages, for example, were infamous. So too were sons who had been reproved by their fathers in wills. If a king or judge "publicly says to someone that he should lead a better life than he has lived" or "warns an advocate or any other man . . . that he should be careful not to accuse anyone wrongfully," the recipient of this advice was infamous (7.6.2).[23] Another title, dealing with royal responsibilities, emphasized that kings should be especially careful not to defame others, to injure their reputations and thereby render them *enfamados* (2.4.4). As in Roman law, *infamia* also fell upon those who practiced certain professions. Brothel keepers, jugglers, clowns, and other professional entertainers were infamous, but the rules allowed a few notable exceptions: "Those who play instruments, or sing to comfort themselves or to please their friends, or for the pleasure of kings or of other lords, shall not be considered infamous on this account" (7.6.4). Usurers and those who fought other people or animals for money were *enfamados*. So too were men who committed the *pecado contra natura* (sin against nature, or homosexuality); in these cases, the *Siete Partidas* instructs that "a man is *enfamado* solely because of his deed even though no sentence may have been issued against him" (7.6.4).

In the second variety of infamy, that of infamy of law, people were declared infamous by a judicial sentence. Anyone convicted of treason, forgery, adultery, theft, robbery, fraud, or bribery was infamous. Judges who failed to enforce the laws were dismissed and marked *enfamados* (2.31.2). Prison guards who committed any number of misdeeds were removed from office and made infamous, as were guardians who defrauded their charges (7.29.12; 6.18.4).

The *Siete Partidas* of Alfonso X thus gave *infamia* a wider scope than had the *Visigothic Code*, for although the list of infamous deeds resembled Visigothic and, to an even greater extent, Roman law, the *Siete Partidas* branded a greater variety of malefactors with infamy.[24] Alfonso's code also suggests that the infamous suffered a greater range of legal and social disabilities. Whereas the Visigothic legislation focused almost exclusively on the right to give testimony, the *Siete Partidas* painted a more expansive view of the

22. The distinction was, to some extent, implicit in Roman law. From Gratian on, canon lawyers developed an increasingly precise notion of the differences between *infamia iuris* and *infamia facti*. See Peters, "Wounded Names"; Migliorino, *Fama e infamia*, 13–14. For this distinction in canon law, see Tatarczuk, *Infamy of Law*, and Frank J. Rodimer, *The Canonical Effects of Infamy of Fact: A Historical Synopsis and Commentary* (Washington, D.C.: Catholic University of America Press, 1954).

23. Compare earlier Roman legislation cited in Rodimer, *Infamy of Fact*, 6.

24. Like the *Visigothic Code*, the *Siete Partidas* (7.6.6) stipulate that some corporal punishments would not inflict infamy.

consequences of infamy. *Infames* were prohibited from occupying offices requiring dignity, a prohibition important in Roman and in canon law but one that the *Visigothic Code* had largely ignored. In a rule describing how people should take pleasure in the *bona fama* of their king and be grieved by his *mala fama*, the *Siete Partidas* stated that murder and defamation were equally serious offenses: "As the wise men who made the ancient laws said, there are two misdeeds which are like equals: to kill a man or to accuse him of wrongdoing (*enfamarlo de mal*), because after a man is made infamous, even if there is no guilt, he is dead to the good and honor of this world. And, his defamation (*enfamamiento*) may be such that death would be better to him than life" (2.13.4).

The Castilian code was thus more explicit in its definitions of *fama* and *infamia* and more thorough in tracing their consequences. Where Visigothic law assumed an understanding of *fama* and *infamia*, the *Siete Partidas* defined its terms carefully, distinguishing between disgrace (*valer menos*), bad reputation (*mala fama*), and infamy (*infamia*). The terms and concepts were, according to the lawmakers, closely related but not identical. In many cases, one who was infamous also labored under a bad reputation, but whereas *nombradia mala* (bad name) or *mala fama* was a social condition, *infamia* was a legal one. The legislators confessed that *mala fama* and *infamia* "seem to be only one thing," but they made an important distinction. Infamy was subject to repeal. A bad reputation, on the other hand, was permanent:

> After the tongues of men have placed a bad name on someone, he never loses it, although he may not deserve it. But the infamy (*desfamamiento*), which we discussed above as it relates to the punishment which a man receives from it, can be taken away by the law. This would occur when an emperor or a king pardons anyone for a crime he has committed by which he was *enfamado*—in this manner, he loses his *mala fama*. (7.6.6)

This is one of several passages in which the *Siete Partidas* showed special sensitivity to the challenges of translating social categories into legal ones.

The *Visigothic Code* and the *Siete Partidas* were the most extensive and influential law codes promulgated in Christian Spain during the Middle Ages but they were not the only legislative projects to wrestle with the delicate problems of witness testimony, reputation, and proof. The twelfth-century *Usatges de Barcelona* provided less systematic guidance about witnesses than did the *Visigothic Code* or the *Siete Partidas,* but they did instruct that some witnesses were more credible than others: "We also order that more honorable [of higher status] witnesses shall be given more credibility than that of less honorable ones." The *Usatges* also allowed disputants to challenge their opponents' witnesses: "And if one is admitted to give testimony and is refused, let the person who refuses him say so and demonstrate why he does not want to admit him. Let witnesses be selected from this territory and one other, unless the case must be investigated further than the boundaries of the county."[25] The *Usatges* did not, however, suggest the likely grounds for such a challenge.

The *Vidal mayor*, a thirteenth-century Aragonese code, similarly acknowledged that the *bona fama* or *mala fama* of both those who came before the law and those who administered it were important concerns. Those more than seven years of age were to be accepted as witnesses, unless "infamy is proven against them."[26] Another rule cautioned that avarice might so distort the judgment of some people that they would ignore the judgment of God and would not "fear falling into *mala fama*" (4.13). Another rule suggested that the king had the ability to restore to *bona fama* those who were defamed with a bad reputation (*diffamado de mala fama*) (6.28). Judges were cautioned to be concerned about the maintenance of their own *bona fama* (6.29).[27]

Many of the *fueros* (municipal charters) also discussed witness testimony and infamy, although never in the same detail as the *Visigothic Code* and the *Siete Partidas*. The *Fuero de Baeza* instructed that false witnesses were to be barred from giving any future testimony and that their *mala fama* was to be widely published.[28] According to the *Fuero de Jaca*, the testimony of signatories to a bad document was prohibited,[29] as was the testimony of homicides, thieves, and false witnesses.[30] The *Fuero de Teruel* stipulated that anyone who denied the contents of a document that he had signed as a witness was forbidden to give testimony.[31] The *Fuero de Novenera* precluded

25. *The Usatges of Barcelona: The Fundamental Law of Catalonia*, trans. Donald Kagay (Philadelphia: University of Pennsylvania Press, 1994), 99. For other rules related to witness testimony, see no. 17 and no. 90.
26. *Vidal mayor: Traducción aragonesa de la obra In excelsis Dei thesauris, de Vidas de Canellas*, ed. Gunnar Tilander, 3 vols., Leges Hispanicae Medii Aevi (Lund, Sweden: H. Ohlssons, 1956), 9.7 (hereafter *Vidal mayor*).
27. The *Vidal mayor*, like many other codes, also discussed the use of *fama* as a form of proof; see *Vidal mayor* 9.49: "Et otrosí fama es quoando todos saben sin dubda aqueilla malfeitría feita, et todos o fasquas todos qui fablan d'aqueilla materia dizen, firmando, que tal o tales fizieron aqueilla malfeitría. Et quoando aqueilla pena peccunjaria no es toda de la cort mas en partida, non puede la cort demandar nin prouar sin quereillant." See also 9.19.
28. *El Fuero de Baeza: Edición, estudio y vocabulario*, ed. Jean Marie Victor Roudil (The Hague: van Goor Zonen, 1962), no. 877, p. 229. The *Siete Partidas*'s distinction between *mala fama* and *infamia* is not at all apparent here.
29. *El Fuero de Jaca: Edición crítica*, ed. Mauricio Molho, Fuentes para la Historia del Pirineo I (Saragossa: Instituto de Estudios Pirenaicos, 1964), no. 214, pp. 120–21.
30. *Fuero de Jaca*, no. 254, under the rubric "Quals non deuen estart testimonjs": "Les homiziers y les mals faytors e les layrons maniffestes, les criminos, les pozonadors y aquels que alguna uetz firen fals testimonj non deuen esta recebutz en ninguna testimonjança." See also "De pena de qui diz fals testimoni," ibid., no. 273.
31. *El Fuero de Teruel*, ed. Max Gorosch, Leges Hispanicae Medii Aevi (Uppsala: Almquist and Wikseels, 1950), no. 100, p. 131.

any person from testifying who had become *enfamado* for perjury or false-hood.[32] The *Furs de València* instructed that those convicted of usury, theft, rape, homicide, adultery, and other similar crimes (*d'altre crim consemblant a aquests*) were infamous.[33] The same code specified that the infamous could not serve as witnesses (*Furs de València* 4.9.3). The condition of in-famy was not, however, necessarily hopeless or permanent. Jaume I ruled that some malefactors who fully discharged the criminal sentences im-posed upon them would no longer suffer under infamy (2.7.1; 2.7.2). The keeping and losing of good names was thus a recurrent concern in me-dieval legislation. Many legislators used the category of infamy to exclude the testimony of those who labored under bad reputations.

The *Visigothic Code* and *Siete Partidas* contained the most sophisticated approaches to the question of reputation and proof, but a great deal of Iberian legislation addressed the problem of lending a legal form to a so-cial condition. The framers of the *Siete Partidas,* who were characteristi-cally lucid on this point, acknowledged that the distinction between *infamia* and *mala fama* was hard to maintain in practice. Infamy, based sometimes on a legal sentence and sometimes on public knowledge about one's way of life, was an element of the law of proofs that provoked the concern of jurists but allowed lawyers and disputants considerable procedural flexibility. Judges had to balance the need for efficiency in court (why expend the court's energy proving what is universally known to be true?) with the need for proofs that were precise and unequivocal. The related problems of *infamia* and *fama* provoked the interest and concern of legal thinkers. Thomas of Piperata's "Treatise on *Fama*" (*Trac-tatus de Fama*) was, for example, inspired by the ambiguities and uncer-tainties he saw in legal thought about *fama*.[34] Legal and moral authorities were ambivalent about how to use these concepts. It was clearly desirable to disqualify dishonest witnesses but, as Augustine cautioned, "[the apos-tle Paul] did not wish man to be judged by man on the basis of suspicious opinion."[35] Canonists recognized the ambiguities in legal traditions re-lated to public knowledge and infamy. There is no reason to think that disputants, whose engagement with the law was perhaps less abstract, did not.[36]

32. *Los Fueros de la Noverena,* ed. Gunnar Tilander, Leges Hispanicae Medii Aevi (Uppsala: Almquist and Wiksells, 1951), no. 232: "Nuill ombre que enfamado sea de periurio o false-dat aya testimoniado, ni est por testimonia ni por ferme nin por fiaduria ni por feyto ninguno non deue seer creydo."

33. *Furs de València,* ed. Germà Colon and Arcadi Garcia, 4 vols. (Barcelona: Barcino, 1970–83), 2.7.5 and 2.7.6.

34. Migliorino, *Fama e infamia,* 67.

35. Hermann, "Establishment of a Rule," 23.

36. Migliorino, *Fama e infamia,* 48–49.

The Law in Practice

The *Visigothic Code,* the *Siete Partidas,* and other law codes articulated no-tions of judicial infamy involving a range of disabilities that fell upon *in-fames.* It is not immediately apparent, however, what these codes can tell us about the social worlds of seventh-century Toledo or thirteenth-century Castile. Law codes rarely yield especially rich or vivid pictures of social life. They hardly ever provide the sort of thick description that would enable us confidently to reconstruct such vital but ephemeral social phenomena as reputation, honor, disgrace, or humiliation. Historians use Justinian's *Digest,* the *Visigothic Code,* the *Laws of Cnut,* the *Fuero de Cuenca,* or Gratian's *Decretum* not because they offer especially accurate representations of real people embroiled in delicate social and political negotiations, but because in many cases they offer the only representations.[37]

It is difficult to reconstruct the nuances of medieval legislation and the impulses that motivated it, and it is harder still to discover how the law re-flected, informed, or governed the attitudes and actions of judges, crimi-nals, and property holders. The social, political, financial, and legal consequences of infamy were serious, but how serious? How closely related were social ostracism and legal infamy? At least some people approached the question of *infamia* strategically, even under those legal regimes in which the consequences of infamy were the most sweeping. Suetonius, for example, reports that some Roman matrons willingly brought infamy upon themselves by enlisting themselves as prostitutes to avoid the harsher penalties for adultery to which prostitutes were not subject.[38]

Charters from the high Middle Ages yield no evidence of such sophisti-cated matrons, but records of judicial hearings can afford us some sense of how the jurisprudence of infamy inflected the daily social life of me-dieval people.[39] Eleventh-century Catalonia provides some especially rich clues about the relationship between reputation, testimony, and infamy, given that the northeast corner of the Iberian Peninsula enjoyed a lively attachment to the written law during the tenth and eleventh centuries. Pro-fessional judges at Vic, Barcelona, Urgell, Girona, and elsewhere studied the *Visigothic Code* carefully and often cited the *Code* during legal proceed-ings.[40] This regional enthusiasm for the *Code* was selective, however. The

37. There are, for example, virtually no narrative sources recording the world of seventh-century Iberia in which the *Visigothic Code* was drafted. The only possible exceptions are ha-giographical texts that pose their own interpretive dilemma.

38. Gardner, *Being a Roman Citizen,* 147.

39. Charters and cartularies, of course, have limitations as sources just as law codes do. They are primarily concerned with property rather than reputation. They shed light primar-ily on only one feature of infamy: disqualification as a witness. The loss of the ability to testify may or may not have been the most distressing consequence of infamy to those marked with *nota infamie.*

40. Several historians have noted the use of Visigothic law in charters from Catalonia and

judges who turned to the *Code* for guidance in adjudicating disputes and governing property transactions found some of its 527 rules more appealing than others. Most tenth- and eleventh-century citations of Visigothic law were related to one of three legal themes: the irrevocability of gifts (especially gifts to churches), the freedom of property-holders to alienate their property without hindrance, and the notion that property transactions carried out through force or intimidation were not valid. Each of these, supported by more or less scrupulous citations of rules from the *Code,* recurred often in charters. The vast majority of the rules in the *Code* (dealing with arson, theft, murder, adultery, Jews, treatment of foreign merchants, personal injury, kingship, and a host of other issues) were simply ignored. Between 900 and 1100, only a dozen rules from the *Code* appeared in charters with any frequency. Quantitative assessments of this sort are an admittedly crude index of the way in which people understood the law, but the figures do show that the *Code* was only used selectively. The tenacity of certain elements of Visigothic jurisprudence is impressive, but just as impressive is the discrimination with which scribes and judges employed the *Code*'s rules.

Judges paid attention to some of the *Visigothic Code*'s rules governing procedure and proof. Often, for example, they cited rules emphasizing the value of written proofs in property disputes. Courts also regularly relied on a Visigothic procedure for replacing lost or destroyed documents. But what about infamy? Did judges and disputants pay attention to Visigothic rules about testimony, infamy, and proof?

The evidence is scattered, but a handful of cases suggests that the law of infamy as formulated by the *Visigothic Code* played a role in legal proceedings. In 994 the abbot of the monastery of Saint Mary at Arles came before Countess Ermengard of Cerdanya and her son, Bishop Berenguer of Elne. The abbot complained that the monastery's neighbors were infringing on the monastery's rights. After hearing the great complaint (*magnam querimoniam vel clamorem*) made by the abbot and his monks, the countess consulted with the judges and lords who were present. The judges cited, in a somewhat garbled fashion, a rule from the *Visigothic Code* relating to testimony that stated that it was not less blameworthy to suppress the truth than to tell falsehoods. According to the rule, those who withheld testimony were *infames*.[41] The countess ordered an investigation into the boundaries

---

Languedoc. For a closer examination, see Jeffrey A. Bowman, *Law, Conflict, and Community around the Year 1000: Property Disputes in the Province of Narbonne* (Ithaca, N.Y.: Cornell University Press, forthcoming).

41. Bibliothèque Nationale de France, Coll. Baluze, fols. 313v–315: "Praedicti vero iudices ei dixerunt: In lege reperimus scriptum quia non est minor reatus vera supprimere quam falsa configere, & si ammonitus quisquam a judice de ea rem que noverit testimonium perhibere noluerit, si nobilis persona est, nullus homo non debet ulterius testimonium recipere;

of the disputed properties. Three of the oldest and most knowledgeable (*et plus sciunt veritatem de praedictos terminos*) members of the community swore an oath not to conceal the truth and then circumambulated the disputed property, noting for the written record natural and manmade landmarks: walls, churches, fields, rocks, and streams. The countess and her court were discriminating about the witnesses they chose, having sought witnesses who were especially well-informed about the property's boundaries. The judge invoked the Visigothic rule that branded reluctant witnesses with infamy, but it is not clear why. In this case, he seems to have done so not because anyone was withholding testimony or because any witnesses were suspected of being *infames,* but merely to emphasize the importance of having reliable witnesses.

A document from Urgell also raises the question of infamy and witness testimony. In November 1013, when a priest named Martin became gravely ill, he made an oral will that conformed to Visigothic testamentary law. Martin died of his illness and shortly thereafter his executors offered sworn testimony regarding an impressive array of bequests, including money, land, wax, relics, wine, cows, and books. Given the richness of Martin's estate, it is not surprising that some controversy surrounded the disposition of his property. Despite challenges from those disappointed by the terms of Martin's will, the judge accepted the testimony of Martin's executors. Emphasizing his confidence in their testimony and trying to avert any future challenges to the terms of Martin's will, the judge also cited the *Visigothic Code's* rule setting a six-month limit on calling witnesses *infames.*[42] An oral will in Sant Cugat's cartulary similarly mentioned that six-month term.[43]

In 1051 a dispute at Vic involving a challenged bequest also raised the issue of infamous witnesses. According to the bishop of Vic, a man named Geribert had given the see a property that included fields, vineyards, and appurtenances. After Geribert's death, three men challenged the donation, saying that Geribert had changed his mind about the bequest and had decided not to give the property to the see. The two judges hearing the case, Adalbert and Salomon, asked the bishop if he could produce witnesses to confirm the documents that he had already presented. Three wit-

---

si vero mino ingenua persona est, & dignitate & testimonio debet carere & centum flagella infamatus suscipere."

42. "Els documents . . . conservats a l'Arxiu capitular de la Seu d'Urgell," ed. Cebrià Baraut, *Urgellia* 4 (1981), no. 328: "Et ego Oliba iudice vidi altercatione inter Bonushomo et Requille et iustum iudicium et inveni sicut est in lege permisum, si infra sex menses non potuerit vicia testium querere et eorum infamia coram iudice comprobare transactis .vi. mensibus nulla ultra temporis spacium dabitur, sed quod testimonium eorum extiterit alligatum valebit perpetuo modis omnibus inconvulsum."

43. *El Cartulario del 'Sant Cugat' del Vallès,* ed. J. Ruis Serra, 3 vols. (Barcelona: Consejo Superior de Investigaciones Científicas, 1946), vol. 2, no. 524 (hereafter *Sant Cugat*).

nesses (Wifrid, Seniofred, and Bernat William) confirmed the bishop's account, swearing on the altar of Saint John that they had seen Geribert transfer the disputed property into the bishop's care by handing him a piece of wood.[44] The judges turned to the three men challenging Geribert's bequest and asked whether they could reasonably contradict the testimony of these witnesses or could impeach them on grounds of infamy.[45] The challengers were evidently unable to impeach the witnesses or to refute their testimony, which the judges accepted. The three challengers, however, seem to have remained unconvinced of the justice of the bishop's claim, for they left the court abruptly and "contemptuously."

A property dispute in 1032 involving the monastery of Sant Cugat near Barcelona provides a final example of the ways legal practice echoed legislation relating to infamy. As in the case at Vic, it involved a disputant who refused to accept a court's decision. Abbot Witard of Sant Cugat and Mir Geribert both claimed fortifications (including buildings, lands, and fishing rights) south of Barcelona. By the time of this dispute, Witard had been litigating aggressively and successfully on Sant Cugat's behalf for decades.[46] Mir, a spirited magnate with ties to Barcelona's vicecomital family, was a worthy opponent for the shrewd abbot. Mir said that the property rightly belonged to his son, arguing that his son's great-grandfather (Galindo) had established a claim to the land through *aprisio* (a type of grant that guaranteed property rights to those who cleared, cultivated, and exploited land). The abbot replied that he knew nothing about any such claim but he did know that Frankish kings and counts of Barcelona had confirmed the property into the monastery's possession with royal and comital privileges. Witard further claimed that the monastery had established rights to the property by bringing it into cultivation, despite difficulties and dangers. Witard thus based his claim both on written proofs—royal and comital privileges—and on having developed the land.

The royal privilege that Witard invoked as proof of his monastery's rights, however, no longer existed. Instead of presenting the document, Witard said that he could present witnesses who knew about the (now missing) document and its contents. Mir, on the other hand, wanted to prove his claim by *aprisio* with witnesses who knew that Galindo had developed the disputed property. The judges preferred to receive the abbot's wit-

44. Arxiu Capitular de Vic, Calaix 9, Episcopologio II, doc. 51: "prefatus episcopus ad conprobare rei veritatem infra scriptos legitimos optuli teste qui sufficienter et legaliter professis sunt testimonium in parte predicti episcopi ad vocem sancti petri et eis cannonicae." Paul Freedman mentions the case in *The Diocese of Vic: Tradition and Regeneration in Medieval Catalonia* (New Brunswick, N.J.: Rutgers University Press, 1983), 200 n. 15.

45. "Predicti iudices conmonuerunt prescriptorum causantes Dalmacius et Guilelmus atque Adalgerus et requisierunt ab illis si habebant quod rationabiliter contradicere predictos testes accusare potuissent causa infamationis."

46. For other disputes, see *Sant Cugat*, vol. 2, nos. 427, 429, 452, 479, 496.

nesses rather than Mir's, because the opinion of the decree (which Louis, king of the Franks, father of King Lothar, made of these churches to Sant Cugat by *aprisio*, and which the petitioner claimed were made by Galindo, the great-grandfather of this Galindo) was anterior. Since the order had been destroyed in the sack of the city of Barcelona, witnesses testified on Witard's behalf for the restoration of the lost document. They said that they had seen it and heard it read. Among other things, they heard that it indicated that the property from which this tension (*intencio*) sprang had been Sant Cugat's possession for sixty years and more.[47]

Mir did not complacently accept the judges' decision in favor of the monastery. He left the court displaying a contempt similar to that exhibited by the three disputants at Vic. Mir then appealed to a prominent Barcelona judge, Bonfill Marc. In a series of flamboyant accusations, he attacked the credibility of the witnesses who had testified on Sant Cugat's behalf. He claimed that the first of these witnesses had apostasized, abandoned his monastic habit, sought out concubines, and conceived children with them. In Mir's account, the second witness had committed adultery, and the third and final witness had deviated from the Christian faith, imitating the Muslim faith by performing circumcision. Mir's accusations were notably not that the monastery's witnesses were misinformed, dishonest, or unreliable, but that they were *infames*.

After hearing Mir's assault on the monastery's witnesses, the judge asked him whether he had witnesses who could verify his accusations. Despite the enthusiasm judges displayed for written proofs, Judge Bonfill Marc knew that there could be little in the way of written proof to show, for example, that the monastery's third witness had been circumcised. To substantiate allegations like these, one would have to rely on other witnesses. Mir promised to produce "witnesses who would confirm the infamy of those witnesses [the monastery] brought against him."[48] In the meantime, he presented two witnesses and asked the judge to verify his claim to the disputed property by *aprisio*. Judge Bonfill was willing to hear Mir's claims but he maintained rigorous procedural standards and, if he were to entertain the notion that Sant Cugat's witnesses had skeletons in their closets that would disqualify their testimony, he was going to follow procedural rules scrupulously. He told Mir that he would consider evidence about Sant Cugat's witnesses but refused to issue a decision in favor of Mir's *aprisio* claim,

---

47. *Sant Cugat,* vol. 2, no. 527. In another case during the same period, the abbot again protested that the monastery's documents relating to a disputed property had been destroyed in the fire at Barcelona. It was because of this loss that the abbot offered documents relating to the surrounding properties to substantiate his claim. See *Sant Cugat,* vol. 2, no. 479. For other disputants relying on similar claims, see Bowman, *Law, Conflict, and Community.*

48. *Sant Cugat,* vol. 2, no. 527: "dixit se inquirere alios illis meliores quibus infamiam a se obiectam, contra se, prolatis testibus, comprobasset."

offering two reasons for his refusal. The first was procedural: he insisted that disputants pursue only one complaint at a time, while Mir was trying both to prove that Sant Cugat's witnesses were unreliable and that his own claim was legitimate. The judge advised Mir first to do something "regarding the infamy of the witnesses against him," before he would consider Mir's claim of *aprisio*. The judge's second reason was that he had his own reservations about the reliability of the witnesses Mir had presented, for the first was "gravely oppressed with infirmity" and the second was "decrepit with age."

Over the protests of Abbot Witard and the viscount of Barcelona, Judge Bonfill allowed the case to remain unresolved until further proofs could be gathered and all witnesses heard. The abbot protested that Mir had forfeited any right to charge his witnesses with *infamia* because the period of six months allowed by Visigothic law had elapsed.[49] Despite the judge's willingness to wait, Mir failed to appear with the promised witnesses and his absence convinced the judge that Mir "could legally and rationally neither impeach [*infamare*] the monastery's witnesses nor prove that they had given false testimony."[50] Because of the monastery's documents—some of which no longer existed—and Mir's failure to substantiate his allegations, the judges awarded the contested lands to the monastery.[51]

This case between Witard and Mir Geribert is especially interesting because both parties were resourceful litigators; both knew something about the law; and both were remarkably good at improvisation within the law. The abbot, for example, deftly used a rule from the *Visigothic Code* that allowed disputants to "restore" lost documents through witness testimony. A proof in such cases was not so much a matter of producing a physical document as it was of describing a lost document persuasively. Disputants tried to present witnesses who could talk about lost documents consistently and whose reputations were unimpeachable. Witard also argued for the irrelevancy of Mir's claim that the monastery's witnesses were *infames* on the grounds that Mir made it after the six-month period allowed by Visigothic law.

Mir Geribert, for his part, exploited the jumble of overlapping jurisdictions and the multiplicity of legal fora that characterized eleventh-century courts. When one judge issued a decision that displeased him, he simply sought another judge. In the long run, this strategy was not successful—

---

49. *Sant Cugat,* vol. 2, no. 527: "Et quamquam ipsi dicerent quod iniuste eos compellebat reiterare audientiam, quoniam spatium sex mensium infamandi testes iam transierat."

50. *Sant Cugat,* vol. 2, no. 527: "Igitur idem iudex quia pleniter novit quod legaliter atque racionabiliter non potest prenotatus Miro infamare supradictos testes aut falsum dixisse testimonium eos convincere."

51. *Sant Cugat,* vol. 2, no. 529. This document also cites part of the Visigothic rule (2.4.7) limiting accusations of infamy to a six-month period.

the second judge eventually ruled in Sant Cugat's favor—but it did buy him some time. Although he did not win, he slowed down what to most of the region's inhabitants during this period must have seemed like Sant Cugat's unstoppable accumulation of every vineyard, *castra*, salt pan, mill, and orchard in its path.

Mir also relied on the notion of legal infamy to reject the monastery's witnesses. During the dispute at Vic, when asked whether they objected to the witness testimony that the bishop had offered, the three disputants merely left the court sulking. When Bonfill Marc extended a similar invitation to Mir, he rose to the occasion with gusto. He did not suggest that these witnesses were unreliable, misinformed, or biased, but instead tried to undermine them categorically, framing his accusations in accordance with Visigothic rules that would have marked these witnesses with *infamia*.[52] Mir, like Roman jurists and canonists, recognized that the law of infamy was particularly flexible.

The quarrel between Mir Geribert and Abbot Witard came to be dominated by a web of conflicting witness testimony. Three groups of witnesses played vital roles in the dispute, either by their presence or absence. One group testified on the monastery's behalf to restore a royal privilege allegedly destroyed in the sack of Barcelona. According to Mir, however, these witnesses were fornicating apostates. A second group of witnesses testified on Mir's behalf that his ancestor had established rights to the disputed property by *aprisio,* but in one judge's opinion these witnesses were unreliable because of their advanced age and infirmity. A third group, who were supposed to confirm Mir's accusations about the shortcomings of the first group, never materialized despite Mir's promise to present them. The three witness groups dramatize some of the difficulties courts and disputants encountered when relying on witness testimony. The memories of witnesses might be faulty, or witnesses might be partial and dishonest. Judges had to consider that some witnesses were ineligible to testify, even if the accusations leveled against them were far-fetched. Finally, it was not always easy to get witnesses to appear in court.[53]

At its outset, the case had centered on the Abbot Witard's claim to possess the property by virtue of a royal privilege, but this legal question faded from view as the proceedings focused increasingly on the availability, reliability, and alleged infamy of different witnesses. While the participants disagreed about the relative merits of the witnesses who offered testimony, they all (Mir Geribert, the judge, Abbot Witard) agreed that the quality of witness testimony varied considerably, and all agreed that some people

52. *Leges Visigothorum* 3.5.3.
53. See also Yvonne Bongert, *Recherches sur les cours laïques du X au XIII siècle* (Paris: Picard, 1949), 71–72.

were categorically disqualified from testifying. Thus, although the prominence of *infamia* as a legal concern grew mostly during the twelfth and thirteenth centuries, the above cases show that eleventh-century courts had also wrestled with it.[54]

We do not know why Mir Geribert never showed up in court with the witnesses he promised to produce. He may have become convinced that no disputant stood a chance against Sant Cugat; if surviving records are any indication, most reasonable people would have concluded that fighting Abbot Witard in court was a waste of time. Or, he may have been unable to find any witnesses willing to testify to the infamy of the monastery's witnesses. His accusations may have been groundless, and may have discouraged further witnesses from continuing to spread the *mala fama*.[55] Although Mir was ultimately unable to discredit the monastery's witnesses, his attempt does show that fleeting and evanescent things like rumor and reputation were given some structure by the written law of the *Visigothic Code*. Judges insisted on the importance of written proofs in property transactions, but often disputes were resolved by appealing to something that looks very much like a special variety of public opinion. As we have seen, the 994 case in Cerdanya was resolved by appealing to what respected senior members of the community knew about the boundaries between different properties. As they noted the defining streams and walls that divided one property from another, they distilled a certain *publica fama*.

Conclusion

Savvy and possibly desperate litigants like Mir Geribert relied on infamy to discredit their opponent's witnesses. In the centuries that followed Mir's dispute with Sant Cugat, litigants in Spain continued to use accusations of *mala fama* to disqualify the testimony of certain individuals and groups: those who lent money at excessive interest, prostitutes, prostitutes' clients, and those who frequented taverns.[56] Raising questions about the *infamia* of a witness was a powerful legal and social tool because the testimony of the disreputable might well be disqualified. Further, people of dubious reputation, in Catalonia and elsewhere, were more likely to be subjected to judicial ordeals.[57] The *Siete Partidas* acknowledged that the effects of in-

54. Peters, "Wounded Names," 72–74.

55. Chris Wickham, "Gossip and Resistance among the Medieval Peasantry," *Past and Present* 160 (1998): 3–24. "Resistance, to be successful, even in court, needed gossip to legitimate it: agreed truth was constructed through gossip."

56. David Nirenberg, *Communities of Violence: Persecution of Minorities in the Middle Ages* (Princeton: Princeton University Press, 1998), 147 n. 79, 152, 159. See also Serra Ruiz, *Honor,* 194–95.

57. Robert Bartlett, *Trial by Fire and Water: The Medieval Judicial Ordeal* (Oxford: Clarendon, 1986), 30; for Catalonia, see Bowman, *Law, Conflict, and Community.*

famy were of *grant fuerza* (strong consequence), but they were extraordinarily difficult to manage.[58] Infamy was a potent but unwieldy tool. As Edward Peters has pointed out, infamy was "a large and imprecise term."[59] Canonists saw that *fama* as a form of proof and *infamia* as a legal disqualification were vague concepts that were subject to abuse.[60] Mir Geribert's extraordinary accusations against Sant Cugat's witnesses may well have been reckless attempts to discredit upstanding and reliable witnesses, but they were carefully couched in Visigothic law. If his accusations about Sant Cugat's witnesses were just, the case shows that it was difficult for disputants to muster the necessary support for a charge of infamy. If they were fabrications, it shows that even groundless accusations about *infamia* were taken seriously enough to complicate the administration of justice. In either instance, his gestures show that medieval courts took *infamia* seriously and that, once *infamia* had been invoked, it was difficult to predict what would happen.

Litigants, lawyers, jurists, and poets all acknowledged the importance of reputation in the administration of justice. Even in Dante's hell, an alternative venue for the administration of justice, it is hard to calibrate the currents of fame and infamy. Among the false councillors of Malebolge, Dante's pilgrim encounters Guido da Montefeltro, who earned his place of dishonor through fraud, bad advice, and betrayal of his religious habit. Hearing the pilgrim speaking *lombardo*, Guido eagerly asks for news from Italy above. Like many of the inhabitants of the underworld, Guido fails to understand the logic that governs the special trajectory of the pilgrim's journey into and out of the underworld. When the pilgrim asks Guido to identify himself, he responds:

> S' i' credesse che mia riposta fosse
> a persona che mai tornasse al mondo,
> questa fiamma starìa sanza più scosse;
> ma però che già mai di questo fondo
> non tornò vivo alcun, s' i' odo il vero,
> sanza tema d'infamia ti rispondo.[61]

[If I thought my answer were to one who would ever return to the world, this flame should stay without another movement; but since none ever returned alive from this depth, if what I hear is true, I answer thee without fear of infamy.]

58. *Siete Partidas* 7.6.7.
59. Peters, "Wounded Names," 43.
60. On public fame as a proof, see Richard Helmholz, "Crime, Compurgation, and the Courts of the Medieval Church," *Law and History Review* 1 (1983): 13; Migliorino, *Fama e infamia*, 57–59.
61. *The Divine Comedy of Dante Alighieri: Inferno,* trans. John D. Sinclair (Oxford: Oxford University Press, 1961), canto 27, lines 61–66.

What Guido has heard, as the reader well knows, is not true. The pilgrim is just passing through. Guido has grievously miscalculated the rules that govern *infamia*. If in life Guido escaped the infamy which, in Dante's eyes, he richly deserved, the poet ensures that his *infamia* is publicly noted for all eternity. Mir Geribert, Thomas of Piperata, Guido of Montefeltro, and the framers of the *Siete Partidas* might have agreed with Juan Ruiz, archpriest of Hita and author of *El Libro de Buen Amor:*

> De pequeña cosa nasçe fama en la vezindat;
> desque nasçe, tarde muere, maguer non sea verdat,
> sienpre cada día cresçe con enbidia e falsedat;
> poca cossa le enpeçe al mesquino en mesquindat.[62]

[From small events a rumor's born and sweeps the neighborhood; / Once born, it's slow to die, although no part of it be true. / Some people, out of envy, spread great lies, which isn't good. / A little swamps the wretched man in wretchedness and rue.]

In both legal and literary culture, the intertwined ideas of *fama* or *infamia* played an important role in determining one's fate in court and one's place in the world. Murmurs became legal facts. Lawmakers and judges struggled to exclude proofs that distorted the truth and those that besmirched the court's dignity. They gave neither perjurers nor prostitutes a voice in court. But in giving a legal reality to something as ephemeral as reputation, they opened the door to new uncertainties and new deceptions. *Fama* and *infamia,* useful legal tools that they doubtlessly were, invited manipulation; but their would-be manipulators soon discovered that they were difficult to control. *Fama,* as Isidore remarked in his *Etymologies,* "creeps like a serpent through tongues and ears."[63]

62. Juan Ruiz, *The Book of True Love,* trans. Saralyn R. Daly, ed. Anthony N. Zahareas (University Park: Pennsylvania State University Press, 1978), v. 707.

63. *Etymologies* 5.27.26, ed. in Patrologia Latina 82, col. 213: "Hoc quoque et infamium, quasi sine bona fama; fama autem dicta, quia fando, id est, loquendo, pervagatur per traduces linguarum et aurium serpens. Est autem nomen et bonarum rerum et malarum. Nam fama felicitatis interdum est, ut illud est: Illustris fama, quod laus est; malarum, ut Virgilius ait: Fama malum, qua non aliud velocius ullum." Also cited in Peters, "Wounded Names," 45

CHAPTER SIX

Constructing Reputations: Fama *and Memory in Christine de Pizan's* Charles V *and* L'Advision Cristine

LORI J. WALTERS

Reputation preoccupied Christine de Pizan throughout her career, especially a woman's reputation, and particularly her own. As France's first professional woman writer, she was repeatedly subjected to the defamation that typically awaited the woman who dared to take up the pen. This chapter concentrates on Christine's meditations about talk and reputation in two works she composed around the same time. The first, *Le Livre des fais et bonnes meurs du roi Charles V le Sage* (*Book of the Deeds and Good Customs of King Charles V the Wise,* hereafter *ChV*), was completed November 30, 1404. Philip the Bold, Duke of Burgundy, had commissioned her to write his deceased brother's biography, possibly intending it as an instruction manual on responsible leadership for the dauphin, Louis of Guyenne, whose father, the "mad" king Charles VI, had brought France to the brink of civil war. The second work, *L'Advision Cristine* (*Christine's Vision,* hereafter *Adv*), written in 1405, is a dream vision in which Christine relates major current events in France to misfortunes in her own life. I consider how Christine quotes and corrects negative talk about herself and King Charles V in order to fashion a positive reputation for both. I begin my discussion with observations drawn from the *Adv,* one of the few works in which Christine explicitly uses the term *fama.* Since *fama* is one of the major themes of the *Adv,* I limit myself to examining how Christine's definition of the term clarifies her implicit treatment of the notion in *ChV.*

I then apply the concept of *fama,* which Margarete Zimmerman reminds us was synonymous with memory,[1] to Christine's biography of Charles V,

---

1. "Mémoire-tradition-historiographie. Christine de Pizan et son *Livre des fais et bonnes*

king of France from 1364 to 1380. Charles inaugurated a new style of king-ship in several important ways. He amassed a library of over a thousand vol-umes, the core of the modern Bibliothèque Nationale de France; he strengthened the connections between the monarchy and the University of Paris (*ChV* III.3); and he commissioned translations (rather, adapta-tions, in the style of the time) of Latin texts into Middle French, texts cho-sen to support the proper functioning of the monarchy. Topping a list of nine "notable books" that Charles had had adapted into the vernacular, Christine placed Saint Augustine's *De civitate Dei* (*The City of God*), followed, in third place, by his *Soliloquia* (*The Soliloquies*). Like the Bible, these works can be translated in three different ways: as text, as text plus gloss, and as "allegorized" text (*ChV* III.xii).[2] In her works, Christine continues con-sciously to fashion the French cultural memory perpetuated by Charles V, the monarch whom she and her father, the court astrologer and the king's personal physician and adviser, had known and loved.

The high standards of wisdom and eloquence that Charles had set for the French monarchy necessitated a new type of writer capable of com-municating theological insights on government to a public no longer re-stricted to clerics trained in Latin, a public that increasingly included women. In response to Charles's mandate, Christine set out to refashion herself as a female political counselor at the same time as she prepared the public to accept a woman in that position. In *Le Chemin de long estude* (*Path of Long Study*, 1403) Christine described how she had undertaken a long and arduous period of study to qualify herself as a civil counselor equipped to meet the intellectual demands of the new times.[3] In *La Mutacion de For-tune* (*Fortune's Transformation*, 1403) she had amply demonstrated her command of the lessons of history, and that led Philip the Bold to com-mission Charles's biography. In *ChV* and the *Adv*, Christine continues im-plicitly to rehearse the never-ending process of proving that she is eminently capable of filling the role of political adviser. In *ChV* too, Chris-tine opens a place for herself in literary tradition as a female biographer, an unprecedented role for a woman.

Although *ChV* is a biography whereas the *Adv* is an autobiography, these two works have more than one element in common, for both are also mir-rors for princes, manuals written to teach the ruler how to govern his king-dom and himself. Another work the king had had translated for the greater good of the state was John of Salisbury's *Policraticus* (1159), con-

meurs du sage Roy Charles V," in *The City of Scholars: New Approaches to Christine de Pizan*, ed. Mar-garete Zimmermann and Dina De Rentiis (Berlin: Walter de Gruyter, 1994), 158–73.

2. All references to this work will be taken from *Le livre des fais et bonnes meurs du sage Roy Charles V*, ed. Suzanne Solente, 2 vols. (Paris: Champion, 1936).

3. Helen Solterer, *The Master and Minerva: Disputing Women in French Medieval Culture* (Berkeley: University of California Press, 1995), 151–75.

sidered the founding text in the medieval mirror tradition. In this genre, the personal and the universal, the microcosm and the macrocosm, are analogous and interdependent, as is the relationship between the biographer and her subject. Since the worthiness of that subject has to be guaranteed by the biographer's own reliability, Christine had to establish her authority in order to establish Charles's reputation. The mirror genre presupposed that the prince's character, defined in part by his conduct in love, would be reflected in the moral health of the kingdom.[4] In turn, the biographer had to prove that she could govern her own conduct to be considered worthy of giving advice on behavior to members of the royal family. Accordingly, in *ChV* Christine's reputation becomes inseparable from the king's.

ChV and the *Adv* represent Christine's efforts to forge a collective memory worthy of the "ideology of France," an evolving system of royal beliefs and doctrines codified most authoritatively beginning in the thirteenth century in *Les Grandes Chroniques de France* (hereafter *GCF*): the source, as Pierre Nora has claimed, of "a new historical memory" in France.[5] Nora's insights into the crucial role of memory in constructing the idea of a nation are relevant to Christine's project. Christine established her role as a writer of dynastic history and shaper of cultural memory within the context of her views on *fama*. In *ChV* she constructed an exemplary image of Charles that complements his representation in the *GCF*. The general strategies adopted by Christine to deflect criticism from herself and from Charles V were part of her endeavor to establish good names for both, a form of *bona fama* for posterity. Christine participates in constructing a dynastic memory, which had been undertaken earlier by the monastic compilers of the *GCF*. *ChV* and the *Adv* simultaneously draw their strength from and reinforce the legitimacy of those dynastic prose chronicles, rendering both works deeply important for any consideration of talk and reputation in the Middle Ages. They mark a moment in history when an author reinterpreted oral and written sources to serve ideology, thereby to advance the aims of the state. Further, Christine redefines those aims in light of her interpretation of that ideology's founding documents, namely, the Scriptures and their patristic interpreters.

Fama and Political Allegory in the *Advision*

Although Christine employs the term *fama* only in book I of the *Adv* and in its prefatory gloss, it is nevertheless one of the principal themes of her

---

4. Rosalind Brown-Grant, *Christine de Pizan and the Moral Defence of Women* (Cambridge: Cambridge University Press, 1999), 89–127; Kate Langdon Forhan, "Reflecting Heroes: Christine de Pizan and the Mirror Tradition," in *City of Scholars*, 189–96.

5. "Between Memory and History: *Les lieux de mémoire*," *Representations* 26 (1989): 21.

three-part work.[6] In her prefatory gloss, Christine instructs the reader to interpret her dream vision on three interrelated levels: the individual human being, the general world (in the sense of the Creation), and the kingdom of France. The work has three parts, each with a different allegorical character (Libera/France in part I, Opinion in part II, Philosophy/Theology in part III) speaking to the protagonist as she mounts through the hierarchy of knowledge (sensory in part I, rational in part II, and theological/mystical in part III).

Christine's interlocutor in part I, Libera (France), described as a Crowned Lady of high reputation, contrasts her glorious past with the disappointments of the present. She sees France torn apart by internecine rivalries and debased by the immorality of those in power. Although she fears that France will experience the destruction promised to sinful countries in countless biblical prophecies and dreams, Libera enjoins Christine, optimistically, to bring the French princes back to reason.

In part II Christine's dream journey takes her to the University, where she views clerics engaged in scholastic debates dominated by Lady Opinion. Although the world is ruled by the error that comes of Opinion, Christine is promised that her works will be exempt from Opinion's evil effects, provided that they are founded on "law, reason, and true feeling."

In part III Christine recounts to Lady Philosophy the long story of her own life, which she divides into two major periods: a happy childhood and an adulthood marked by endless problems. Among the latter was the charge that she had taken a lover after the death of her husband, a charge to which she pleads innocent. The Boethian Lady Philosophy then transforms herself into Lady Theology, who proceeds to give Christine a sermon inspired to a large degree by Saint Aquinas and Saint Augustine, and in particular by Saint Augustine's *De Trinitate* (*The Trinity*). Christine ends her work by comparing its three parts to the three precious stones that shine in Theology's crown.

Christine's title, the *Advision Cristine,* gives a clue to the work's meaning and function. With etymological roots that link vision and advice, the word *advision* indicates the text's dual character. It is a political dream vision as well as a piece of practical advice, the fruit of the intellectual journey that has qualified Christine to give advice to royalty. But Christine's appeal to the citizens of the very Christian country of France goes beyond being merely an intellectual issue, for it also delves into the realm of faith. By accepting her misfortunes and the slanderous accusations against her, Chris-

6. All quotations are taken from *Le livre de l'Advision Cristine,* ed. Christine Reno and Liliane Dulac (Paris: Champion, 2000), xii–xiv. I have adopted their interpretation of *Fama* as a personification in the three instances in which the term appears in the text (pp. 6, 15, 16). I am grateful to the editors for granting me access to a pre-publication version of their edition.

tine patterns herself on Christ. The stance of loving self-sacrifice that she adopts in imitation of Christ's own reflects the ultimate wisdom that Theology can convey to human beings. Although hoping that those in power will heed her advice to mend their immoral ways and avert further political disasters, Christine intimates that her example as sacrificial victim might turn out to be the wisest one for the French in the even more difficult times soon to come.

The term *fama* appears first in the explanatory gloss that Christine added, in her own hand, to her final, authoritative version of the *Adv*.[7] She begins by recounting how she, as the protagonist of her own life story, was "transported by *Fama*'s cry" from Lombardy to France. Again, in *Adv* I.4, the text being glossed, she reiterates that she had been attracted to Paris ("the second Athens") "by *Fama*'s cries" (p. 15). Christine's personified *Fama* is an energetic lady who proclaims France's glory and honor to the sound of trumpets and horns. Encouraged by *Fama*'s call, Christine's guardians leave their native Italy to serve the Crowned Lady of France. If we read the narrative as its author has instructed us to do in her gloss, that is, as pertaining to Christine herself, we see *Fama* representing the lure of worldly renown, the kind her father responded to when he accepted Charles V's invitation to become his adviser in Paris.

It is significant that Christine uses the Latin term *fama*.[8] The Middle Ages inherited two classical traditions concerning renown. The first came from the *Aeneid,* where Virgil proposes an allegorical representation of *Fama* as a freakish bird whose plumes are covered with eyes, ears, and mouths, and who flies rapidly through the world (IV, verses 173–97). The tradition deriving from this monster, feminine and changeable by nature, figured more widely in French literary culture than in others because of the influential *Roman d'Enéas,* an anonymous adaptation of Virgil (ca. 1155). The second tradition comes from *The Metamorphoses,* where Ovid describes the House of Renown as chaotic, noisy, and a mixture of truth and lies. Ovid's conception reappears in the French *Ovide moralisé,* a version of the *Metamorphoses* with moralizing glosses, and in Chaucer's *House of Fame*.[9]

In the *Adv* Christine transfers many of the negative aspects of *fama* in the

---

7. Reno and Dulac, *Adv,* xlii.
8. See the articles in the volume of *Médiévales* 24 (1993) dedicated to "La Renommée." In "La *Réputation* dans la langue française médiévale: Glossaire onomasiologique du Moyen Français," 45–56, Gilles Roques omits mention of Christine's use of the Latin *fama* and instead enumerates many of the French variants of the term.
9. Jacqueline Cerquiglini-Toulet, "*Fama* et les preux: Nom et renom à la fin du Moyen Âge," ibid., 40; and Thelma Fenster, "La *fama,* la femme, et la Dame de la Tour: Christine de Pizan et la médisance," in *Au champ des escriptures: Actes du IIIe colloque international sur Christine de Pizan* (Lausanne, 18–22 July 1998), ed. Eric Hicks (Paris: Champion, 2000), 462–63, esp. nn. 7 and 8.

two traditions to her personified Opinion,[10] thus creating the possibility of a more positive *fama* associated with reputation. Like the Virgilian monster, Christine's Opinion is inherently undefinable, because she is constantly changing. Opinion can comprise all the things that we mean by talk—rumor, public opinion, hearsay, and the like. She has a double nature: "initiator of all progress and at the same time responsible for the most disastrous illusions."[11] Opinion can be a force for good or for evil: "She is positive in the sense that she urges humans to seek out the truth or to acquire a skill, but negative in the sense that she is only provisional and uncertain, and so can cause humans to make errors of judgement."[12] Christine portrays Opinion as the cause of France's current problems, for she creates dissension among princes and corrupts knights and clerics alike through lust and fraud. Opinion has also caused Christine's present difficulties by involving her in the literary quarrel about Jean de Meun's *Romance of the Rose* (p. 87; hereafter *Rose*)—the immensely popular poem that she had criticized for its immorality and its defamation of the female character[13]—and by circulating derogatory comments about the author and her writings. Whereas in *Fortune's Transformation* Christine had identified the implacable deity Fortune as the cause of mankind's ills, in the *Adv* she blames them on Opinion. The advantage is that Opinion can be manipulated, redefined, then fixed in written form. By substituting Opinion for Fortune, Christine emphasizes the importance of her own determination and the ruler's in combating Opinion's nefarious effects. She implies that both ruler and writer have a responsibility to reshape public opinion to project the image they desire to leave for future generations.

If *fama* as reputation signifies secular glory for Christine, it can also signify a form of renown that transcends one's own time and place. Christine recounts that during her childhood, she was transported in response to the call of *Fama*, "the cry of the blessed prophets," to "the law of God, in which all goodliness is contained" (p. 6). Originally a concept designating worldly renown, the result of favorable public opinion, the *fama* that Christine has in mind here transcends a purely secular status. Christine's wording now suggests that reputation is connected to the institution of human laws, which in turn are consonant with the law of God. Her metaphor of childhood and adulthood, echoing as it does the Pauline epistle (1 Cor. 13) and Saint Augustine's restatement of it (*Trin.* 15.23.44), points to a

---

10. Christine draws her inspiration for the figure primarily from the Platonic tradition of Opinion as an inferior form of knowledge and from Aquinas's definition of Opinion in his *Commentary on the Metaphysics of Aristotle* (VII.15.1610).

11. Reno and Dulac, *Adv,* xviii. All translations into English are my own unless indicated otherwise.

12. Brown-Grant, *Christine de Pizan,* 107.

13. See ibid., 7–51, for a synopsis of the debate.

higher understanding of the relationship between her act of prophecy and her loving self-sacrifice for her country.

Christine helps clarify how reputation can survive after death. Elaborating on a passage from Ecclesiastes that warns, "Take care for your good name, because it will remain longer with you than any precious treasure," she explains:

> Renown [*renom*] properly tends toward lofty things, close to incorruptible ones, because earthly goods are of short duration, with the exception of one's good name, which can attain a certain perpetuity; this is clear to us by our experience without any other proof, in the way that our religion bears witness to the worthy names of the very perfect ones [i.e., the saints] by inscribing them in eternal and indelible memory. (*ChV* 1.4)

Worldly renown can endure after someone's death because it tends toward lofty things like the names of saints, which are inscribed by Christianity in "eternal and indelible memory." Christine draws the *Adv* to a close with a similar insight. When she transforms Philosophy into Theology, it is done to the accompaniment of Boethius's comment that riches, honors, rank, property, beauty, strength, and power fail to provide happiness. Numerous quotations from the Church Fathers affirm that happiness can come only from God.

True happiness includes an enduring reputation, which must be founded on divine authority. Christine locates that authority in the divine monarchy, steward of the French nation. One way in which Christine tries to create an enduring reputation for herself, for Charles V, and for France is to align herself with the tradition of royal political ideology established in the *GCF*, a major source for both *ChV*[14] and the *Adv*.[15] The *GCF* was a vernacular prose history kept by the monks of the royal abbey of Saint-Denis from the 1270s through the mid-fifteenth century. Louis IX (who reigned from 1226 to 1270) had initiated the composition of the *GCF* by having a monk named Primat adapt existing Latin chronicles into the vernacular. Primat presented the first copy of the *GCF* to Louis' successor, King Philip III, in 1274. Rather than simply reproducing the style of their Latin models, Primat and the Dionysian monks who continued his work under subsequent monarchs assimilated elements of the newly emerging practice of vernacular prose history. Surviving in one hundred and thirty manuscripts, the *GCF* in its final form describes a chain of royal lives from the fall of Troy to the reign of Charles VI in the 1380s. The figures of Clovis, Charlemagne, Saint Louis, and finally Charles V, the prototype of the wise Christian king,

---

14. Solente, *Livre des Fais*, I.xli. Christine acknowledges that the *GCF* furnished background information for two of the episodes (I.xxxii; III.lii).
15. Reno and Dulac, *Adv*, xxxvii–xxxviii.

receive special treatment. The *GCF* flourished under Charles V, who wanted the history of his own Valois dynasty to be incorporated into the official history of the Capetian monarchy.

In claiming, as Christine does in the prefatory gloss to the *Adv,* that France's fame still derives from its most-Christian character and its links to the Church, Christine echoes Primat in the prologue to the *GCF.* There, Primat invokes the well-known themes of *translatio studii et imperii,* the displacement of the locus of learning and political power from Greece to Rome to France. *Clergie* (the French equivalent of *studium*) and *chevalerie* (the French equivalent of *imperium*) had settled in France and would stay there as long as France remained worthy of the honor. Primat believes that France enjoys a singular status among nations because, in his words, "the fountain of *clergie,* by which Holy Church is maintained and illuminated, flourishes in Paris." By "Holy Church," Primat and Christine have in mind an ideal akin to Augustine's City of God, which can differ from the concrete form that the Church takes in a particular time and place.

Christine strives to protect the *fama* of the newly emerging French nation from the ravages of Fortune by allying it with royal political ideology and by fixing it for posterity in her texts. Just as Primat had done before her, in *ChV* Christine traces the line of descent of the French from the Trojans to Pharamond, the first crowned king of France. In expressing her hopes for the future of the "noble nacion françoise," Christine's enthusiasm knows no bounds: "Thus was the beginning of this noble French nation crowned with ancient nobility, which—thanks be to God!—from one inheritor to the next, has continued, despite the contrary movements of inconstant Fortune, to grow in goodness. May God grant it increasing splendor until the end of time!" (*ChV* I.v.).

Following the aims of the French royal house as expressed in the *GCF,* Christine championed the myth of the destined ascendancy of the French nation despite its recent setbacks. Charles V worked hard to strengthen the monarchy by supervising the official record of his own reign in the *GCF* and by commissioning his own tomb at Saint-Denis.[16] To these previously existing monuments to Charles's *fama,* Christine adds her own written testimonial. She dramatizes her role as keeper of dynastic memory in *Adv* by having the Crowned Lady ask Christine to take up her writing instruments and record "written memorials" (*des memoires escriptes*) of her dignity (I.vi). Christine's permanent, written form of the Crowned Lady's story constitutes the Lady's *fama,* which, according to official ideology, is France's lot.

Christine does not apply official ideology mechanically; rather, she actively contributes to its formation. Her use of the term *nacion* suggests that

16. Charity Cannon Willard, *Christine de Pizan: Her Life and Works* (New York: Persea Books, 1984), 133.

she may have been a pioneer in shaping notions of French nationhood, since, according to Colette Beaune, it is unusual to find references to the French "nation" before the end of the fifteenth century.[17] Her innovations extend to the *GCF* themselves. Christine may have intended *ChV* to be an alternative to manuscripts of the *GCF* made during the reign of Charles VI. Anne D. Hedeman explains how during Charles VI's reign production of the *GCF* became increasingly dominated by special groups, to the detriment of the interests of the country as a whole. Christine was part of a small but influential group of royalists who encouraged the queen and the princes to keep the peace and to work for the common good. Hedeman considers the tracts and sermons written by members of this group to be successors to the political program of Charles V's *GCF* rather than official copies of the *GCF.* By writing her biography of Charles V, Christine was attempting to circumvent the instability of Charles VI's government by focusing on and even embellishing Charles V's more successful reign; she hoped that her work would inspire leaders to follow his example rather than that of his son.[18] In claiming therefore that Christine's writings "in particular focus on themes that became important in copies of the *GCF* produced during the second half of Charles VI's reign,"[19] Hedeman suggests that Christine was a key player during this troubled period, perhaps even influencing the author-compilers of the *GCF* as well as being influenced by them.

Saint Augustine, *Fama,* and the Rhetoric of Exemplarity

Saint Augustine is one of the most cited authority figures in the *Adv,* appearing frequently in the concluding passages and also in the gloss as one who, along with Saint Paul, had increased the power of the Church and the faith (p. 9). With this pattern of allusion, Christine has Augustine's meditations form a frame to her own.[20] The way that Christine reads them, however, testifies to changing perceptions of Augustine's ideas. When Augustine began his monumental *City of God* in 403, his intention was to defend Christianity against the accusation that it had caused the fall of Rome. In developing the idea that far from having destroyed classical culture, Christianity had preserved it, Augustine was led to make a radical synthe-

17. *The Birth of an Ideology: Myths and Symbols of Nation in Late Medieval France,* trans. Susan Ross Huston and ed. Fredric L. Cheyette (Berkeley: University of California Press, 1991), 5.

18. Willard, *Christine de Pizan,* 115–17.

19. Anne D. Hedeman, *The Royal Image: Illustrations of the "Grandes Chroniques de France," 1274–1422* (Berkeley: University of California Press, 1991), 139.

20. See Lori J. Walters, "La réécriture de saint Augustin par Christine de Pizan: De la *Cité de Dieu* à la *Cité des Dames,*" in *Au champ des escriptures,* 197–215.

sis of classical and Christian thought, one that was subject to reformulation throughout the Middle Ages. Whereas Augustine had stressed the interpretation of human life as a pilgrimage to the City of God, understood as the community of saints, medieval political theorists increasingly applied his ideas to the political order. Augustine had taken an active part in the appropriation and assimilation of the classical legacy—but that legacy later asserted its dominance over its Christian overlay. Augustine's words and authority were often appropriated to speak to arguments that he had never anticipated.[21]

At the beginning of the fifteenth century, many were increasingly inclined to view Augustine as a theologian whose wisdom and eloquence could ever more increasingly be applied to issues confronting the Christian state. Sayings about *fama* attributed to Augustine appear frequently in popular anthologies circulating in France in the fourteenth and fifteenth centuries. The concept of defamatory language as a threat to the commonwealth can be attributed to the Roman model of the functional nature of the speech act transmitted by Augustine to the medieval world. His concern about the effects of defamatory language on reputation, however, seems otherwise at odds with his distrust of worldly fame and glory.[22] This is particularly evident in his unsympathetic attitude toward Lucretia's attempt to uphold her good name.

Perhaps no better illustration can be found concerning late medieval views of the venerable Church Father than what we see in Christine's reevaluation of his account of Lucretia. For him, Lucretia is not a model to be emulated, for she was wrong in committing suicide to clear her name after her rape by King Tarquin's son (*City* I.xix). In recounting Lucretia's story in her *Livre de la Cité des Dames* (*Book of the City of Ladies,* hereafter *Cité*), written in 1405, Christine makes two major points: first, that women who are chaste and lead a moral existence (the majority) do not enjoy being raped; and second, that Lucretia performed a socially beneficial service by denouncing the criminal and by subsequently committing suicide. Because of Lucretia's courageous acts, the Roman people rose up en masse and expelled Tarquin from Rome, and would have killed his son had they found him (II.xliv). For Christine the most noteworthy result of Lucretia's example was that it initiated a far-reaching reform of barbarous conduct by leading to the institution of a severe law against rape.

Unlike Augustine, who upholds the Church's interdiction against sui-

---

21. "Political Augustinianism," in *Augustine through the Ages: An Encyclopedia,* ed. Allan D. Fitzgerald et al. (Grand Rapids, Mich.: Eerdmans, 1999), 657–58; "Renaissance to the Enlightenment," ibid., 718.

22. Solterer, *Master and Minerva,* 149; 248–49 n. 37. She notes that in *City* V.xix Augustine associates the search for a good reputation with the passion for domination (*cupiditas dominationis*).

cide, Christine envisages rape as a sin against the common good and against women that must be denounced. In the *Adv*'s prefatory gloss, Christine ascribes the downward trend in Christian history to the lustful ways of several French kings; she also cites Paris's rape of Helen as the cause of Troy's destruction, which set off the movement of *imperium* from Troy to France (I.xxv); and she lists the rape of Lucretia as one of the sexual transgressions that precipitated the fall of Rome (I.xxv). Christine often returns to the theme of rape, suggesting that if French rulers repeat the sins of their ancestors, they too will lose political and cultural supremacy. The superiority of a country has to be founded on the ruler's personal conduct, especially in the domain of love, which explains why mirrors for princes consistently argue against lechery and why Christine applauds Charles V for having summarily hanged one of his servants for rape. Whereas Christine agreed with Augustine in envisaging rape as a sin against the individual, unlike Augustine she also saw it as a public sin that had to be denounced for society's benefit.

But Christine's most important objection to Augustine was that he had failed to consider how Lucretia's suicide registered a protest against the defamation of her character. As Christine describes Lucretia, the Roman matron proclaimed that she would kill herself so that henceforth no woman would have to live in shame and dishonor because she had been raped (a corrected Eve who in turn implicitly upbraids her male defamers). Lucretia actively constructed her good name, much as Christine tried to do for her own name in *ChV* and in the *Adv*. With the words she ascribes to Lucretia, Christine tacitly responds to Augustine's insinuation that Lucretia's suicide was a mark of her guilt. Lucretia's declaration that she had not been wanton is similar to Christine's own proclamation of innocence for a sexual impropriety. Both acts have implications not only for the individual woman but for all women. Lucretia becomes a type of female Christ who sacrifices her life for the greater good of all women. In the *Cité* Christine takes up Lucretia's story a second time to remark that it was the Roman matron's reputation as a model of virtue that had attracted her rapist (II.lxiv). By proclaiming her innocence and then taking her life, Lucretia becomes again a model of virtue, and an even more compelling one than she had originally been, since by her voluntary self-sacrifice as innocent victim, like Christ, she actively shapes her own *fama* and that of her gender. Her *fama* passes into law to protect all women against rape and against defamation of character.[23]

The differing attitudes of Christine and Augustine regarding Lucretia's suicide suggest that Christine's highest understanding of reputation, rather

23. Pace Solterer, who contends that Christine's socially responsible discourse cannot change social relations between women and men: see *Master and Minerva*, 175.

than stemming from Catholic orthodoxy, should be identified with a conception of the fifteenth-century Christian state that encouraged those in the public eye to maintain an impeccable reputation. Christine's view of Lucretia's conduct, differing as it does from that of Augustine, nonetheless one of her most esteemed *auctoritates,* testifies to the importance of talk and reputation in the medieval period, especially for those who exercised a public function. In a study of reputation's potency as a cultural signifier in the late Middle Ages, Jan R. Veenstra recounts how the wife of Louis of Orleans, Valentine Visconti of Milan, was hounded out of the Court of Burgundy in 1396 by gossip that she had bewitched Charles VI.[24] A society with no official source of information, early fifteenth-century France was, as Thelma Fenster notes, a "culture of surveillance."[25] Even romantic love, which for us moderns is perhaps the quintessential private emotion, was for the aristocracy primarily a way of behaving and a form of self-representation, as C. Stephen Jaeger argues. He claims that the social function of love was "to show forth virtue in lovers, to raise their inner worth, to increase their honor and enhance their reputation."[26] Conversely, conduct in love could not only detract from one's reputation but it also could have political consequences, as shown by the fall of the "Tarquinian dynasty" in Rome. Christine's interpretation of the story shows her consciousness of the public effects of reputation.

In *ChV* and the *Adv,* Christine attempts to mold public opinion through a rhetoric of exemplarity.[27] In *ChV* she explains that just as white is defined in opposition to black, and day in opposition to night, the conduct that the reader should adopt will be obvious through contrast. When evil is blamed, virtue is implicitly praised; conversely, when virtue is praised, sin is implicitly blamed (I.xxvii). In the *Adv* and in the *Cité* she calls this technique reading by *antiphrasis,* which consists in interpreting something negative in a positive light, or vice versa. Christine underlines the importance of this technique by referring to herself as France's *antigraphus,* that is, France's secretary (*Adv* I.v, p. 16). As "antigraphe" of France's "aventures" (p. 16), Christine makes herself analogous to "sainte Sapience divine" (Divine Holy Wisdom), the "antigraffe" of the world's "aventures" (p. 6).[28] Christine ingeniously establishes a parallel between her own work as France's secretary and the work of God and his Evangelists, who served as the

---

24. Jan R. Veenstra, *Magic and Divination at the Courts of Burgundy and France: Text and Context of Laurens Pignon's "Contre les Devineurs" 1411* (New York: Brill, 1998), 81–85.

25. "La *fama,*" 462.

26. *Ennobling Love: In Search of a Lost Sensibility* (Philadelphia: University of Pennsylvania Press, 1999), 6.

27. On the notion of exemplarity, see in particular J.-Th. Welter, *L'exemplum dans la littérature religieuse et didactique du Moyen Âge* (Paris: Société d'histoire ecclésiastique de la France, 1927).

28. See Solterer, *Master and Minerva,* 151–75, on Christine's "sapiential writing."

world's secretaries in writing Holy Scripture. The *antigraphes*—Christine, Divine Sapience, and the Evangelists—all work through *antiphrasis,* the use of positive and negative exempla. Generally speaking, the exemplum is an implicit or explicit moral. Its goal is to change behavior through the eloquent communication of a piece of wisdom. In the concluding passages of the *Adv,* therefore, Christine appeals to her royal addressees by quoting an exemplum made famous by Saint Jerome. She melds her voice to his in enjoining those in her audience to evaluate their conduct in Theology's mirror, a metaphor popular with a future Father of the Church, Aquinas, for whom theology was the highest form of human wisdom.

As Christine puts it in her *Epistre au Dieu d'amours* (*Letter of the God of Love,* 1399), France, the country that had been woman's "shield and defense," has now become a country that flouts the rights of women. Christine's experience as a widow had taught her that lesson only too well. She identifies the prevalence of rape as an index of France's present dissolute state, and suggests, by means of her references to Lucretia, that one solution to the problem is the institution and enforcement of severe laws against it. Christine continues in the spirit of *The City of God* as interpreted by Charles and his translator Raoul, by redefining Augustine's original synthesis of Roman and divine law in a contemporary context. Much of her redefinition has to do with giving permanent written form to ethical notions, whether in the shape of laws, other legal documents, or written texts like her own. Christine creatively interprets Charles V's bidding to make theological works relevant to contemporary politics by "translating" passages from Aquinas into the vernacular in the *Adv* and *ChV,*[29] thus interpreting him for a new age. She takes Aquinas's synthesis of Aristotle's *Metaphysics* and his *Politics* (evident in his prologue to his *Commentary on the Metaphysics*) one step further by applying it to practical problems of governance in early fifteenth-century France. *Fama,* Christine seems to say, must be formed by its reflection in Theology's mirror.

Charles V: The Memory of an Exemplary King and His Exemplary Biographer

In accepting Philip the Bold's commission to undertake the composition of his deceased brother's biography, Christine sought to create a lasting form of memory that would perpetuate Charles V's good name for centuries to come. Her written monument to this particular king would instruct his royal descendents about their duties as rulers while encouraging

29. She translates sections of his *Commentary on the Metaphysics of Aristotle* in *Adv* II.vi.10–II.xii (Reno and Dulac, *Adv,* 170) and paraphrases others in *ChV* (Solente, *Livre des Fais,* I.lxvi–lxvii).

public opinion to accept the monarchy's legitimacy and her role as its spokesperson. Christine thus inscribes *ChV* within a poetics of dynastic memory. In its initial line, which opens with a verse taken directly from penitential Psalm 50, she asks God for the understanding necessary to explain those things that she had conceived in her memory ("les choses conceues en ma memoire"). In thus speaking through the voice of David, considered to be the author of the Psalms, Christine invokes the memory of this Old Testament ruler whom the *GCF* had promoted as a forerunner of the Christian king. At the end of the prologue to Charles V's biography, Christine claims to have undertaken the work for the purpose of "recalling his life and praiseworthy virtues and customs worthy of perpetual *memory*" ("ramentevant sa vie et louables vertus et meurs dignes de perpetuelle *memoire*" [emphasis mine]).

Christine enacts a process by which a personal form of memory—inspired undoubtedly by Augustine's idea in *De Trinitate* (*Trin.* 14.3–5) that "the memory of one's past life is explained by the persistence in the blessed soul of images stored up in the memory"[30]—is transformed into a collective memory through writing. She states that writing is useful because things that are not written down are easily forgotten by "le ventre de la memoire" (the womb—literally: "stomach"—of memory; *ChV* II.xxi). In "remembering" (Old French *remembrer*) Charles, Christine initiates an act of private commemoration (Latin *commemorari*) of Charles's achievements each time her work is read silently and an act of public commemoration each time it is read aloud to others. In the last chapter, describing Charles's death, she restates the object of her endeavor, which is to record "his virtues worthy of being remembered forever" ("des vertus de lui dignes d'infinie memoire"). Christine frames her biography with eloquent statements of *fama* as a textualized form of positive remembrance, thus complementing allusions to Augustine.

Christine uses varied strategies to establish a stellar reputation for Charles. She illustrates first how he resembles exemplary earlier kings, such as David (II.xv), Charlemagne (II.x), and Clovis (I.xxv). The comparison that Christine makes between Charles and Louis IX is her most telling one, for she elevates the image of her patron, and that of the monarchy in general, by placing the king in a direct line to Christ by way of the saintly Louis. That is, when Christine shows Charles worshiping at the Sainte Chapelle, she implicitly brings out his resemblance to Louis, and she informs her readers that Charles had a particular veneration for Saint Louis (I.xxxiii). She further evokes other memories of Charles as a holy king when, in the chapter on his final hours, she first has him apostrophize the crown of thorns (enshrined in the Sainte Chapelle by Louis) and then, only secondarily, the

---

30. "Memory," in *Augustine,* ed. Fitzgerald, 554.

royal crown. In his last moments Charles expresses the realization that the crown of thorns, symbol of Christ's suffering and death, is superior to the crown of earthly glory (III.lxxi). As it was for Christ and Saint Louis, Charles's failings, sufferings, and defeats are but a reflection of the true victory that he achieved both in heaven and on earth, in the moral legacy that he left behind. Christine creatively exploits the traditional image of the crown to make it a potent symbol for the nascent nation of France. Her pattern of imagery, which extends from the description in book I of the nation "crowned with ancient nobility," to her opposition of the two crowns during the king's dying moments, and finally to her evocation of Theology's crown at the conclusion of the *Adv,* gives concrete form to the overarching themes of *fama* and kingship. In this way Christine uses her eloquence to reinforce the power of the monarchy, for the monarchy could not maintain its power nor could God's will be made known on earth without the aid of the writer-statesperson to help the monarchy interpret that will to the people.

As her second strategy, Christine replies directly to charges made against Charles. She discusses the monarch's failings: "Here is described how King Charles achieved many victories in his wars, even though he did not go there in person, and the reason why he did not go" (II.x). She then counters criticism that Charles was weak and cowardly in battle by stating that he had indeed led troops in battle before becoming sickly, and that he was not naturally cowardly but avoided combat only after he had contracted a serious illness. Christine then moves from defense to offense. She cites the observation made by Vegetius in another work that Charles had had translated,[31] that military enterprises governed by reason are more admirable than those led by force. She reasons that by devising military strategies instead of relying on brute force, Charles had accomplished more for the people than any king since Charlemagne: just as Charlemagne's prowess had made him worthy of being called "Charles the Great," so should Charles V be called "the Wise" because of his courage and wisdom. Christine thus has found a clever way to turn Charles's apparent weakness into a strength, since the comparison with Charlemagne serves to legitimize the later King Charles. At the same time she has proved herself to be as good a strategist as Charles, since the substitution of warrior king ideal with that of the wise king redefines kingship for her contemporaries.

Besides trying to clear Charles of the charges leveled against him by the public, Christine launches into a reevaluation of his four brothers and then his sons, starting with King Charles VI. She is not above using Christ himself to deflect criticism from Philip the Bold, Charles's brother and her

31. Christine refers to this in III.xii as *De chevalerie* (On Chivalry).

patron (*ChV* II.xiii). Although her rhetoric is obvious propaganda, the impulse can be explained and even justified by reference to the ideological position underlying her statement: she is trying to strengthen French resolve against encroachment by the English. Her reasoning is that if France is to realize its glorious destiny to guide Christendom and thus the world, it has to resist being taken over by outside forces. By rehabilitating Charles's brothers, all uncles of the present king, as well as the king himself, Christine does her best to strengthen the monarchy at a time when it is subjected to extreme internal and external pressures.

Christine then constructs her own reputation along the same lines as Charles's. She opens the section that functions as a prologue to book II with rebuttals to the derogatory comments that have been circulating about her (II.ii). She says that she wants to prevent envious or evil-speaking people, who often want to diminish the reputation of authors, from accusing her of lying or of not keeping her promises. Christine returns to the idea of carrying out her duty in the section "Where Christine answers certain criticisms that could be made about her" (II.xviii). She devotes this chapter to replying to two major criticisms about her work that had come to her attention: first, that her praise of some royal family members makes no mention of their vices because she wants to win their good graces or other forms of gain; second, that she should not praise people who are still alive, since it is impossible to know what they will do in the future. She responds that she was not motivated by gain but simply wanted to produce the work that had been requested of her by Philip and is thus employing her God-given talents to further monarchical aims. To speak the truth even when it is praiseworthy, she contends, is never flattery. Although her aim is to praise the virtues of her subjects, criticism of their corresponding vices is implicit, and, she asks rhetorically, are vices not condemned when virtues are praised? Finally, she reasons that it is not good to criticize rulers in front of their subjects. In sum, her answers, couched in the language of *antiphrasis,* illustrate once again her conception of the public nature of her role as royal biographer.

Anticipating other criticisms of her work in II.xxi, she reports that gossipmongers (*reprimeurs de louange*) have accused her of ignorance and presumptuousness because she, a woman, has written a book on military matters. They could further say: "This woman has no personal knowledge of what she explains in her book; she only recopies word for word what other authors have said." Christine's answer is that although she borrows from other authors, she uses those borrowings to express her own ideas. Some might also ask, "What presumption moves this ignorant woman to dare to pronounce on such a lofty thing as the discipline of chivalry and what comprises it?" In reply, Christine cites Hugh of Saint-Victor's opinion that a statement is to be judged by its wisdom, not by the stature of the person pronouncing it, and she points out the example of Minerva, a mythological woman involved in government and warfare and the inventor of military equipment. That Minerva was more familiar as the personification of wisdom served only to strengthen Christine's argument.

Christine's molding of talk and other forms of common knowledge to her own designs is related to the first-person presentation of her material. These two techniques determine the shape of her biography at least as much as written sources and the testimony of others do. Although it is not always apparent, Christine is the work's most important eyewitness. She bases her biography to a large extent on her firsthand knowledge of the king. In the *Adv* she recounts how in December 1368, when she was a very young child, she was presented to Charles V at the Louvre. Having grown up close to the royal court, Christine feels able to paint the king's portrait: "Here is said and described the physiognomy and build of King Charles" (I.xvii). In another instance Christine makes it clear that, as the king's biographer, she is to a large extent testifying to the truth of her own experience. She says that she knows Charles surrounded himself with the most qualified philosophers and advisers "because experience taught me the truth of it" (I.xv); in other words, because Charles had her own father summoned from Italy to become one of his advisers. As a direct consequence of Charles's act, she herself was "translatez" (transported) to France, which, she assures us, can be verified by many people still alive. Although Christine does not state it directly, her use of the first person and her signature provide the best guarantee of eyewitness testimony.

In writing the biography of a king of exemplary virtue in the first person, Christine resembles former biographers of Saint Louis. Jean de Joinville and Guillaume de Saint-Pathus, for instance, had reported what they had seen and heard Louis do and say. Their testimonials to Louis sanctity are additionally based on the statements of first-person eyewitnesses who testified in Louis canonization proceedings.[32] Christine's need to defend her own reputation in writing a biography of the king acquires another dimension: Since the eligibility of a candidate for sainthood is established by eyewitness accounts, the person testifying has to be recognized as reliable; it therefore follows that if Christine wants to establish that Charles V's character borders on the saintly, she has to prove her own qualifications to testify on his behalf.

Christine spells out many of the intellectual operations involved in writing history to her readers. Jacques Le Goff has explained that history in the Middle Ages implied a rearrangement and reworking of lived experience—primarily the subject's but also the biographer's, if the biographer

---

32. Jacques Le Goff, *Saint Louis* (Paris: Gallimard, 1996), 337.

knew the subject personally—according to paradigms that had been invested with authority.[33] Christine expresses the desire to tame talk by having it enter the very fabric of her written text and be subject to her revisions. Talk, a form of living language, becomes part and parcel of the dynastic history being written out before readers. Christine stresses that her compilation takes into account not only written but also oral sources, including the reports of reliable witnesses and various types of talk. By correcting and appropriating what is said for her ongoing construction of dynastic memory, Christine facilitates a dialogue while speaking in her own voice as a person who has lived through many of the events recounted. In creating a "lieu de mémoire" for Charles by writing his biography, Christine herself becomes in a very real sense a living "lieu de mémoire." Her conception appears to be a tribute to Augustine's belief that memory "is the mind, it is the very self" (*Trin.* 10.17.26).[34]

Yet another view of memory, that of Mary Carruthers, "signifies the process by which a work of literature becomes institutionalized—internalized within the language and pedagogy of a group."[35] Pointing out that the medieval person would have rehearsed a whole series of exemplary stories, Carruthers defines the medieval self in general (not just the writer) as the "subject who remembers." From that perspective, the Christine of *ChV* becomes the subject who compiles and shapes oral and written testimony to create a permanent repository of cultural memory. Christine's archive of *ChV* contains the exemplary life of that king, which completes and extends the story of other model rulers such as David, Charlemagne, Clovis, and Louis IX. In so doing, Christine simultaneously bases herself on and reinforces the authority of the *GCF*, which celebrate these very same figures in the vernacular[36] and in prose, the two seen as the language of truth. Following the lead of the *GCF*, Christine addresses a lesson to the French people in proposing the exemplary figure of Charles V to them in a language understandable to all. By citing what people said, she is able to respond to them, turning her narrative into an extended conversation. In *ChV* Christine seems to mold reputations from memory before our very eyes and ears out of the three-way discourse that she stages among

33. Jacques Le Goff, *History and Memory*, trans. Steven Rendall and Elizabeth Claman (New York: Columbia University Press, 1992), 68–79.
34. "Memory," in *Augustine*, ed. Fitzgerald, 554.
35. Mary Carruthers, *The Book of Memory: A Study of Memory in Medieval Culture* (Cambridge: Cambridge University Press, 1990), 9.
36. For more on Christine's use of the vernacular, see Lori J. Walters, "The Royal Vernacular: Poet and Patron in Christine de Pizan's *Charles V* and the *Sept Psaumes allégorisés*," in *The Vernacular Spirit: Essays on Medieval Religious Literature*, ed. Renate Blumenfeld-Kosinski, Duncan Robertson, and Nancy Warren (New York: Palgrave, 2002), 145–82, and "'Translating Petrarch': *Cité des dames* II.7.1, Jean Daudin, and Vernacular Authority," in *Christine 2000: Studies on Christine de Pizan in Honor of Angus J. Kennedy*, ed. John Campbell and Nadia Margolis (Amsterdam: Rodopi, 2000), 283–97.

the Divinity, the French people, and herself as intermediary and spokesperson.

Like Father, like Daughter: Charles V, Thomas de Pizan, and Christine

In *ChV* Christine constructs portraits of Charles and of herself as his royal biographer on the paradigm of the "humanist saint,"[37] a model combining wisdom and eloquence.[38] Whether known primarily as a writer who gave advice to world leaders or as someone who counted on the advice and rhetorical skills of others to help rule, he or she was proficient in both domains. Christine is careful to foreground the king's rhetorical skills. Because Charles writes and speaks well, and because he commissions "translations" of Latin works into Middle French, he becomes a more effective monarch. His mandate as ruler offers Christine the possibility of creating her own role as political counselor and biographer. She shrewdly uses Charles's translation campaign to authorize her transformation of the idea of kingship. And in redefining contemporary French kingship in terms of wisdom, she ingeniously allows a place both for herself and for her father as wise advisers to the monarch. Charles's translation campaign also legitimizes Christine's transformation of him from individual king to exemplary ruler, a prime example of the ideal of the writer-statesperson that he had fostered in keeping with the model bequeathed to him by the monkish keepers of the *GCF*. The French monarchy's idea of *translatio* in turn authorizes Christine to mold her own image on Charles's exemplary melding of wisdom and eloquence.

Christine's *translatio* involved acquiring a new set of "fathers" in Paris, the first being Charles. When Christine adds to the *fama* of her gender and her country through her display of learning and her cultivation of *sagesse* as an intellectual, ethical, and theological ideal, she is shaping her persona on the king's. She perpetuates the image of the country as a fount of *studium* or *clergie* that she had helped to construct in writing his biography. Charles V cultivated his descent from Charlemagne, who had reinvigorated the study of Latin and stimulated the copying of manuscripts. Charles recognized France's superiority in the world of learning by strengthening links between the monarchy and the University of Paris. Christine celebrates France's status as an intellectual center by calling Paris

---

37. Lori J. Walters, "The Humanist Saint: Christine, Augustine, Petrarch, and Louis IX," forthcoming.

38. I would emend Solterer's formulation, *Master and Minerva*, 175, that Christine's writing combines "Minervan wisdom and Roman eloquence" to read "vernacular eloquence," an eloquence designed to adapt the grace and authority of its Ciceronian model to the character of the Middle French language and to the needs of contemporary French society.

"a second Athens." The city's reputation for learning accounts for her father's decision to accept Charles V's offer to come to Paris rather than to join the court of Louis II of Hungary. In the terms of the *Adv*'s allegory, Tommasso di Benvenuto da Pizzano's desire to acquire *fama* by going to Paris marked the metaphorical birth of his daughter Christine as an intellectual being.

Christine's rebirth signaled the construction/reconstruction of her persona in light of the "fathers" that she found in her newly adopted country and according to her own father's figure. In presenting herself as architect of Charles's biography, she likens herself to Charles as redesigner of the Louvre and builder of many public edifices (I.x). To borrow a medieval term, Christine models her own *ordonnance* (that is, her division of the biography into sections, chapters, etc.) on the king's *ordonnance*—the order that Charles instituted and maintained in the kingdom, in its laws, regulations, fiscal and administrative matters, and in the very buildings that he had designed, redesigned, and constructed from scratch. One of Christine's answers to her detractors (II.xxi, discussed above) is that although she borrows from other authors, she uses those borrowings to express her own ideas. She compares her originality to that of architects who employ stone and other materials not of their own making to construct a building that conforms to their conception. With this metaphor, Christine implies that she composes the king's life much as Charles constructs both his kingdom and his personal life, which she describes as "ordonnee," as befits a virtuous prince (I.xv). The way in which Charles as king puts order in his own life dictates how Christine as writer orders the composition of his life, a *vita* of a latter-day "humanist saint." In constructing Charles's biography, she is, to apply her metaphor to her own writing, reinforcing the foundations of her autobiography.

Christine's second father was her biological father. Tommasso was rechristened in Paris as Thomas de Pizan, a Gallicized form of his name that symbolized his new identity at the French court. As Charles's personal physician, he cared for the king's bodily needs, and as his adviser and counselor he ministered to his more political and spiritual concerns. In turn, Thomas was nurtured by the intellectual atmosphere provided by the king. Thomas transcends the status of biological father to become his daughter's intellectual mentor, who was formed by the main secular intellectual mentor of his time, Charles V, as well as contributing to the king's physical and moral formation. Although Thomas was renowned during his lifetime, shortly after his death Opinion was to begin to tarnish his *fama*. As Veenstra explains, astrology, promoted by Charles V as a means of understanding the true significance of history, had come under strong attack in early fifteenth-century Paris through its association with sorcery and court scandals. Christine felt the need to shore up France's "intellectual dynasty" by rehabilitating astrology, and with it, her father. This she does primarily by associating both with Christianity. She contends that her father's knowledge of astrology made him famous throughout Christendom (I.xv). In a chapter on Charles's devotional practices—a chapter whose number, thirty-three, has overwhelming Christological and Augustinian Trinitarian overtones—Christine places her father among a group of advisers who supported the authority of a relic of the Holy Blood through natural science and through the judgment of the "docteurs" (I.xxxiii). Christine cunningly assimilates her physician father to the Church doctors to rehabilitate him for an early fifteenth-century public and to strengthen *her* legitimacy as self-appointed doctor to the body politic.

If in the *Advision* Christine becomes, in Rosalind Brown-Grant's words, "a female exemplar for the princely reader,"[39] this is to a large extent possible because she had already fashioned herself on the example set by Charles V, intellectual mentor to all Christendom and reflection of the suffering Christ. *ChV* functions much like a piece of evidence in a trial for Charles's "canonization" as "humanist saint." Christine's biography proves that Charles was successful at his job as sovereign, which set the example to be followed by the French, as it had been communicated to them in the copies of the *GCF* dealing with his reign that he had supervised. Additionally, the persona that Christine creates for herself in the act of writing the biography illustrates that the king was worthy of the act of memorialization that Christine performs for him, for his example as statesman and master "translator" had made it possible for her, his loyal subject, to be transformed into the writer-philosopher needed by the monarchy. In turn, Christine had to justify her new persona by continuing, long after Charles's death and for the benefit of his successors, to function as a political counselor who put her wisdom and eloquence at the service of the state. In making extensive use of the first person to present an exemplary self for emulation by the *Adv*'s royal readers, Christine provides as it were *living* proof that her conception of *fama* has performed the exemplary function that the divinity conceived for it and that she had helped, and would continue to help, transmit to the polis on behalf of the monarchy.

The *Fama* of the Fathers and Mother Church: Saint Thomas, Saint Augustine, and Christine

In the *Adv* Christine acquires a third spiritual father in the person of another Thomas, the venerable Church Father Thomas Aquinas. Christine brought *her* new identity to fruition in Paris—where, as we recall, *fama* is established according to the law of God and the blessed prophets—both

39. Brown-Grant, *Christine de Pizan*, 89.

by seeing her father's evolution under Charles's watchful eye and by contact with the thought of Saint Thomas Aquinas. Christine's *Adv* is a synthesis of the major intellectual currents of her time, with particular emphasis on the relationship between sense experience, wisdom, and governance in the thought of Saint Augustine, Aristotle, and Saint Thomas Aquinas. Christine translates passages of Aquinas in *ChV* and the *Adv,* and Aquinas's thought, perhaps to a greater extent than Augustine's, dominates the *Adv.* Christine's discussion of Aristotle's correction of earlier philosophers by his ideas about first causes, one of the concepts through which Aquinas had integrated Aristotle into a Christian framework, paves the way for her transformation of Lady Philosophy into Lady Theology. The ending of the *Adv* recalls Aquinas's comments on a knowledge more perfect than dialectic.[40] Whereas the *Adv* supplies evidence of Christine's mastery of the intellectual treasury of her times, her final gesture, like Aquinas's, is one of love that goes beyond the greatest human intellectual capacities. Christine's holy trinity of fathers—Charles V, Thomas de Pizan, and Thomas Aquinas—reinforces the Augustinian Trinitarian thematics and structure of the *Adv.* Christine's theological meditations extend and develop Aquinas's thirteenth-century interpretation of Augustine, itself founded on Augustine's system but respectfully differing from it on essential points.

Christine establishes her authority according to the hierarchy of human transmitters of sacred doctrine set forth by Aquinas: the authority of the authors of Holy Scripture was the highest, followed by that of the church doctors, which, unlike the first, was open to revision, and finally, the work of the contemporary theologian, whose authority was not as great as that of the church doctors. According to Aquinas, the contemporary theologian had to interpret God's word for the times, basing that interpretation primarily on preceding Christian tradition but drawing from the best of pagan philosophers as well.[41] Christine makes herself over as a type of female theologian on the model of the contemporary theologian proposed by Aquinas. She refines the position of the university-trained theologian by trying to recover theology for the "simple person" like herself and like many in her lay audience who had not received training in theology in Latin.[42] Since her self-appointed role as a woman qualified to enter into theological speculations had little or no precedent, she seems to borrow some of her authority from the female character of the metaphor "Mother

40. *Commentary on the Sentences,* 35.2.1. Quoted by David Knowles, *The Evolution of Medieval Thought* (New York: Vintage, 1962), 268.

41. "Thomas Aquinas," in *Augustine,* ed. Fitzgerald, 829–32.

42. Benjamin Semple, "The Critique of Knowledge as Power: The Limits of Philosophy and Theology in Christine de Pizan," *Christine de Pizan and the Categories of Difference,* ed. Marilynn Desmond (Minneapolis: University of Minnesota Press, 1998), 108–27.

Church." When she implicitly enters into the debate, begun by Augustine and continued by Aquinas, on whether woman reflected the *imago Dei* directly or indirectly (by reflecting the male's),[43] she positions herself as a "Church Mother." In the *Cité*, completed roughly a year before the *Adv*, Christine alludes to Augustine in the following way: "Saint Augustine, the holy Father of the Church, who was converted to Christianity by his mother's weeping. . . . it was thanks to the tears of a woman that Saint Augustine, this holy luminary, now shines his light down from the altar and illuminates the whole of Christendom" (*Cité* I.10).[44]

With this seemingly ingenuous aside, Christine poses a simple (but not simplistic) response to the often acrid theological debates over the *imago Dei*. Her answer is grounded in Aristotle's ideas on sense experience and in Augustine's emphasis on the importance of sight to knowledge. These insights justify the value of experience to all humans, including those lacking the university education of a philosopher. Even the simplest person can see that sons follow the example set by their mothers. In the humble here-and-now, as evidenced by Augustine's own moving testimonial to Monnica, no man, not even a glorious Church Father, would be able to achieve exemplary status if his mother did not lead the way through her own example.

Christine's *Fama* in Theology's Mirror

By citing Monnica's contribution to the development of Saint Augustine's piety, Christine gently rebukes the pride of male theologians, a gesture that cannot fail to recall Aquinas's own respectful criticism of his great predecessor Augustine. The ending of the *Adv* suggests that Christine realized that her womanly wisdom was in reality a bittersweet pill. The ironic view of the human condition with which she brings her work to a close has implications for her take on *fama* in general and for her own *fama* in particular. The *Adv* celebrates the triumph of human reason *and* reveals its ultimate inadequacy before the mysteries of faith.

Let us first consider the ending as a victory of human wisdom and eloquence before turning to the way that it subverts its own pretensions to human authority. The dream vision, traditionally metaphorized as a mirror, has over the course of Christine's narrative become one with Theology's mirror. This mirror reflects upon the monarchy, the writer-adviser, and the working symbiosis of the two. What Lady Theology sees in the mir-

43. Kari Elisabeth Børresen, *Subordination and Equivalence: The Nature and Role of Woman in Augustine and Thomas Aquinas, A Reprint of a Pioneering Classic* (Kampen, the Netherlands: Kok Pharos, 1995), 26–30, 164–70; reprint of original French *Subordination et équivalence: Nature et rôle de la femme d'après Augustin et Thomas d'Aquin* (Oslo: Universitetsforlaget, 1968).

44. Rosalind Brown-Grant, *The Book of the City of Ladies* (New York: Penguin, 1999), 26–27.

ror she holds in her hand is her own face topped by her crown, the zenith of all the crown imagery that has preceded it. The *Adv*'s final image is of the three jewels in Theology's crown—a diamond, a cameo, and a ruby—which, the author tells us, stand for the three parts of her text. Christine regales the readers of her three-part work with a series of three *mises en abysme,* namely, Theology's mirror, Theology's crown, and finally the three jewels in the crown, each of which is more powerful than the preceding one. Christine thus ends her dream vision with the image of three mirrors that appear to telescope each other, a beautiful rendering of the mystery of the Trinity—which complements her references, placed strategically at the beginning of part III—to the other great mystery of the Christian faith, the Incarnation.[45] Christine's stunning rhetorical tour-de-force, coming at the conclusion of her text, reinforces the spiritual themes that she has heretofore articulated through overtly didactic and poetic means. Her implicit contrast of Jean de Meun's metaphor of the *Rose* as a mirror for lovers with Dante's ruby as a metaphor for divine love[46] seems calculated to show that eloquence in the service of theology can outdo eloquence in the service of purely secular aims.

If the mirror of Theology that Christine had created in writing her *Adv* proclaims her *fama* as self-made theologian, a *fama* that she had hoped to secure against the slings of outrageous Fortune, she as human author and transmitter of knowledge finds herself caught in its perplexing reflections. The three gems in the crown hold an enigmatic message for all observers, and no one is more intrigued by that enigma than Christine herself. The jewels consist of a cameo depicting a human head, flanked by a diamond and a ruby. Christine portrays the diamond as "hard and piercing; and although it is clear when not in a setting, when it is set and put in gold, it seems obscure and brown" (p. 142). Although this image belies the sparkle that we now associate with diamonds mounted in gold, the medieval setting described here clouds the gem's brightness. The diamond's obscurity in its setting recalls the Pauline epistle (1 Cor. 13–14) repeatedly invoked by Christine in speaking of *fama,* which introduces reflections on prophecy appropriate to an *advision* that unites dream vision with advice. Sight that is obscured in this life is contrasted with the promise of clear vision in the next, when each one will see God, the Exemplar of exemplars, face to face.

The last, and culminating, precious stone in the series is the ruby, which is "clear and shining and without dark shadow." Its clarity becomes more pleasing as one contemplates it. Blood-red, it evokes Christ's sacrifice, which bridged the gap between the human and the divine. As I see it, the

---

45. Semple, "Critique of Knowledge," 123.
46. See *Paradiso* IX, 69, where Dante also uses the metaphor of the mirror, and *Paradiso* XXX, 66.

cameo set between the diamond and the ruby could stand for Christine's sermon-like method of instruction by means of *exempla*. Just as the cameo traces the white imprint of a human physiognomy on a brown background, the image that Christine has constructed of herself as female theologian would necessarily include a dark counterpoint. The negative of her bright silhouette, her imagistic *antiphrasis* as it were, would lie in the recognition that despite all human efforts to give permanent and immutable expression to one's *fama*, it is never entirely exempt from change. This lesson applies equally to Church Mothers and to Church Fathers. In this world even theologians are condemned "to see through a glass darkly." Christine had not moved *fama* as far away from the Virgilian monster, nor from the Janus-faced Lady Fortune, as she had hoped.

Part 3

FAMA AND SPEECH

CHAPTER SEVEN

Sin, Speech, and Scolding in Late Medieval England

SANDY BARDSLEY

Relieving England of between one-third and one-half of its population, the Black Death of the mid-fourteenth century was once thought to have ushered in a "golden age" for the English peasantry.[1] To the consternation of landowners and the appreciation of peasants, wages rose and prices fell in the decades following the plague. But as historians have recognized more recently, the shift in social and economic relations in the century following the Black Death was neither dramatic nor automatic. Recent scholarship examining post-plague England has, therefore, explored not only social, cultural, and economic changes, but also political and cultural continuities, hegemonic forces that prevented demographic crisis from prompting a successful social revolution. Deprived of a significant chunk of their labor supply, landowners fought desperately to keep wages low and even to reinstate traditional manorial fees and dues that they had allowed to lapse.[2] Similarly, the monarchy, lacking one-third of its pre-plague tax base, imposed new taxes and dealt harshly with peasant and urban rebels. Priests and poets fumed about disruptive and disrespectful peasants who demanded higher wages or better working conditions. In this essay, I propose an additional vehicle for minimizing social disruption after the plague: from the mid-fourteenth century, the pre-plague clerical discourse on Sins of the Tongue was

1. See, for example, James E. Thorold Rogers, *Six Centuries of Work and Wages: The History of English Labour* (New York: G. P. Putnam's Sons, 1903); idem, *A History of Agriculture and Prices in England,* 7 vols. (Oxford: Clarendon, 1866–1902).
2. See Barbara A. Hanawalt, "Peasant Resistance to Royal and Seigniorial Impositions," in *Social Unrest in the Late Middle Ages,* ed. Francis X. Newman (Binghamton, N.Y.: Medieval and Renaissance Texts and Studies, 1986), 23–47.

increasingly employed to reinscribe traditional social hierarchies and discourage disruptive and inflammatory speech. Invoking *fama* and reminding everyone of its importance, in other words, helped to ensure that elite worlds were not turned as far upside down as they feared.

As Edwin Craun has noted, the thirteenth and fourteenth centuries witnessed increasing concern about the power of speech, particularly within the church, and this concern was manifest in both ecclesiastical and secular writings of the following centuries.[3] I build on Craun's argument by proposing that—especially from the late fourteenth century—the discourse spread not only from clerical to lay participants, but also to nonliterate, nonelite English men and women. That is, the discourse on Sins of the Tongue was popularized as well as laicized, and appropriated to serve the interests of those who sought to assert or to emphasize power at a local level. I examine evidence for the popularization of the discourse on Sins of the Tongue in the late fourteenth and fifteenth centuries, focusing especially on three types of deviant speech: barratry, cursing, and scolding.

A Popularization of the Discourse on Sins of the Tongue

As Craun has noted, the late medieval discourse of evil speech was grounded in the church. After the Fourth Lateran Council of 1215 had established that all Christians were required to attend confession at least once a year, texts identifying and categorizing vices proliferated. To hear confessions and dispense appropriate penances, priests needed something of a taxonomy of sins, locating each in relation to others in a hierarchy of evil. Among these closely scrutinized and annotated sins were the Sins of the Tongue, regularly granted a chapter or more in the expansive and encyclopedic pastoral manuscripts that proliferated starting in the early thirteenth century. In England, the church enforced its jurisdiction over speech not only from the pulpit and in the confessional but also by means of its courts. Among supplementary constitutions passed at the Council of Oxford, convoked in 1222 to promote the decrees of the Fourth Lateran Council within the province of Canterbury, was one that excommunicated anyone who falsely and maliciously accused another of a crime. This measure, which was subsequently adopted throughout the dioceses of thirteenth-century England, was supposed to be read aloud in parish churches at regular intervals. Ecclesiastical law firmly asserted the church's jurisdiction over crimes of defamation and was likely familiar to the laity.[4]

3. Edwin D. Craun, *Lies, Slander, and Obscenity in Medieval English Literature: Pastoral Rhetoric and the Deviant Speaker* (Cambridge: Cambridge University Press, 1997).
4. R. H. Helmholz, "Introduction," in *Select Cases on Defamation to 1600*, ed. R. H. Helmholz, Publications of the Selden Society, vol. 101 (London: Selden Society, 1985), xiv–xv.

Although much late medieval concern about evil speech was focused within the church, secular legislators soon picked up on these heightened anxieties. In 1275 and 1276, for instance, English statutes specifically prohibited rumors and slanders concerning the king or great nobles and expressed concern that justice in royal courts was impeded by "barrators" who indulged in wasteful litigation. During the late Middle Ages, the jurisdiction of royal courts over speech crimes was solidified by a series of statutes not only against treason but also against rumors and lies about the aristocracy.[5]

Until this point, concern about speech was focused mostly within the strong central institutions of church and government. But during the fourteenth and fifteenth centuries—especially from the late fourteenth century onward—the discourse on dangerous speech was further elaborated on and popularized by authors of treatises, poetry, ballads, and plays, and by manuscript illustrators, wood and stone carvers, and painters of church walls and windows. Especially from the early fourteenth century, many Latin treatises on vices were translated into English, and by the late fourteenth century the pastoral discourse on Sins of the Tongue had been thoroughly co-opted by vernacular writers and craftspeople.

Fourteenth- and fifteenth-century literature and art demonstrated much concern both with speech in general and with the instruments of speech, the mouth and the tongue, in particular. The entrance to hell, for example, was often represented in wallpaintings, stained-glass windows, carvings, manuscript illuminations, and even stage props in mystery cycle plays as a gigantic mouth that consumed sinners. Although hellmouth images had been around since the eleventh century, they became increasingly popular and detailed in the fourteenth and fifteenth centuries, complete with glaring eyes, gaping jaws, and sharp teeth. In wallpaintings and stained-glass windows, part of the material environment with which ordinary parishioners interacted daily, hellmouths appeared in scenes of the Last Judgment, in which the worthy ascended to heaven and the damned were cast into the inferno through the mouth of hell, propelled by demons of all shapes, sizes, and colors. Some sinners were rounded up with ropes and dragged toward the hellmouth, others were pushed in wheelbarrows or threatened with pitchforks.[6] Hellmouths could have multiple meanings

---

5. *Statutes of the Realm,* 9 vols. (London, 1810–22), 1:35, 44.

6. Examples of hellmouths on bench-ends can be seen at Horning (Norfolk), Southwold (Suffolk), and Freckenham (Suffolk). Hellmouths were frequently incorporated into wallpaintings that depicted the scene of the Last Judgment (and were thus known as dooms). Examples can be found in the Church of Saint Thomas of Canterbury in Salisbury and the Guild Chapel in Stratford-upon-Avon. A wonderful stained-glass window incorporating a hellmouth survives at Fairford (Gloucestershire). For discussion of hellmouths throughout northern Europe, see Pamela Sheingorn, "'Who Can Open the Doors of His Face?': The Iconography of Hell Mouth," in *The Iconography of Hell,* ed. Clifford Davidson and Thomas H. Seilor (Kalamazoo, Mich.: Medieval Institute Publications, 1992), 1–19.

for those who viewed them, and the discourse on Sins of the Tongue was not the only reason for their increased representation: in her work on hell-mouth images in late medieval mystery plays, Patricia Dignan has suggested that hellmouths gained popularity in the same period as increased importance was placed on the sacrament of the Eucharist. From the thirteenth century, she has noted, the mouth became especially important both as a site of virtue (the gateway for the Eucharist) and as a site of sin (the home of the sinful tongue).[7] Edwin Craun has also pointed out that both the mouth and the tongue were foci of concern in late medieval England. Constructed as powerful, very often phallic, weapons, tongues were described as having "slain more people than did King Alexander." Medieval vernacular proverbs cautioned that "the tongue breaks bone though itself has none," that "the tongue of an evil man is worse than a spear," and that "tongues are worse than swords."[8] Chaucer's Pardoner tells the pilgrims en route to Canterbury that one of his methods for humbling an enemy is to "sting him smartly with my tongue."[9] Elsewhere in the *Canterbury Tales*, tongues are described as cutting through bonds of friendship and as being sharpened or polished in readiness for attack.[10] Poems that sought to instruct children in proper manners thus advised them to "be of good tongue" and cautioned that "thine own tongue may be thy foe."[11]

By the late fourteenth century, anxieties about speech made their way into local courts and organizations. Ordinances against abusive speech were passed in many manorial and borough courts, and anyone who insulted court officials was increasingly likely to be prosecuted. In the villages of Wolveston and East Merrington (Durham) in 1379, for instance, tenants were warned against harming others in either words or deeds.[12]

7. Patricia Grace Dignan, "Hellmouth and Villains: The Role of the Uncontrolled Mouth in Four Middle English Mystery Cycles" (Ph.D. diss., University of Cincinnati, 1994), esp. 1–3.

8. "See Much, Say Little, and Learn to Suffer in Time," in *Religious Lyrics of the Fifteenth Century*, ed. Carleton Brown (Oxford: Clarendon, 1939), 279–80, at 279; Bartlett J. Whiting and Helen Wescott Whiting, *Proverbs, Sentences, and Proverbial Phrases from English Writings Mainly before 1500* (Cambridge: Belknap Press of Harvard University Press, 1968), 602–3 (note especially T384, T392, and T395). Latin proverbs employed similar metaphors. For a discussion of Latin and English proverbs that depicted the tongue as a sword, and some of their biblical antecedents, see Paul Sheneman, "The Tongue as a Sword: Psalms 56 and 63 and the Pardoner," *Chaucer Review* 27 (1993): 396–400.

9. "The Pardoner's Prologue," Group C, line 413, in *The Riverside Chaucer*, ed. Larry D. Benson (Boston: Houghton Mifflin, 1987), 195. All translations from *The Canterbury Tales* are my own.

10. See, for instance, "The Manciple's Tale," H 340–42, ibid., 286; "The General Prologue," A 712–13, ibid., 34.

11. See, for instance, "How the Good Wife Taught Her Daughter" and "How the Wise Man Taught His Son," both in *The Babees' Book: Medieval Manners for the Young Now First Done into Modern English from the Texts of Dr. F. J. Furnivall*, ed. Edith Rickert (Colchester: Chatto and Windus, 1908), 31–42, 43–47.

12. *Halmota Prioratus Dunelmensis: Containing Extracts from the Halmote Court or Manor Rolls of the Prior and Convent of Durham*, A.D. 1296–A.D. 1384, ed. W. H. D. Longstaffe and John Booth, Surtees Society Publications, vol. 82 (Durham: Andrews, 1889), 153–54.

Guilds passed similar ordinances prohibiting dissension or rebellious speech among members, fining and even expelling those who transgressed.[13] Ordinances from a guild at Watlington (Norfolk) in the 1380s, for instance, insisted that any conflicts that had arisen between members be settled at fraternity feasts, and that conversation at feasts should be "all of peace and love."[14]

At the same time as they worried about evil tongues and mouths in general, vernacular moralists and legislators also investigated specific types of dangerous speech. New terms emerged for describing particular verbal transgressions. "Backbiters," for instance, emerged in the thirteenth century as those who spread false or unkind rumors. "Janglers" and "jangleresses," appearing in English texts from the fourteenth century, chattered too much, particularly in inappropriate situations, such as during church services. "Praters," first mentioned in surviving texts from the early fifteenth century, talked excessively or boasted or spoke evil.[15] Each term had a history and a literature of its own, yet each was also part of the widening late medieval discourse about the evils of speech and the threat that evil speech posed to *fama*. Indeed, the risks were dire: as noted by the early fourteenth-century Roberd of Brunne, a backbiter was responsible for slaying three people before God: himself or herself; the person whose reputation was damaged; and the person to whom he or she told the tale.[16] Three crimes that stand out as subject to particular popular concern in late medieval England were barratry, cursing, and scolding. The generalized discourse of Sins of the Tongue played a role in the development of each crime, and each in turn contributed to this same generalized discourse.

Barratry

In the late thirteenth century, a new kind of speech crime emerged. Associated first with the general extension of royal jurisdiction, barratry originally involved the offense of pursuing spurious court cases that wasted the time of judges. The Middle English noun *barat* or *baret* meant both deception and trouble or fighting. Those who brought litigation before the courts without sufficient cause were regarded as both deceitful and trouble-making: they created social tension, deceived the court with weak claims, and subverted judicial attention from more important issues. During the thirteenth to fifteenth centuries, however, the meaning of barratry

---

13. *English Gilds*, ed. Joshua Toulmin Smith and Lucy Toulmin Smith, Early English Text Society, vol. 40 (London: N. Trübner, 1870): 4, 104, 315.

14. Gervase Rosser, "Going to the Fraternity Feast: Commensality and Social Relations in Late Medieval England," *Journal of British Studies* 33 (1994): 430–46, at 441.

15. I rely primarily on the *Oxford English Dictionary*, 2nd ed., for early uses of these words.

16. Robert Mannyng, *Handlyng Synne*, ed. Frederick J. Furnivall, Early English Text Society, vol. 119 (London: K. Paul, Trench, Trübner, 1901), 55.

expanded, both through the behavior it described and the social classes to whom the label was applied. By the early sixteenth century, barratry could mean "trouble-making" in the most general sense, both within courts and within the community at large.

Two statutes passed in the mid-1270s expressed concern that barrators were impeding justice by clogging the royal courts with lengthy cases and usurping the king's jurisdiction by claiming authority to pronounce judgments. The Statutes of Westminster of 1275, for instance, instructed sheriffs: "No sheriff shall suffer barretors [or maintainers of] quarrels in their shires. Neither stewards of great lords, nor any other unless he is attorney for his lord, may make suit or give judgment in the counties or pronounce the judgment unless he be specially required and prayed of all the suitors, and attorneys of the suitors, who shall be at the court."[17] The intention of this law was to regulate ways in which members of the nobility might use the royal courts in their dealings with each other. Barratry, then, signified upper-class litigiousness and legal meddling. Over the next century, however, the meaning expanded. A statute of 1361 empowered specially appointed magnates in the countryside with the power to restrain "offenders, rioters, and other barrators," and in 1396, Richard II, fearing "conspiracy of the people," sent a commission into Cheshire in search of "barrators and rioters."[18] Barratry was thus no longer a crime committed primarily by members of the elite in their constant struggles against each other but could also imply any kind of local disturbance, of which verbal offense and riot were two instances. By the late fourteenth century, regulations against barratry were also enforced at strictly local levels. Boroughs and guilds sought to protect their courts and their communities from barrators, and the meaning of barratry expanded further. The term "common barrator," with its implications of a threat to the "common peace," entered popular parlance. Several guilds whose regulations were surveyed by the king in 1389 prohibited barratry to protect their reputations and limit their liability in supporting members who pursued court cases. A London guild, for instance, set out that "if any brother . . . become of evil fame . . . as thief or common barretor or common questmonger . . . that anon he be put out of the fraternity."[19] Barretors attacked the *fama* of others and brought bad *fama* upon themselves and their associates.

17. *Statutes of the Realm*, 1:35. See also ibid., 1:44.

18. Ibid., 1:364. See also John Capgrave, *The Chronicle of England*, ed. Francis Charles Hingeston, Rolls Series, vol. 1 (London: Longman, Brown, Green, Longmans and Roberts, 1858), 264.

19. *A Book of London English, 1384–1425*, ed. R. W. Chambers and Marjorie Daunt (Oxford: Clarendon, 1931), 43 and 75. A similar rule governed members of the Gild of the Lord's Prayer in York: "It is forbidden that any brother of the gild shall, in the belief that he will have help from his brethren, be forward in getting into lawsuit or quarrel, or in upholding any cause whatsoever, upon pain of losing all help and friendship, or every relief, from the gild"; see *English Gilds*, ed. Smith and Smith, 138.

Surviving court cases from early fifteenth-century London also indicate that barratry encompassed a wider range of behavior. No longer an elite offense, barratry could be pursued and punished at all social levels. Sir John Scarle, parson of Saint Leonard's in Fasterlane, for instance, was described in a secular court in 1421 as a barrator, a scold, and a common ribald of his tongue. Among John Scarle's many verbal offenses, the court record claimed, was his habit of revealing the confessions of his female parishioners if they did not agree to commit adultery with him. The next year John Kempe, a carter, was presented as a barrator and a scold, and in 1423 Lambo the Boatman was accused of being a chider, a barrator with his neighbors, and a rebel against the king's officers.[20] As tradesmen, Kempe and Lambo were of inferior social status to Scarle, the parson. Their prosecution demonstrates that, by the early fifteenth century, the notion of barratry was applied to a range of social levels and a range of situations.[21] The presentations of Scarle, Kempe, and Lambo—each charged with multiple verbal offenses—also suggest that the meaning of barratry was no longer confined to litigiousness. Rather, it implied a more general verbal disorder.

Just as the concept of barratry was applied more frequently by courts in the late fourteenth and fifteenth centuries, so too was it invoked more often by authors of prescriptive literature. As evil people who should be avoided, barrators were grouped by contemporaries alongside felons, bawds, thieves, usurers, traitors, and liars.[22] By 1579, William Lambard's collection of instructions for justices of the peace defined a barrator as "a common quarrellour, or [person] otherwise of evill name and fame, Or a Maintainour of quarrels, or an Embraceour of Juries." A barrator, he claimed, was "a spotte in the common wealth."[23] Another sixteenth-century guide for jurors in local courts described common barrators as "Scolds [or] Brawlers, to the noyance and disturbance of their neighbours" and insisted that they should be punished.[24] From its earliest meaning as the practice of bringing false quarrels before the courts, barratry, by the sixteenth century, implied a more general disruption of both the judicial sys-

20. *Calendar of Plea and Memoranda Rolls, 1413–37,* ed. A. H. Thomas (Cambridge: Cambridge University Press, 1943), 127, 141, 155.
21. Marjorie McIntosh noticed a few presentments for barratry in fourteenth- and fifteenth-century local courts of smaller communities. See Marjorie Keniston McIntosh, *Controlling Misbehavior in England, 1370–1600* (New York: Cambridge University Press, 1998), 60 n. 10.
22. See, for example, *Jacob's Well, an English Treatise on the Cleansing of Man's Conscience,* ed. Arthur Brandeis, Early English Text Society, vol. 115 (London: K. Paul, Trench, Trübner, 1900): part 1, 15; *The Book of the Knight of La Tour-Landry,* ed. Thomas Wright, Early English Text Society, vol. 33a (London: K. Paul, Trench, Trübner, 1906), 53.
23. William Lambard, *Eirenarcha: or of the Office of the Iustices of Peace* (London, 1582).
24. John Kitchin, *Jurisdictions: or, the Lawful Authority of Courts Leet, Courts Baron, Court of Marshalseys, Court of Pypowder and Ancient Demesne,* 5th ed. (London, 1675), 20.

tem and local peace. The contexts in which the term might be invoked had broadened similarly: while originally pertaining primarily to disputes among members of the elite, the charge of barratry by the fifteenth and sixteenth centuries was also pursued at local levels and against ordinary folk.

Cursing

Whereas barratry was always a secular crime, even in its origins at elite levels, the verbal offense of cursing remained more closely allied with the church. Cursing was regarded as an offshoot of blasphemy, a crime that theologians defined as speech that misrepresented God's nature by adding to or subtracting from his properties or by ascribing his properties to a created being. To blaspheme was thus to attack the *fama* of God, a risky enterprise indeed, and blasphemers did this by complaining, for instance, that God was cruel or neglectful or wrong.[25] One particular variety of blasphemy condemned in multiple fourteenth- and fifteenth-century exempla, poems, and artistic representations, however, was the practice of cursing by a part of God's or Christ's body. A swearer might, for instance, exclaim "by Christ's foot!" "by God's bones!" or "by the heart of Christ!" According to a common exemplum, each time such a curse was uttered, the body of Christ in heaven was literally injured. In this way, claimed priests, poets, and artists, those who cursed harmed Christ's body every bit as much as had the Jews who allegedly nailed him to the cross. If those who cursed did not cease to swear and did not repent for their previous oaths, they might expect similar bodily pains throughout eternity.

Poems, stories, wallpaintings, and stained-glass windows attest to the wide circulation of this tale at popular levels from the fourteenth century onward. Roberd of Brunne mentions an early version in 1303, but the tale was increasingly popularized in the late fourteenth and fifteenth centuries.[26] In an early fifteenth-century wallpainting from Broughton (Buckinghamshire), for instance, the body of the adult Christ lies across his mother's lap as in representations of the Pietà. Unlike Pietà representations, however, Christ's body in the Broughton painting shows visible signs of the swearers' words: his right foot and right hand have been dismembered, and his bones can be seen through his flesh. Surrounding Christ and his mother are nine men, each with a symbol of his own verbal transgression. One man holds up a dismembered hand, another holds Christ's head, a third holds a heart, a fourth a foot and some bones, a fifth a communion wafer and bones, while a sixth and seventh man each hold bones

25. See Edwin D. Craun, "'Inordinata Locutio': Blasphemy in Pastoral Literature, 1200–1500," *Traditio* 39 (1983): 35–62; David Lawton, *Blasphemy* (Philadelphia: University of Pennsylvania Press, 1993).
26. *Handlyng Synne*, ed. Furnivall.

only.[27] Another early fifteenth-century wallpainting, in the church at Corby (Lincolnshire), represents a similar theme, with the Virgin and her Son again in the center. In this painting, however, the eight young men who surround the Pietà are each accompanied by a devil who inflicts on him the punishment appropriate to his curse. Scrolls issuing from the mouths of the men record their blasphemous utterances, but the inscriptions on these scrolls are too decayed to read.[28] Several poems listed sample punishments doled out to recalcitrant swearers in hell, which might give some idea of the scrolls' contents:

> By goddes body I swore ever in ire,
> Therefore I skorken [am scalded] and burn in fire.
> For swearing by God's side this pain have I,
> Therefore you swearers beware hereby!
> By the heart of God I swore in vain,
> Therefore I suffer this grievous pain.[29]

The exemplum of the curser's fate continued to be popular into the sixteenth century. One tale, for example, told of a gentleman who went hunting on a Sunday (a sin in itself) but failed to catch anything. Miserable, he retreated to a tavern, and began to curse at his bad luck, muttering, "By god's blood, this day is unhappy!" Before too long, his nose began to bleed, which caused him to curse further, swearing by "god's passion," "god's wounds," "god's flesh," and "god's nails." Such blasphemy resulted in the gentleman hunter bleeding in great streams from his ears, eyes, wrists, navel, hands, and elsewhere. At the same time, his tongue, which was black

27. The other two men, seated below Christ and his mother, are playing some kind of board game, and one strikes the other on the head with his sword. The relationship of these last two men to the scene is unclear, except that poems and exempla often represented dice players or other game players as habitual swearers and sometimes coupled warnings against swearing with warnings against gaming.

28. For a representation of the Corby wallpainting, see Conway Library photograph negative #176/3 (16) at the Courtauld Institute, London. It has been suggested that a third wallpainting, now lost, also represented the theme of Christ and the swearers. The wallpainting, at Walsham-le-Willows church in Suffolk, was photographed before it was destroyed, and a copy is reproduced in Christopher Woodforde, *The Norwich School of Glass-Painting in the Fifteenth Century* (London: Oxford University Press, 1950), facing p. 186. See also idem, "A Medieval Campaign against Blasphemy," *Downside Review* 55 (1937): 1–6. On the left-hand side of the Corby wallpainting is a naked woman seated on a red-horned beast, holding an unidentifiable object in her left hand and uttering something recorded on a scroll. Woodforde has suggested that she may represent lust, but her absence from exempla, poems, and other artistic representations concerning cursing, plus her peripheral placement in the wallpainting, may indicate that she was included as a space filler rather than as an integral part of the scene. Alternately, she may represent a tapster.

29. *Mittelenglische Dichtungen aus der Handschrift 432 des Trinity Coll. in Dublin,* ed. Rudolf Brotanek (Halle, Germany: M. Niemeyer, 1940), 99–102. See also John Mirk, *Mirk's Festial: A Collection of Homilies,* ed. Theodore Erbe, Early English Text Society, vol. 96 (London: K. Paul, Trench, Trübner, 1908), 113.

as pitch, shot out of his mouth in "a marvelous horrible, ugsome [loathsome] and fearful manner." And thus the gentleman continued, bleeding and cursing, until he died, while those around him watched in horror.[30]

By the fifteenth and sixteenth centuries, then, cursing had moved beyond the umbrella of blasphemy to become a crime of its own, easily recognized at the local level in popular poems, stories, and artistic media. Through the exemplum of the curser's fate, the crime of cursing became increasingly concrete and the negative potential of words was further underscored.

Scolding

By the second half of the fourteenth century, a new crime had appeared in the borough, manor, and church courts of England. Thousands of men and women—especially women—were charged with the crime of "scolding," which involved attacking the *fama* of others by means of public (and typically loud) insults.[31] Incidents of scolding were often described as constituting a disruption of the "common peace" or "King's peace," and offenders were punished by fine, or, occasionally, by being strapped into a "cucking stool" and dunked in a pond, river, or water-filled pit.[32] Like barratry and cursing, the crime of scolding also broadened significantly in meaning during the late fourteenth and fifteenth centuries. While the term *scold* was used occasionally in literary and religious texts from as early as 1275, it was not widely adopted as a legal category until the late fourteenth century, following the Black Death.[33] A handful of scolds can be found in pre-plague court records, but their numbers pale in comparison

30. This story, reproduced in Gerald R. Owst, *Literature and Pulpit in Medieval England* (Cambridge: Cambridge University Press, 1933), 423–24, originally appeared in Brother Whitford of Sion's *Werke for Housholders* (London, 1533). Another tale, from the same source, involved the death of a young London apprentice who habitually cursed "by the bones of god" and suffered an incurable "great marvelous sickness" which involved the flesh and skin of his arms, fingers, legs, feet, and toes dividing in half, as if cut with a knife, so that his bones were revealed.

31. Elsewhere I deal in more depth with the gendered nature of scolding; see my "Scolding Women: Cultural Knowledge and the Criminalization of Speech in Late Medieval England, 1300–1500" (Ph.D. diss., University of North Carolina at Chapel Hill, 1999), chap. 4.

32. Fines and duckings in cucking stools applied only in secular jurisdictions. In theory, scolds, along with brewsters and bakers who cheated their customers, were fined for their first three offences, and subject to physical punishments thereafter. But although cucking stools were supposed to be owned and maintained by every manor and town, most jurisdictions failed to do so in the fourteenth and early fifteenth centuries. When scolds were punished by church courts, they were subject to the range of ecclesiastical punishments.

33. The earliest surviving mention of scolding in English in the late medieval sense of the word appears in a late-thirteenth century version of a series of proverbs likely compiled in the mid-twelfth century; see "The Proverbs of Alfred," in *An Old English Miscellany*, ed. Richard Morris, Early English Text Society, vol. 49 (London: N. Trübner, 1872), 127. See the *Middle English Dictionary*, ed. Hans Kurath (Ann Arbor: University of Michigan Press, 1952–), s.v. "scold"; *Oxford English Dictionary*, 2nd ed., s.v. "scold."

to those of the late fourteenth and fifteenth centuries. Unlike barratry, however, nationwide statutes never mentioned scolding. Local jurisdictions that adopted the legal category of scold did so as a result of a dialogue between the increasingly popularized discourse on Sins of the Tongue and political dynamics at local levels.[34]

Even while the legal category of scolding was still evolving, prosecution of many kinds of crime involving speech seems to have been on the increase in mid- to late fourteenth-century manorial and borough courts. One local-level crime that presaged scolding was that of falsely raising a "hue and cry." Raising the hue and cry was a traditional means of community policing in medieval English villages. When someone saw an offense being committed, they were expected to shout out to their neighbors to pursue the offender, and anyone within earshot who did not respond to the hue and cry could be punished in the local court. But local courts also considered the legitimacy of each hue raised: if it was decided that the hue was not justified, the raiser was punished. Each person who was able to speak—whether a woman, a man, or a child, whether of high or low status—could muster others in pursuit of an alleged offender. Each had the opportunity to malign the *fama* of others in a mode that demanded immediate communal response. But once the pursuit was over, the *fama* of the hue-raiser was also adjudicated in the manorial or borough courts. Hue-raising as a means of communal policing declined in popularity throughout England from the late fourteenth century, precisely the period in which scolding presentments began. Village reconstructions suggest that hues and cries, both "just" and "unjust" (or "false"), were particularly frequent between the famine of the 1310s–20s and the immediate aftermath of the Black Death, but declined during the second half of the fourteenth century, and had disappeared in many jurisdictions by the early 1400s, the period in which scolding prosecutions became more common.[35]

34. I focus here especially on the emergence of scolding in manorial and borough courts, because scolding cases were heard in these local courts far more often than in the king's courts or in ecclesiastical courts. While scolding cases sometimes appeared in church courts and king's courts (such as sheriff's tourns or eyre courts), the charges brought in these sessions were much more likely to be "secondary" charges. By "secondary" charges, I mean that individuals were charged with some other crime, civil or moral, and the scolding charges were added on to the original accusation. For instance, Ruth Karras has noted that of 161 prostitutes charged in the Middlesex and Barking church courts between 1489 and 1492, forty-five were charged at the same time as common scolds, common defamers of their neighbors, or both. The function of listing multiple accusations, she has suggested, was to emphasize the perception that a particular individual was out of control. See Ruth Mazo Karras, *Common Women: Prostitution and Sexuality in Medieval England* (Oxford: Oxford University Press, 1996), 139.

35. J. Ambrose Raftis, for instance, reported increasing numbers of hues in the court of Warboys during the first half of the fourteenth century but only occasional hues in the early fifteenth century; see his *Warboys: Two Hundred Years in the Life of an English Mediaeval Village*

Not only did the frequency of false hue presentments change but so too did their format. In the thirteenth and early fourteenth centuries, most people whose hues were judged unjust were presented for very particular and bounded offenses: they were stated to have raised an unjust hue against a specified person on a specified date. In the late fourteenth and early fifteenth centuries, however, when courts began to prosecute scolds, the lines between hue-raising and scolding began to blur. In addition to specific cases of unjust hue-raising, some courts started to prosecute individuals as "common hue-raisers" in the same way that scolds were beginning to be presented as "common scolds." In Chedzoy (Somerset) for instance, individuals were prosecuted throughout the fourteenth century for specific instances of raising false hues. In 1372, however, Alice, wife of Richard Raules, was presented as a "common hue-raiser and disturber of the peace of the lord King and of her neighbors." Alice's offense was constructed not as a specific behavior, but as an identity, an ongoing part of her personality that had negative consequences for the people of Chedzoy. Two years later, the first scolding presentment was heard in Chedzoy, constructed along very similar lines to Alice's case: Joan, wife of John Frend, was prosecuted as a common scold who disturbed the peace of the lord.[36] In Chedzoy, an expanding interpretation of false hue-raising seemed to anticipate the first prosecution of scolding. The sheriff's tourn held at Northwich (Cheshire) in 1410 drew a more explicit connection between hue-raising and scolding. Robert of Pomiale and Thomas, Robert's son, were accused of raising an "enormous hue" on Hugh of Knottesford without any cause, calling him a thief and "many other vile names." Robert and Thomas were judged to be scolds, responsible for sowing discord among their neighbors.[37] Similar slippage between the two crimes is suggested by

(Toronto: Pontifical Institute of Mediaeval Studies, 1974), 218–20, 224. Edward Britton's study of Broughton found similarly that the use of hues increased significantly over the period 1288–1340, but he did not consider the later period; see his *Community of the Vill: A Study in the History of the Family and Village Life in Fourteenth-Century England* (Toronto: Macmillan of Canada, 1977), 121. A similar pattern was found at Holywell-cum-Needingworth by Edwin Brezette DeWindt: hues and cries were reported for nearly every year of surviving court rolls until 1396, but only one hue (in 1403) was reported in sixteen years of surviving court rolls between 1400 and 1457; see his *Land and People in Holywell-cum-Needingworth: Structures of Tenure and Patterns of Social Organization in an East Midlands Village, 1252–1457* (Toronto: Pontifical Institute of Mediaeval Studies, 1972), 272–73. The most comprehensive analysis of hue-raisings to date has been carried out by Sherri Olson for the villages of Upwood and Ellington (Huntingdonshire). Olson found that the average number of hue citations per court roll increased markedly in both villages from the 1280s to the 1350s, but dropped off thereafter, with "an ambiguous and uneven withering away" in the early fifteenth century; see her *Chronicle of All That Happens: Voices from the Village Court in Medieval England* (Toronto: Pontifical Institute of Mediaeval Studies, 1996), 92–98.

36. British Library, Additional Charters, 16054, 16065a.

37. Public Record Office (hereafter PRO) CHES 19/3, m. 27v. At nearby Colburnford in the following year, Avilla, wife of Robert de Moston, was charged as a scold who raised an "enormous hue" on Henry de Croghdon, calling him a "strong thief" against the peace of

the fact that individuals prosecuted for scolding were often in trouble for false hue-raising at the same time or on a later occasion. Of ten people prosecuted for scolding in Bridgwater between 1378 and 1380, three were also judged guilty of raising a false hue; of five Nottingham scolds in 1395–96, two were simultaneously charged with raising a false hue; and of seven Ramsey presentments of scolds between 1387 and 1422, three were also deemed false hue-raisers.[38]

A second speech-related crime that overlapped with scolding by the late fourteenth century was abuse of community officials and institutions.[39] In the second half of the fourteenth century, local officials seem to have been especially concerned about attacks on their fragile *fama*. In her study of the small town of Ramsey (Huntingdonshire), for instance, Anne DeWindt suggested that the late fourteenth and early fifteenth centuries saw a significant increase in charges of "rebelliousness" against town officials. Some Ramsey townspeople were also charged with the crime of "being rebellious and contrary" toward officials and their neighbors. In 1429 and again in 1430, ordinances were passed in Ramsey ordering "that no one is to be rebellious to the Constables, under penalty of 6s.8d." Offenses involving disrespect did occur in earlier and later periods (in 1294, for instance, a Ramsey man accused of forestalling was deemed in contempt of court for saying "outrageous things" to the jurors), but the last decades of the four-

---

the lord (PRO CHES 19/3, m. 30r.). In both the case of Robert and Thomas and the case of Avilla, the raising of an "enormous hue" was considered akin to scolding; they were labeled *both* raisers of enormous false hues *and* scolds.

38. *Bridgwater Borough Archives,* vol. 2, ed. Thomas Bruce Dilks (Somerset, Eng.: Somerset Record Society Publications, 1938): 3, 15, 49, 52, 104; *Records of the Borough of Nottingham,* vol. 1, ed. W. H. Stevenson et al. (Nottingham, 1882), 294–95, 304–5, 308–9; *The Court Rolls of Ramsey, Hepmangrove, and Bury, 1268–1600,* ed. Edwin Brezette DeWindt (Toronto: Pontifical Institute of Mediaeval Studies, 1990), 539, 615, 618, 652, 701. Because no court series is complete, these figures are minimum numbers; in other words, more scolds may have been false hue-raisers and vice versa.

39. Social and economic historians have long debated whether the Black Death resulted in a breakdown of communal harmony, manifested in increased local conflict and disrespect for community officials. Some, such as J. A. Raftis and Edwin DeWindt, have suggested that, after the plague, local tensions increased, personal pledges appeared less frequently in manorial court records, and village administration depended less on social ties than on impersonal bylaws. See especially Raftis, *Warboys,* and DeWindt, *Land and People.* The "breakdown" view has also been articulated by Barbara A. Hanawalt's *The Ties That Bound: Peasant Families in Medieval England* (New York: Oxford University Press, 1986), in which she juxtaposed the stability of the family unit against an eroding community structure. Other historians have been more skeptical about the extent of communal disintegration. Zvi Razi, for instance, has argued that social ties and village administration underwent little change during the fourteenth century. Similarly, Christopher Dyer has argued for relative continuity over the fourteenth century, pointing out that while late medieval communities were never egalitarian, they could still function in cohesive and unifying ways, both before and after the plague. See Zvi Razi, "Family, Land, and the Village Community in Later Medieval England," *Past and Present* 93 (1981): 3–36; Christopher Dyer, "The English Medieval Village Community and Its Decline," *Journal of British Studies* 33 (1994): 407–29.

teenth and first decades of the fifteenth centuries seem to have been a period of particular hostility *toward* local officials, particular sensitivity *by* local officials, or both.[40]

The types of behavior considered disrespectful varied. A manorial official in the village of Halton (Cheshire) objected, for example, when two local men allegedly called him a thief as he collected rents for the lord in 1357.[41] In nearby Middlewich in 1361, William, son of Thomas Luycesonne, was presented for having obstructed and abused the bailiff as he carried out his duties. In the following year, the same court heard three similar cases involving abuse of the bailiff, and it fined another man 12d. for lying in court.[42] In other jurisdictions, such as Walworth (Surrey) in 1369, individuals were described as rebels against the constables of the local lord.[43] Disrespectful behavior was often described in the context of the courtroom: individuals were charged with contempt of court or were punished for gossiping during court sessions. In Halton in 1394, for example, Thomas le Heuster was fined 2d. for having gossiped (*garulauit*) in court, despite frequent admonitions to be silent. Thomas de Lyne, also of Halton, was fined 2d. in 1402 for having gossiped in court and having threatened William Fisherman in the presence of the bailiff and in contempt of the lord. In nearby Wydnes in the same year, Henry Dankynson was fined 3d. for gossiping in court, in spite of the bailiff's warnings.[44] And in Ramsey in 1422, a disgruntled John Webster was dealt a fine of 6d. for saying in court that the jurors were false (which in this context meant that they were liars).[45]

While disruptive speech in the courtroom and toward local officials was

40. Anne Reiber DeWindt, "Local Government in a Small Town: A Medieval Leet Jury and Its Constituents," *Albion* 23 (1991): 627–54, at 635–37.

41. PRO DL30 1/21.

42. PRO SC2 156/2.

43. PRO SC2 205/24. Raftis found that villagers at Warboys were charged as "rebels" much more regularly after the Black Death than before; see his *Warboys*, 221.

44. PRO SC2 155/84; PRO DL30 3/42. In many instances, the Latin words used to describe inappropriate speech in court were closely related to words used to describe scolding, suggesting that the offenses were constructed in similar ways. In Chedzoy in 1379, for example, John Cogan was fined 6d. for having gossiped (*garulauit*) in contempt of court. At the same court, four women and one man were fined either 3d. or 6d. for being common scolds or gossips (*communes garulatores*). Six men were in trouble in Methwold (Norfolk) in 1369 for offenses closely related to scolding: two were fined for "tumult and gossiping etc." ("tumultum et garul' etcetera") and four for "murmuring and gossiping etc." ("murmere et garul' etcetera") (PRO DL30 104/1471). The Latin word *maledicere* (ill-speaking) was also used sometimes to describe both scolds and those who gossiped during court sessions. William Adeson and Roger de Newal of Bradford (Yorkshire), for instance, were fined for ill-speaking (*maledicunt*) in contempt of court in 1355. At the same court, Agnes de Baksholt was presented as a "common ill-speaker" (*maledictrix*) of people (PRO DL30 1957/129). The term *maledicere* was used to describe contempt of court even before the plague: at Chilton in 1344, John le Rove was fined 1d. for having "maledixit" Roger Syward in court (PRO SC2 203/27).

45. Anne DeWindt, "Local Government," 635.

presented throughout the fourteenth century, and perhaps especially during the decades immediately following the plague, it was not prosecuted as frequently by the mid-fifteenth century. The increasing recognition of scolding as a legal category may have come to incorporate contempt of court and of local officials, just as it seemed to overtake charges of false hues. As Karen Jones and Michael Zell discovered in their study of scolding in Fordwich (Kent) between 1450 and 1570, scolding prosecutions sometimes seem to have grown out of verbal conflicts involving individuals in positions of authority.[46] Like prosecutions for the raising of false hues, presentments involving abuse of officials and inappropriate speech in court anticipated, overlapped with, and were eventually superseded by prosecutions of scolds.

In addition to hue-raising, abuse of officials, and contempt of court, some crimes involving speech were quite specific and not widely replicated. At Pleshey (Essex) in 1344, for instance, Margery, wife of William of Berwyk, and Little Juliana found themselves in trouble for a crime that might later have fallen under the category of scolding. The court heard that they were guilty of gossiping at night in the village, so that other villagers could not sleep, and they were fined a total of 6d. In Pleshey, problematic or disruptive speech was already deemed punishable before the plague, but it had not yet acquired the label of scolding. Margery and Little Juliana might be regarded as "proto-scolds," individuals who could have been charged as scolds had the legal construction and vocabulary existed.[47]

The post-plague novelty of scolding as a legal category is also suggested by the fact that when scolds *were* presented in the mid-fourteenth century, the ways in which their offenses were recorded were anything but uniform. Lacking an established tradition of correct procedures on how to record crimes, scribes translated the term *scold* as best they could, drawing from any one of a number of Latin terms that described inappropriate speech. Often they chose different words and constructions at different times, even when the context suggested that a similar crime was being committed. The court rolls of Bradford between 1355 and 1361, for instance, contain three different Latin words for "scold," plus several constructions of the offense. Agnes de Baksholt was presented in 1355 for having hit Robert Dickson, and it was noted that she was a *communis maledictrix gentium,* or "common speaker of evil about people." Two years later, Robert was fined as a *communis litigator et objurgator inter vicinos,* or "common scold among his neighbors." Both the terms *litigator* (or the feminine version *litigatrix*) and

46. Karen Jones and Michael Zell, "Bad Conversation? Gender and Social Control in a Kentish Borough, c. 1450–1570," *Continuity and Change* 13 (1998): 11–31, here 20–21, 25.
47. PRO DL30 63/801, m. 22r.

objurgator (or *objurgatrix*) translate as scold, and if any distinction existed between them in the fourteenth century, it has been impossible to discern it. In 1359, for instance, three Bradford women were presented as *communes et notoriis objurgatrices* (common and notorious scolds), and remanded to the next court session, in which they were described as *communes litigatrices* (common scolds.)[48] Jurors from the village of Allerton, under the jurisdiction of Bradford, presented Agnes de Wyndhill as a *communis litigatrix,* or "common scold," in 1361, and in the same year Bradford jurors presented Christina Jacdoghtre and Agnes Bastholpt as *communes litigatrices cum vicinos suis* (common scolds with their neighbors).[49] In other words, scolds presented in the Bradford courts between 1355 and 1361 might be described in Latin as *maledictrices, objurgatrices, litigatrices,* or a combination of these terms.[50] They might be recorded as "common" offenders or as "common and notorious" offenders, and they might or might not be described as scolding with or among their neighbors.[51]

The absence of scolds yet the presence of "proto-scolds" in samples of pre-plague courts, the lack of uniformity in early scolding presentments, and the rise and fall of other crimes that seem especially to have anticipated scolding (hue-raising and disrespect toward officials) suggests that prosecution of scolding was largely, if not entirely, a post-plague development. Although the concept of scolding had existed since the late thirteenth century, its presence in popular discourse did not translate immediately into its prosecution in the courts. Yet once it entered the courts, thousands of women and men faced punishment as scolds. By no means every local jurisdiction prosecuted scolds on a regular basis, but those that did found it a useful, and sometimes profitable, way to undermine insubordinate speech. In the borough court session held on 23 July 1426 in Middlewich, for example, nine women and one man were accused of scolding. Eight of these (all women) were deemed guilty and the court collected 8s. 5d. in fines.[52] Ten scolding accusations was an unusually high

48. In fact, they were described in the first presentment as *communes and notoris obiugatrices et [ ]satrices* (the first part of the last word is illegible). PRO DL30 1957/129.

49. Agnes Bastholpt may well be the same Agnes de Baksholt presented in 1355. Medieval spellings of surnames were by no means standardized. PRO DL30 1957/129.

50. Or the masculine forms of these: *maledictores, objurgatores,* or *litigatores.*

51. A similar variety of terms was recorded at Congleton in 1369–70. Scolds were recorded as common *rixatrices* (or *rixatores*) or *litigatores* (for some reason, even women in Congleton in these years were described with the masculine form of the noun): PRO DL30 1/21. In other fourteenth-century courts, scolds were described as *garulatrices* (or *garulatores*), a word that stems from the Latin for *gossip* and is related to the modern adjective *garrulous.* Ecclesiastical courts often presented scolds as *communes diffamatrices* (or *diffamatores*), or "common defamers," reflecting the church's jurisdiction over matters of defamation. Another frequent ecclesiastical court term was *suscitatrices* (or *suscitatores*) *dissensiones,* or "sowers of dissension."

52. PRO SC2 156/5, m. 11r.

number for a single court session—most jurisdictions that prosecuted scolds saw only a few cases a year—but perhaps the threat of being accused of scolding, implicit in the high number of accusations, influenced others to guard their tongues. Although most alleged scolds (between 75 and 95 percent) were women, the category was remarkably flexible; those accused of scolding could come from any social rank below that of gentry, and could be single, married, or widowed. The words that constituted scolding could be the traditional slurs of "whore" or "thief" or "liar" or they could be more imaginative and tailored insults such as "wedded man's whore" or "child murderer." The legal category of scold proved remarkably resilient: the cucking stool owned by the town of Leominster (Herefordshire) was last used in 1808 or 1809 to dunk a "very disorderly old woman," one Jenny Pipes, alias Jane Curran; and, as late as 1824, the town of Congleton (Cheshire) punished a scolding woman by making her wear a scold's bridle.[53] The category also proved portable, accompanying settlers to Puritan New England.[54]

Why the Fourteenth and Fifteenth Centuries?

Scolding, barratry, and cursing were each Sins of the Tongue with a distinctive chronology and dynamic. Barratry, a secular crime, originated with the central government and spread to local courts and organizations. Cursing, an offshoot of blasphemy, remained closely tied to the church, even as it was depicted and discussed at popular levels. And scolding arose in the local manorial and borough courts, anticipated by crimes such as false hue-raising and abuse of officials, and remained closely tied to local dynamics. None of these crimes was driven solely by concern about speech: barratry, especially in its earliest form, also involved a concern with wasteful litigation; cursing implied disrespect for God; and scolding tapped into longstanding concerns about the power of women. But each crime was simultaneously a component and a consequence of the increasingly popular discourse on Sins of the Tongue.

Why did such a discourse become popular at local levels in the four-

53. Another woman, also probably a scold, was paraded through Leominster in 1817 but was not ducked because the river was too low; see T. N. Brushfield, "On Obsolete Punishments, with Particular Reference to those of Cheshire. Part II: The Ducking Stool and Allied Punishments," *Journal of the Architectural, Archaeological, and Historic Society, for the County, City and Neighbourhood of Chester,* 1st series, 2 (1861): 203–34, at 233. For Congleton, see Vernon Mortimer, "The Tongue Can No Man Tame," *Cheshire Life* (March 1975): 72–73, at 73. Mortimer does not cite his source for the 1824 punishment of Anne Runcorn with the scold's bridle.

54. See, for instance, Jane Kamensky, *Governing the Tongue: The Politics of Speech in Early New England* (Oxford: Oxford University Press, 1997). A "gossip" character conducts tours for visitors at Old Sturbridge Village, Sturbridge, Massachusetts. One of the songs included in Old Sturbridge Village's music program also makes a reference to a wife as a scold.

teenth and fifteenth centuries? Part of the answer doubtless lies with its earlier ecclesiastical incarnation as the discourse identified by Craun in his
book. But it was by no means inevitable that the thirteenth-century discourse on Sins of the Tongue would cross over from Latin to the vernacular, from elite and ecclesiastical to local. Although elite and popular
cultures were perhaps not so starkly binary, few ecclesiastical discourses
were taken up with such enthusiasm at local, popular levels. Thirteenth-
century sermon manuals and exempla collections were filled with morali-
ties that did not make their way into wallpaintings and were not translated
into crimes punished by local, secular courts. The discourse on Sins of the
Tongue succeeded in becoming especially popular because it resonated
with particular groups of people in particular ways and at a particular time.

While the popularization of the discourse on Sins of the Tongue began
before the mid-fourteenth century, the Black Death of 1348–49 was an important force in underscoring its resonance at all social levels. The Black
Death, which killed between a third and a half of the English population,
resulted in serious social and economic disruption. A changing ratio of re-
sources to people encouraged peasants and townspeople to question established systems of authority, much to the horror of their social superiors.
In this strained relationship between tenants and landowners in the
decades following the Black Death of the mid-fourteenth century, control
over speech and regulation of *fama* proved something of a touchstone. Before the plague, England's landowners enjoyed low labor costs and high
crop prices. After the plague, however, the labor force shrank dramatically
and, with fewer mouths to feed, the demand for grain dropped.[55] Individual peasants found that they had considerably more bargaining power
with their landowners than before the demographic crisis and could demand higher wages and lower rents. Landowners, however, fought back:
they legislated and tried to enforce a wage freeze, reinstated old manorial
dues that had been allowed to lapse, and resisted all efforts by serfs to rid
themselves of the bonds of villeinage. The power of peasant voices in
spreading resistance to seigneurial demands was demonstrated by the
"Great Rumour" of 1377, which prompted peasants from more than forty
villages in the south of England to refuse to bring in the harvest because
they claimed freedom from labor services to landowners.[56] Tensions came
to a head in the revolts of 1381, during which peasants and townspeople,

55. Immediately following the plague, grain prices rose because of the shortage of harvest
workers. By the 1370s, they had begun to fall because production did not drop as sharply as
population. See David Farmer, "Prices and Wages, 1350–1500," in *The Agrarian History of England and Wales*, vol. 3: *1348–1500*, ed. Edward Miller (Cambridge: Cambridge University
Press, 1991), 431–525.
56. Rosamund Faith, "The 'Great Rumour' of 1377 and Peasant Ideology," in *The English
Rising of 1381*, ed. Rodney H. Hilton and Trevor H. Aston (Cambridge: Cambridge University Press, 1984), 43–73.

primarily from Essex and Kent, marched on London, beheaded the archbishop of Canterbury and other important officials, and demanded to
speak with the king. The revolt was quickly put down, but contemporary
chronicles suggest that the direct and forceful threat to the hierarchy of
landowners over peasants frightened the ruling classes. When outraged
members of the nobility and clergy described the events of 1381, they expressed horror at the rebels' audacious actions and deplored the audacity
and illegitimacy of their voices. Some chroniclers linked peasant rebels
with heretics, suggesting that the "disasters, plots, disputes, strife, and sedition" of the revolt were a result of Lollardy, a heretical movement that had
developed in the late fourteenth century.[57] Others characterized participants in the uprising as members of an uncontrollable, bestial mob, who
bleated like sheep, bayed like wolves, or spoke with the devilish voices of
peacocks.[58] By characterizing peasants' voices as animal-like, chroniclers
and poets cast rebels not only as inferiors but also as traitors to the naturally ordained order of things. Like animals, peasants did not possess legitimate voices, and by implication they belonged at home in the pastures,
not involved in affairs of governance.

While contemporary writers cast the clash between landowners and
peasants as a contest over legitimate speech, regulation of speech also
played a crucial role in the fourteenth- and fifteenth-century expansion of
the administrative classes. These nascent bureaucratic classes were located
primarily at the local level, focusing their efforts on governing the manor,
borough, and parish.[59] Control over the speech of subordinates was essential to these efforts to attain and maintain respectability. It was in this
context that local leaders in some late fourteenth- and fifteenth-century
boroughs and guilds passed bylaws forbidding scolding, barratry, and
defamation of mayors, members of town councils, and local officials.[60]

57. This quote is from Adam Usk's *Chronicle,* cited in Margaret E. Aston, "Lollardy and
Sedition, 1381–1431," *Past and Present* 17 (1960): 1–44, at 6. For other works that address
links between Lollardy and the events of 1381, see Margaret E. Aston, "Corpus Christi and
Corpus Regni: Heresy and the Peasants Revolt," *Past and Present* 143 (1994): 3–48; Charles
W. C. Oman, *The Great Revolt of 1381* (1906; reprint, Oxford: Clarendon, 1969), 19–21; *The
Peasants Revolt of 1381,* ed. R. B. Dobson (London: Macmillan, 1970), 367, 373–78; Michael
Wilks, "*Reformatio Regni:* Wyclif and Hus as Leaders of Religious Protest Movements," *Studies
in Church History* 9 (1972): 109–30, at 126–27.

58. Ralph Hanna III, "Pilate's Voice/Shirley's Case," *South Atlantic Quarterly* 91 (1992):
793–812, at 800–801. See also Paul Strohm, *Hochon's Arrow: The Social Imagination of Fourteenth-Century Texts* (Princeton: Princeton University Press, 1992), 33–56.

59. For discussion of England's rising local elites, see especially Robert C. Palmer, *English
Law in the Age of the Black Death, 1348–1381: A Transformation of Governance and Law* (Chapel
Hill: University of North Carolina Press, 1993), and McIntosh, *Controlling Misbehavior,* esp.
129–36.

60. See, for instance, bylaws recorded in the villages of East Merrington and Wolveston
(Durham) in 1379 (cited in note 12 above). For the bylaws of London in 1419, see *Liber Al-
bus: The White Book of the City of London,* ed. and trans. H. T. Riley (London, 1861), 226, 287,

Like relationships between landowners and peasants, those between local-level administrators and subordinates were often articulated through conflicts over the legitimacy and appropriateness of speech.

The discourse on Sins of the Tongue was thus popularized because it was convenient to do so. Local-level efforts to control speech, accompanied as they were by the moral backdrop of the ecclesiastical discourse, proved remarkably flexible. For a few, however, such as Henry le Vernon of Middlewich, the discourse on Sins of the Tongue may have been a little too popular and flexible. Henry was convicted as a scold in 1434, toward the end of what was probably a long life. Neither the fact that he came from a well-established local family, nor that he had served the town as bailiff, juror, and chamberlain, nor that he owned several properties was enough to prevent him from being gored by the same discursive sword that he, as a member of the local leadership, had helped to forge. The plight of Henry le Vernon, fined 10d. and presumably subject to considerable humiliation, demonstrates the ever-slippery nature of the newly popularized discourse on the evils of discourse.[61]

394–96. For the bylaws of Worcester in 1467, see *English Gilds*, ed. Smith and Smith, 384–85. For the bylaws of Hereford in 1486, see *Borough Customs*, 2 vols., ed. Mary Bateson, Selden Society Publications (London: B. Quaritch, 1904–1906), 1:79–80.

61. For Henry le Vernon's prosecution, see PRO SC2 156/6. Other information about Henry has been compiled from records of borough courts, sheriff's tourns, eyre courts, account rolls, and land deeds.

CHAPTER EIGHT

Romancing the Word: Fama *in the Middle English* Sir Launfal *and* Athelston

RICHARD HORVATH

The aristocratic ethos out of which medieval romance grew makes its pre-occupation with *fama,* as reputation, seem perfectly generic. Given the centrality of oath-making to the feudal contract, and, likewise, the threats that slander and gossip posed to the maintenance of courtly affiliation, it is no less natural that the capacity of speech to make and dismantle the social status of individuals, a more discrete conception of *fama,* should figure so prominently in this literary tradition. Other contributors to this volume show how *fama* in these respects—as forms of talk or as reputation, the social product of discourse and action—shapes cultural developments across the European Middle Ages. Medieval romance, as it evolves into an increasingly popular social discourse toward the fifteenth century, both participates in and reflects this phenomenon. The imaginative dimensions of this literature, moreover, make it a unique context for exploring the discursive mechanisms of talk and their cultural consequences. Complementing the studies of historical and legal *fama* in this volume, my interest centers on the activity of speech—that is, speech as action—in certain exemplary Middle English romances, as a narrative device and a theme in its own right.

Coming from the same region of England but with interesting differences in perspective, the late-fourteenth-century texts *Sir Launfal* and *Athelston* are apt case studies for a consideration of *fama* as both the medium and subject of Middle English romance. Both belong to the late-fourteenth-century tail-rhyme school of the East Midlands, a nonaristocratic literary movement with strong roots in oral tradition.[1] While the

1. Stylistically, tail-rhyme romances feature a twelve-line stanza with a concatenating

familiar "herkeneth" formulae in romances of this type were almost certainly vestigial tropes, they point up more demonstrative and performative types of utterance within these particular narratives. The poems' social horizons help us gauge the workings of romance *fama* in another vein as well. As a descendant of Marie de France's *Lanval, Sir Launfal* exemplifies not only the adaptation of the Breton lay tradition into Middle English but also the passage of French courtly romance into an English climate that transforms the social dynamics of the inherited tradition.[2] Complementarily, *Athelston*'s narrative independence and native English ethos sharpen the differences between courtly and noncourtly perspectives, its central conflict between royal, ecclesiastical, and baronial power extending the politics of *fama* into an urban arena, outside the court.[3]

More to the point, the exemplarity of these texts rests on their interest in talk and its social consequences. With implications for the cultural workings of *fama* assessed elsewhere in this volume, both poems dramatize the capacity of transgressive speech acts, chiefly slander and lies, to disrupt social order. As do many other romances, *Sir Launfal* and *Athelston* respond to this threat by seeking to codify and thereby control the spoken word—itself a kind of speech act. The resultant circuit of transformations embodies significant anxieties about the capacity of *fama* to shape individual identity and communal relations, including those between authors and audiences. Growing out of the tension between speech and writing deeply embedded within romance convention, the solutions these texts engineer to the *fama* of dangerous utterances remain sui generis, however ironic, provisional, and problematic they may be. For *fama* as reputation, the consequences of the narrative dynamics I examine below reflect similarly across the genre as a whole, given medieval romance's ubiquitous obsession with the past and its own origins. At the same time, the speech-act

---

rhyme scheme, a formulaic vocabulary, and sporadic alliteration. The proposition that twenty-three such texts comprise a coherent, localized school is A. M. Trounce's, in "English Tail-Rhyme Romances," *Medium Aevum* 1 (1932): 87–108, 168–82; 2 (1933): 34–57, 189–98; 3 (1934): 30–50. On the popular disposition of the tail-rhyme movement as well as its stylistic features, see also A. J. Bliss, ed., *Sir Launfal* (London: Thomas Nelson and Sons, 1960), 31–36.

2. A. J. Bliss's reductive characterization of the Middle English Breton lays as the work of traveling minstrels targeting not "a sophisticated aristocratic audience versed in the code of courtly love" but "simpler, less sensitive listeners in market-square or inn-yard" (*Sir Launfal*, 1) seems outmoded now in a number of respects. Conversely, my discussion of *Sir Launfal* discerns a rather sophisticated impulse to codify and textualize speech, particularly the types of disruptive talking that circulate freely in many French courtly romances.

3. Although Trounce surmises the existence of an unrecovered French original in his edition (*Athelston: A Middle English Romance*, Early English Text Society, o.s., 224 [London: Oxford University Press, 1951]), the consensus remains that *Athelston* has no known direct source (Ronald B. Herzman, Graham Drake, and Eve Salisbury, eds., *Four Romances of England: King Horn, Havelock the Dane, Bevis of Hampton, Athelston* [Kalamazoo, Mich.: Medieval Institute Publications, 1999], 341).

economies that structure these texts in such fundamental ways resonate with nonromance discourses as well, including the self-conscious discourse of late-medieval authorship at large.

I

Insofar as this discussion focuses on narrative acts of speech and their textual embodiment as particular forms of romance *fama,* it assumes some familiarity with the conflict between speaking and writing at the heart of medieval romance poetics and with speech-act theory. A brief overview of both topics will clarify the foundations of my poetic analysis. On the most obvious level, the first issue involves the self-reflexive authorial theatrics that characterize so many romance prologues and epilogues, from Chrétien de Troyes' courtly meditations in the twelfth century through the ossified, belated tropes of fifteenth-century Middle English works. Whereas Chrétien's emphasis on the elaborately textile nature of his compositions (*entrelacement* and *conjointure*) conveys respect for the fixed status of books and derision for the popularizing activity of minstrel tellers, Marie de France's *translatio* of her *Lais* advertises the authenticity of oral traditions as their basis.[4]

In the Middle English romance tradition, as in the Continental, the relationship between speaking and writing grows more complex as narratives begin to mirror such authorial concerns and lend them thematic weight. While early works like *Sir Orfeo* (late thirteenth century) conflate the romance poet and hero through speech, the phenomenon reaches its quintessence a century later in *Sir Gawain and the Green Knight:* Here, a narrative obsession with artifice plays out the poet's design, announced in the prologue, to transform an oral lay into a textual artifact, a "stori stif and stronge," and Gawain's preference for discourse over action grounds his heroism in the ability to speak effectually.[5]

Such examples move past the orality-textuality opposition that has governed much discussion of medieval romance to reveal that acts of speaking become constitutive narrative events in this literature. As authorial speech begets the quests for self-validation that virtually define the medieval romance tradition (so far as it can be defined), it produces—or per

4. See Chrétien's prologues to *Erec et Enide,* lines 20–22, and *Cligés,* lines 17–23, in *Les Romans de Chrétien de Troyes,* vol. 1 (*Erec et Enide*), ed. Mario Roques, and vol. 2 (*Cligés*), ed. Alexandre Micha (Paris: H. Champion, 1955, 1957); and Marie's "Prologue," lines 33–38, *Les Lais de Marie de France,* ed. Jean Rychner (Paris: H. Champion, 1966).

5. *Sir Gawain and the Green Knight,* ed. J. R. R. Tolkien and E. V. Gordon, rev. Norman Davis, 2nd ed. (Oxford: Clarendon, 1967), line 35. For a synthetic account of Middle English romance development, charting demarcations between high and low forms, see Derek Pearsall, "The Development of Middle English Romance," *Mediaeval Studies* 27 (1965): 91–116.

forms—the very stuff of romance adventure: chivalric endeavor, heroic struggle, conflict between private and public experience, social alienation and integration. Indeed, across a wide range of narratives, *fama* structures the relations between individual and society so integral to romance ideology, to its notions of personal identity and community. Although self-declarative acts of speaking reify the heroic self and strengthen communal bonds in works such as the early Middle English *King Horn* and *Havelock the Dane* (late thirteenth century),[6] the capacity of speech to rend individual reputations and the social fabric at large is exemplified readily enough by the circuit of transgressive talk in Chrétien's *Erec et Enide,* or the lies and slander that propagate throughout Marie's *Lais.*[7] As instrumental as such motifs are for narrative development, the negotiation between self and society through performative speech becomes a central romance conflict in its own right.

On an intuitive level, this notion of performance is analogous to the demonstrative performance of deeds in other medieval cultural frameworks. Several contributions to this volume illustrate the crucial role of audiences in verifying the performance of a deed, as well as the active nature of the demonstration itself.[8] In identifying the importance of witnesses and social convention for an understanding of linguistic performance in romance texts, this analogy, in turn, suggests the aptness of a speech-act approach to romance *fama*. From a sociolinguistic perspective, the conventionality of performative utterances rests on the communal dynamic of all spoken language.[9] J. L. Austin's original discussion of performative speech highlights the crucial role of social conventions in giving

6. See John Ganim, *Style and Consciousness in Middle English Narrative* (Princeton: Princeton University Press, 1983), 16–54.

7. On verbal restraint in the *Lais,* see Michelle A. Freeman, "Marie de France's Poetics of Silence: The Implications for a Feminine *Translatio,*" *Publications of the Modern Language Society* 99 (1984): 860–83.

8. See particularly the essays by Chris Wickman, Jeffrey A. Bowman, and Madeline H. Caviness and Charles G. Nelson. Outside this volume, pertaining to medieval English legal practices, see Charles Donahue, "Proof by Witnesses in the Church Courts of Medieval England," in *On the Laws and Customs of England: Essays in Honor of Samuel E. Thorne,* ed. Morris S. Arnold et al. (Chapel Hill: University of North Carolina Press, 1981), 127–58.

9. The founding articulations of speech-act theory are J. L. Austin's *How to Do Things with Words,* 2nd ed., ed. J. O. Ursom and Marina Sbisà (Cambridge: Harvard University Press, 1962), and John Searle's *Speech Acts: An Essay in the Philosophy of Language* (Cambridge: Cambridge University Press, 1969). Application to literature is based largely on Mary Louise Pratt, *Toward a Speech-Act Theory of Literary Discourse* (Bloomington: Indiana University Press, 1977). On this see also Richard Ohmann, "Speech Acts and the Definition of Literature," *Philosophy and Rhetoric* 4 (1971): 1–19, and "Literature as Act," in *Approaches to Poetics,* ed. Seymour Chatman (New York: Columbia University Press, 1973), 81–107. For theory and praxis, see Stanley Fish, "How to Do Things with Austin and Searle: Speech Act Theory and Literary Criticism," *Modern Language Notes* 91 (1976): 983–1025. Sandy Petry, *Speech Acts and Literary Theory* (New York: Routledge, 1990), offers a useful overview and a reasoned endorsement of the theory's relevance for literary analysis.

any utterance "illocutionary" force, defined as an effect on the audience.[10] To the extent that the audience's expectations about and response to an utterance are governed by convention—as with a bet or promise, quintessentially for Austin—performative speech generates its own referent, a conventional social reality distinct from any independent reality.[11] The chief implication of this move—that truth and falsehood are social conventions rather than objective states, representing "only . . . a general dimension of being a right or proper thing to say as opposed to a wrong thing, in these circumstances, to this audience, for these purposes and with these intentions"[12]—resonates as strongly with the romances I discuss below as with the examples cited above.

As a whole, medieval romance seems a virtual model for the contention that fictive discourse mirrors other performative language in creating its own referents and invoking conventional social expectations. The Austinian notion that all speech is in some sense performative, that every utterance does or enacts something conventional, focuses attention in all manner of romances on the variety of contextual, illocutionary effects triggered by even the simplest direct utterances. The obsession of many works with dramatic and aberrant speech acts, especially boasts, troths, secrets, and lies, suggests that talk is more than a narrative mechanism in this literature. Rather, it serves as both the means and locus for the processes of transformation that inform the genre as a whole. The brief examples above suggest that the circulation of speech in Middle English romances establishes internal verbal economies that test the boundaries between private and public experience even as they assert the *fama* of the poems' heroes, and seek to convert poets into heroes themselves. If the narrative dynamics through which romances such as *Sir Launfal* and *Athelston* convert speech into writing constitute a kind of romance magic, perhaps it is a magic with pertinent consequences for the development of authorship in late medieval England.

II

Extant in a single manuscript (British Museum MS Cotton Caligula A.II) and self-attributed to an author, Thomas Chestre, about whom virtually

10. Austin's definition of illocution is discursive: "performance of an act *in* saying something as opposed to performance of an act *of* saying something" (*How to Do Things,* 99–100); "a conventional act: an act done as conforming to a convention" (105); "An effect must be achieved on the audience if the illocutionary act is to be carried out" (116).

11. In eroding his original distinction between constative and performative utterances (those that *say* or *describe* something versus those that *do* something), Austin effaced the opposition between truthfulness, associated with the former, and production, associated with the latter (*How to Do Things,* 133–47; see also Petry, *Speech Acts,* 22–41).

12. Austin, *How to Do Things,* 145.

nothing is known, *Sir Launfal* interpolates several versions of a popular story about a disenfranchised knight.[13] The resultant lay unfolds, as do many tail-rhyme romances, by de-centering courtly authority and disrupting conventional romance junctures between fantasy and social realism. From the fractious arena of Arthur's court, the narrative moves outward to the middle realm of the town (Karlyoun, 88–120) and then to the threshold of the faerie world, where Launfal decamps under a tree and meets a magical mistress.[14]

To a significant extent, the agent of these and later disjunctions is *fama*, as both reputation and talk. A quick overview of the poem's architecture reveals the verbal economy at its core, whereby dialogue more so than event becomes the main agent of the narrative. Vague rumors about Queen Gwennere's marital unfaithfulness (46–48) precipitate Launfal's departure from Arthur's court, insofar as Launfal's disregard for her on those grounds (44) seems behind her refusal to give him gifts. This affront provokes Launfal's cryptic report that a letter relating his father's death (never detailed, much less read) has summoned him home (74–78). Once Launfal reaches the town, colorful conversations with the mayor (95–126) and the mayor's daughter (194–210) illustrate the popular flavor of not only this work but also tail-rhyme romance generally.

This dialogue presages the pivotal conversation in the woods between Launfal and the faerie mistress Tryamour (301–66), an intimate exchange that contrasts sharply with the public challenge that the Italian knight Syr Valentyne issues to Launfal later, via letter (523–39). Launfal's demeanor throughout these central episodes is taciturn, as he hardly speaks to Tryamour; laughs "full stylle" at Valentyne's challenge; and, in the following scenes, resists the queen's advances and refutes her slander, both that he "lovyst no woman, ne no woman the" (689) and that he tried to seduce her (772–83). The discourse concluding the story sustains a legalistic tone, with the queen's rash oath that she will have her eyes put out if Launfal can produce a fairer mistress (808–10), with the wrangling among the knights and barons about Launfal's sentence (787–806, 835–82), and finally with Tryamour's formal pronouncement to Arthur resolving Launfal's predicament (991–1005).[15]

13. Chestre drew on two known sources, chiefly the early- fourteenth-century, Middle English *Sir Landevale*, an adaptation of Marie de France's *Lanval* (second half of the twelfth century); and also the anonymous Old French Breton lay *Graelent* (closely related to *Lanval*). He used at least one unknown source as well, an analogue to an episode in Andreas Capellanus's *The Art of Courtly Love* (ca. 1185). See Bliss, *Sir Launfal*, 24–31, and Anne Laskaya and Eve Salisbury, eds., *The Middle English Breton Lays* (Kalamazoo, Mich.: Medieval Institute Publications, 1995), 201–2.

14. All textual references, cited parenthetically by line numbers, are from the edition noted above by Laskaya and Salisbury, in *Middle English Breton Lays*, 201–62.

15. A related index of the poem's preoccupation with speech and the conventionality of

The hyperbolic moments that disrupt the narrative illusion involve problematic utterances that push the limits of romance decorum. Overall, twin circuits of transgressive utterance revolving around the figures of Queen Gwennere and Tryamour impel and ultimately unify the narrative. While the antagonism between these women is plain enough, their performance as speakers is perhaps less obvious. In instigating and then resolving the male hero's dilemma through conspicuous, though very different speech acts, the queen and the faerie mistress raise questions about the same romance conventions their words engage. A closer examination of their roles as antagonistic hubs of *Sir Launfal*'s discourse, framing Launfal's ambiguous behavior as the hero, exposes significant anxieties about speech as a social mechanism no less than a literary one.

Throughout the poem the queen is defined by and through speech. The object of loosely circulating gossip at the outset—"For the lady bar los [bore reputation] of swych word / That sche hadde lemmannys under [lovers besides] her lord, / So fele [many] ther nas noon ende" (46–48)—she remains at the center of a web of transgressive and socially disruptive *fama* that threatens not only Launfal but the stability of the whole court. Earl R. Anderson has charted the pattern of lies ("lesynges") across Chestre's version of the story, progressing from seemingly harmless fibs (Launfal's dubious excuse for leaving Arthur's court [76–78] and the cover-up of Launfal's poverty by his friends Jon and Huwe [160–74]), to petty excuses (the mayor's self-interested claims that he has no room for Launfal at his inn [109–14] and that he had intended to invite Launfal to his feast [403–8]), and finally to the queen's malicious accusations about Launfal's deviant sexuality and treachery. As Anderson observes, only the final, serious lies are part of the inherited *Lanval* story.[16] Chestre's development of this motif, thus, has the dual effect of accentuating Gwennere's unfaithfulness as a *function* of her speech and of thematizing the act of lying itself.

Calling the queen's words "lies" in the first place implies that they are constative utterances—which is to say, capable of falsity because they embody truth value. In fact, the narrative reveals that they are to be understood more properly as performative or illocutionary utterances, speech acts bound by their conventionality within specific contexts (both the ro-

---

its discourse involves the unusually frequent formulaic oral tags that advertise the narrator's truthfulness (e.g., "wythout lesyng," "forsothe to say," "wythouten fable"). On the effect of this convention in thwarting the audience's identification with *Sir Launfal*'s fictional events in favor of a more contingent reality, the circumstances of writing and reading, see Timothy D. O'Brien, "The 'Readerly' Sir Launfal," *Parergon* 8 (1990): 35–37. Though O'Brien does not adopt a speech-act perspective, his reading discloses the illocutionary function of these formulae quite well.

16. Earl R. Anderson, "The Structure of *Sir Launfal*," *Papers on Language and Literature* 13 (1977): 116–18.

mance genre and the *Lanval* story) rather than by independent criteria. We recognize this in part by noting the lack of narrative consequence for the earlier, relatively trivial lies. What matters for these types of utterances, their narrative rationale, as it were, is the pattern they establish and the expectations they raise, a set of *conventions* for interpreting the more serious lies that follow. In turn, this conventionality—a social construction of the poem itself but also of romance writing at large, insofar as other works (including *Athelston*) share in this manner of speaking—governs what the queen's lies are and how they operate.

From the perspective of speech-act theory, judgment of both the trivial and the serious "lesynges" in the poem depends on their "felicity" or success rather than their seeming falsity, truthfulness being an irrelevant category (Austin, *How to Do Things*, 14). On the one hand, Launfal's white lie about his father's death and his friends' misrepresentation of his situation effect his separation from Arthur's court, an event necessary to his heroic development and the story's progress. Contextualized thus, which is to say, conventionalized by their speakers' intentions and hearers' expectations, these lies prove felicitous rather than "false." Queen Gwennere's accusations, on the other hand, are unsuccessful or infelicitous (rather than false) because they do *not* bring about their intended, conventional results. The first charge, an impetuous, spiteful curse—"'Fy on the, thou coward! / . . . Thou lovyst no woman, ne no woman the—/ Thou were worthy forlore!'" (685–90)—fails in two senses, procuring neither Launfal's acquiescence to her earlier come-on (676–81) nor ocular proof (at this juncture) that Launfal does love a woman. Though motivated likewise by spite, her second "lie" is a more formal speech act, a public accusation to Arthur that Launfal "'besofte me of shame [propositioned me shamefully]—/ My lemman for to be'" and then boasted "'That the lothlokest [most loathly] mayde that [Tyramour] hadde / Myght be a Quene above me!'" (716–20). The queen's caveat that her earlier, private proposition of Launfal was spoken in jest ("'I spak to Launfal yn my game'" [715]) does not affect the viability of her utterance; what matters here is the accusation's failure to bring about its intended, rigorously conventionalized results: Launfal's judicial punishment. In the erosion of that expectation (or at least possibility) over the remainder of the narrative, through legal discourse and then Tryamour's appearance, this second speech act proves infelicitous quite spectacularly.

The construction of the queen across the poem as the object and subject of speech contrasts strikingly with Launfal's characterization. His behavior involves looking more than talking, most notably in the tryst with Tryamour. The poet's lavish account of Tryamour's pavilion and seminude body notwithstanding, Launfal's gaze is what gives the scene its voyeuristic charge: "Hys eyn wer carbonkeles bryght—/ As the mone they schon anyght, / That spreteth out ovyr all" (271–73).[17] The visual basis of Launfal's demeanor makes his silence with Tryamour unsurprising. To Tryamour's thirty-eight lines of speech, he speaks only four in reply (311–12, 335–36), and his love-play is wordless (347–50). Most significantly, when she enjoins him, in the poem's most emphatic speech act, to "'make no bost of me . . . And yf thou doost, I warny the before, / All my love thou hast forlore!'" (362–65), he says nothing in response. We presume Launfal's consent, but instead of returning a vow he retreats into a cryptic interiority: "Launfal tok hys leve to wende [go]. . . . Tho [then] was the knyght yn herte at wylle [at ease]; / In hys chaunber he hyld hym stylle [kept silent] / All that underntyde [afternoon]" (367–75). The erasure of Launfal's oath is conspicuous given the narrative's obsession with speech in other respects, and it becomes problematic when Launfal eventually imperils himself by violating Tryamour's decree (694–99).[18]

While Launfal does speak in that key instance, to be sure, his words prove markedly infelicitous. His boast about Tryamour is both an exasperated retort to the queen's accusation that "'Thou lovyst no woman, ne no woman the'" (689) and a declaration of his virility, foregrounded by his just-completed brawl with Valentyne.[19] Considering the infrequency of Launfal's speech in the poem, his delivery here bears note:

> The knyght was sore aschamed tho [then];
> To speke ne myghte he forgo . . .
> "I have loved a fayryr woman
> Than thou ever leydest thyn ey upon
> Thys seven yer and more!"
> (691–96)

The failure of restraint signals Launfal's awareness that his utterance will violate Tryamour's prohibition, even if his assent to it was unspoken. How-

17. A psychological measure of Launfal's passivity would note his self-consciousness at becoming the object of others' gazes, dramatized best in the scene where he falls off his horse while leaving Karlyoun and rides away "for to dryve away lokynge" (218). Concerning Launfal's subjection to the gazes of other characters as well as the story's authors, read as a species of Freudian anxiety, see A. C. Spearing, "The Lanval Story," in *The Medieval Poet as Voyeur: Looking and Listening in Medieval Love-Narratives* (Cambridge: Cambridge University Press, 1993), 97–119.

18. *Sir Landevale* similarly implies, rather than denotes, Launfal's consent to Tryamour's condition (*Middle English Breton Lays*, ed. Laskaya and Salisbury, lines 153–66, p. 427). Marie de France records Lanval's agreement indirectly: "Il li respunt que bien tendra / Ceo qu'ele li comaundera" ("He answered that he would do / exactly as she commanded"). *Les Lais de Marie de France*, ed. Rychner, lines 151–52; *The Lais of Marie de France*, trans. Robert Hanning and Joan Ferrante (Durham, N.C.: Labyrinth, 1978).

19. On the theme of Launfal's manhood, reconceptualized in Chestre's version of the story, see Anderson, "Structure of *Sir Launfal*," and Anne Laskaya, "Thomas Chestre's Revisions of Manhood in *Sir Launfal*," in *Retelling Tales: Essays in Honor of Russell Peck*, ed. Thomas Hahn and Alan Lupack (Rochester, N.Y.: Boydell and Brewer, 1997), 191–212.

ever dubious the offense, casuistically, its consequence is certain. Launfal's not altogether rash utterance turns out, in fact, to be the most infelicitous illocution in the poem, provoking the queen's juridical accusation and depriving him of Tryamour's help. Her abandonment of the hero during his greatest crisis plays out the terms of their pledge, however wordless his affirmation; in keeping with the conventions the illocutions engaged, their mutual interpretation is all that matters.

Launfal's second pivotal speech act is his defense to Arthur and the baronial court against the queen's charge (772–83). His most formal and extensive talk in the poem, it carefully refutes Arthur's accusation of treachery for "'yelpyng [boasting]'" and telling a "'fowll lesynge'" about Tryamour, and for supposedly propositioning the queen (761–68). That Arthur mentions the latter offense almost in passing (766–68) highlights Launfal's boast as his only real act. Though his rebuttal is a model of legal propriety, the practical conventions of this court render it infelicitous. The twelve knights impaneled as jurors agree to acquit Launfal not on the basis of his testimony but through their own familiarity with rumors of the queen's infidelity. Mimicking the first allusion to the gossip at the beginning of the poem, their words demonstrate the textual circulation of the queen's *fama*: Compare "For the lady bar los of swych word [bore the reputation] / That sche hadde lemmannys under her lord" (46–47) and "All they seyde ham betwene, / . . . / The Quene bar los of swych a word / That sche lovede lemmannes wythout her lord [besides her lord]" (787–91). When Tryamour does not appear and Arthur commands the barons to pass judgment (836–37), Launfal's testimony becomes less than a memory, erased by legalistic squabbling—conventional stuff indeed: "Some dampnede Launfal there, / And some made hym quyt and skere [acquitted and innocent]—/ Har tales were well breme [heated]" (880–82).

Although Launfal remains an alienated and oddly reticent hero throughout the romance, the dramatic failure of his words to consolidate and ensure his courtly status owes less to his own deficiency than to the instability of the society he is never quite able to join. As testimony to his disenfranchisement, his speeches diagnose a serious breakdown in the social and judicial conventions of the Arthurian court, one that estranges virtually all of its members. Of greatest consequence, Launfal's words expose the unreliability of speech as a mechanism of genuine social exchange in such a culture, perhaps the culture of romance at large. In transgressing a promise that he never actually made, verbally—in abrogating an absent speech act, as it were—Launfal comes to understand that even what one says in self-defense and good faith can become illicit, with dangerous consequences to the individual and corporate body both.

If the anxieties about *fama* raised by the queen and Launfal threaten to unsettle the court as well as the poem, the figure of Tryamour stands as the means of resolving, or at least mollifying, those apprehensions. A courtly outsider, she is the most powerful and enlightened speaker in the work. Professing commitment to Launfal as her "swetyng paramour" (306) and bestowing riches and magical protection on him through a (literally) fantastic speech act (311–36), she understands too the capacity of words to undo desire as swiftly as they construct it. Her decree that Launfal "make no bost of me" (362) respects the power of utterances that aggrandize the self and publicize intimacy to rend the social fabric. When her commissive illocution fails under the pressure of the queen's slander—Gwennere's linguistic bad faith—the delicate counterpoise between individual and communal prerogative nearly collapses.

In repairing this rift, Tryamour employs a special type of magic. From a speech-act perspective her unexpected arrival at the end of the poem, saving both Launfal and the court, is more than a convenient romance convention, a deus ex machina trope that absolves Launfal's transgression and glosses the poem's conclusion with generosity and justice. For if Tryamour's public appearance before the barons raises questions about her own linguistic sincerity, given her warning to Launfal, it also subverts the conventions that had governed the court's verbal economy to this point. The barons' raucous talk dissipates when Tryamour's maidens parade her into the court, and as "ech man hadde greet desyre / To se har clothynge" (890–91), they trade their judicial duty for overawed spectatorship. Indeed, the faerie's reemergence at the poem's most suspenseful juncture is a visual more than oral performance, nearly forty lines of voyeuristic imagery (925–66) that convert the barons' wrangling into a prurient silence.

The formulaic, thoroughly conventional rhetoric of the description highlights the radiance of Tryamour's body: similes such as "jolyf as bryd on bowe" (931), "bryght as blosme on brere" (934), "As rose on rys [twig] her rode [complexion] was red; / The her schon upon her hed / As gold wyre that schynyth bryght" (937); the crown of gold and precious stones and the ermine robe adorning her body (940–43); the saddle-cloth "ypaynted wyth ymagerye" (951). This embellishment affords Tryamour a physical substantiality quite different from her earlier aspect, in the attenuated relationship with Launfal (277–300). That was a private display, considerably briefer and lacking a description of her clothing altogether, even before she disrobed. While the nudity solicits an imaginative response, from readers along with the poet and Launfal, presumably, the paucity of other detail, especially pertaining to her attire, enforces our distance and underscores the voyeuristic nature of the scene. We watch but remain excluded.

With her reappearance, the poet transforms Tryamour. The highly rhetoricized description of her procession into the court remakes her into a visual spectacle before a public audience. As conventional as the portrait is, adhering to the top-down structure prescribed by rhetorical treatises, it is calculated to elicit an equally conventional response, from the poem's readers no less than the barons.[20] The latent fascination with her unadorned body in the earlier scene becomes now an invitation to inspect and "read" her decorated appearance, quite literally—not just in the audience's imagination but on the very surface of the page. This type of display expects a public reception; her earlier privacy, the coy self-exposure to Launfal and the reticence about being viewed by others, serves here as an ironic gloss on the remarkable luminescence of Tryamour's embellished body and the implacable desire that it be seen, a desire she obviously shares. Her transformation, thus, consists of a highly public process of illumination, one that exploits the rhetorical conventionality of romance (little different in today's popular versions of the genre) to re-make the heroine into a visual icon, a body clothed and paraded for all to view.

From a speech-act vantage point, the success of the poet's elaborate rhetorical utterance lies in negotiating conventions within and outside the poem. Internally, the familiar lineaments of Tryamour's portrait reconfigure the existing narrative conventions, establishing a new context that potentially resolves the problems occasioned by infelicitous speech acts. By consolidating what was forbidden to say about Tryamour into an illuminated text, by enshrining prohibited speech in an iconographic image, the portrait manages to articulate a silent "boast" that undermines not merely Tryamour's injunction but also, more importantly, the unjust accusations against Launfal. As such, the poet's description is the most successful speech act in the romance. Beyond the narrative borders, the visual splendor of the portrait bespeaks an authorial power to shape conventions and audience response through textuality rather than talk. The poet's primary accomplishment here is to turn romance tradition not so much upside down as on its edge, employing stock motifs to explore the seams between literary and social experience. Real magic, this romance implies, derives not so much from *faerie* as from the text's power to materialize, control, and preserve speech in writing—in effect, the power to control *fama*.

The most self-conscious romance marvel of all, this transformation of speech into writing rewrites the whole work in its wake. Although Tryamour's corporeal re-emergence resolves the central narrative conflict, its

20. Typical references are Matthew of Vendôme's *Ars versificatoria* (ca. 1175) and Geoffrey of Vinsauf's *Poetria nova* (1208–1216). For outlines see James J. Murphy, *Rhetoric in the Middle Ages: A History of Rhetorical Theory from Saint Augustine to the Renaissance* (Berkeley: University of California Press, 1974), 163–73. Bliss stresses the stock quality of this and other descriptions throughout the poem, "part of the furniture of a [romance] world well known to the audience" (*Sir Launfal*, 44–45).

ultimate consequence is to remove both her and Launfal from Arthur's court, from the text, and—insofar as "Seththe [afterwards] saw hym yn thys lond noman, / Ne no more of hym telle y ne can" (1036–37)—from the romance world altogether. Just as the spectacular image of Tryamour overwhelms the courtly audience within the narrative, so does it silence the poem's author and readership alike. Fame (*fama*) itself, the fullest sort of success in this romance idiom, obviates any other presence, and so the heroes' joint exit seems entirely more natural than Tryamour's entrance. Chestre's version naturalizes the departure in particular by altering Tryamour's destination, from the fictive Avalon of Marie's *Lanval* (and *Sir Landevale*) to the actual island of Oléron, off Brittany (1021–23), a place-name publicized during this period in the code of maritime law, the *Rooles ou Jugemans d'Oléron.*[21] This salient change helps dislocate the story from the domain of fantasy and inscribe it in real social space.

Tryamour's blinding of the queen, also unique to Chestre's version, has a similar effect. While the faerie's power may seem autonomous, the breath conveying her curse (1006–8) merely fulfills the queen's rash vow, some two hundred lines earlier, that she would be blinded if Launfal presented his mistress (809–10). With marvelous logic Tryamour's wordless utterance seals off the circuit of slander and impolitic speech begotten by the queen, not through legalistic retribution but through a perfectly felicitous conversion of speech into action. Within the poem's revised context, Tryamour's speech-less acts seem entirely more conventional than ironic.

The series of speech-act conversions I have been tracking reaches an end with the most peculiar utterance in the poem, the self-naming of Thomas Chestre in line 1039: "Thomas Chestre made thys tale / Of the noble knyght Syr Launfale" (1039–40). As ephemeral as he remains, the curious literalism of Chestre's transpiration as the poem's maker contends with the superficial bias toward magic and disbelief across the poem. One effect of Chestre's belated appearance here is to ironize the prologue's advertisement of the tale's origin as a Breton lay (4). In drawing attention to the poem's "made-ness," its crafted textuality, Chestre's self-attribution undermines the postured orality that for so many readers consigns this type of poem to an unsophisticated popular tradition.[22]

Through its peculiar verbal and social logic, then, re-calibrated by a nameless poetic authority, *Sir Launfal* asks its readers to revise a number of

21. See Bliss, *Sir Launfal*, 89–90 n. 278. While the text offers no detail about Tryamour after her departure, it does acknowledge Launfal's fame in the penultimate stanza, with the rumor of his horse's yearly reappearance (lines 1024–32).
22. As O'Brien observes, "The late fourteenth and early fifteenth centuries are a time of fashionable interest in the Breton lay as a literary artifact, and this sort of interest can complicate the tone of a poem *apparently* 'meant for simpler, less sensitive listeners in market-square or inn-yard'" ("'Readerly' *Sir Launfal*," 35).

beliefs: in Launfal's silence rather than his prowess as a hero or lover; in Tryamour's spectacular materiality over the illicit talk that threatens the court; and, above all, in the power of romance poetics to codify and control speech. With the breakdown of legal discourse into skirmishing and then into a lingering gaze, the last scene stages the conflict between talk and writing that lies at the very heart of romance convention. Insofar as Tryamour is summoned back by neither Launfal nor her own wishes, but by the collective readerly desire of the baronial court and the poem's audience, her spectacular re-inscription augurs the triumph of poetic over faerie magic. Considering that Launfal's escape from the court and his ensuing *fama* depend on the conventional response of several audiences to the physical embodiment of his patroness, the materialized text, more than the absent poet, stands as the primary agent of narrative success.

III

While mirroring *Sir Launfal* in several formal respects, *Athelston* thematizes *fama* to a less assured but ultimately more provocative conclusion. A product of the same tail-rhyme movement, extant also in only one manuscript (Gonville and Caius College, Cambridge MS 175), it distinguishes itself by a narrative perspective that extends well outside the court. This broader social perspective fosters a preoccupation with textual transmission and reception beyond the codification of speech. The anonymous poet advertises as much at the outset, when he identifies the four main characters as messengers "that wolden yn Yngelond lettrys bere, / As it wes here kynde" (14–15).[23] Their swearing of brotherhood under a linden tree a few lines later (23–24) may resemble Launfal's magical conversion in the woods rather palely, but as a speech act it shapes the characters and plot just as directly. The transformative effects are immediate: When one of the four, Athelston, inherits the throne of England from his uncle in the following scene, he swiftly promotes his sworn brothers to aristocratic rank, making Wymound the Earl of Dover, Egeland the Earl of Stone, and Alryke the Archbishop of Canterbury (37–60).

Messengers, letters, and "messengering" stand as both the subject and vehicle of the romance, metaphors for the metamorphosis of speech into texts and the enterprise of sending, receiving, and reading them. Virtually all the narrative action occurs through the transmission of letters. Three epistolary quests, positioned symmetrically near the beginning, middle, and end of the poem, account for roughly one-quarter of its total length.

---

23. All textual references to *Athelston,* cited parenthetically by line numbers, are from the edition in *Four Romances of England,* ed. Ronald B. Herzman, Graham Drake, and Eve Salisbury (Kalamazoo, Mich.: Medieval Institute Publications, 1999), 341–84.

The first (182–240) involves King Athelston's summoning of Egeland, at the instigation of the envious Wymound's "false lesyngys" (83, 131) that Egeland is a traitor (121–68). In the second envoy, Athelston's queen aims to repair the brewing catastrophe by requesting Archbishop Alryke to intercede with her husband on Egeland's behalf (297–416). The final episode completes the circuit of deception, when Alryke lures Wymound back to court with a duplicitous letter reporting that Egeland has been executed (701–58).[24]

The most interesting link between the letter journeys is their agency. The figure who conveys each letter, supervises its reading, and then accompanies the addressee on the return trip is a foundling who shares the name of the messenger-who-became-king, Athelston (184–86). Just as the quixotic details surrounding this fifth and most efficacious messenger make him the story's most intriguing player, his errant horseback journeys with the letters figure him as the proper hero of the romance—a bourgeois hero at that. His vivid dialogue with the letters' addressees, practical self-regard, and improvisational wit shape his subplot into a public, middle-class drama that counterpoints "common imperfect reality against the figuration of reality in the main romance plot."[25]

The messenger's orchestration of the three epistolary journeys becomes productive in its own right, insofar as the narrative encompasses not just the documents he delivers but also the dramatic scenarios growing up around their conveyance. For example, though the first letters to Egeland and his wife are ambiguous, the messenger controls the presentation by delivering them to the earl (202–4), disposing his response while describing the contents: ("'This lettre oughte to make the blythe . . . / The kyng wole for the cuntas [countess's] sake / Bothe thy sones knyghtes make'" [206–8]), and then leading Egeland into his wife's chamber, "to rede the lettrys before that hende" (224). The manner in which this vignette turns the act of reading into a topic[26] and the messenger into the

---

24. On the poem's analogies to English history and legend, see Laura A. Hibbard, "*Athelston*, A Westminster Legend," *Publications of the Modern Language Society* 36 (1921): 223–44; and *Mediaeval Romance in England* (New York: Oxford University Press, 1924), 143–46.

25. Derek Pearsall, "The Development of Middle English Romance," 31. The text acknowledges the messenger's mixed status twice through apposition, "the messanger, the noble man" (199, 339; see also 360–62). A. Inskip Dickerson, citing Chaucer, notes that the medieval messenger, though an office of rank, was one of the few accessible to commoners and nobility alike ("The Subplot of the Messenger in *Athelston*," *Papers on Language and Literature* 12 [1976]: 117).

26. Further exemplifying the poet's fondness for homonymy, the word *rede* takes on three denotations across the narrative: giving advice (210, 661), reading a text (203–4, 224, 366, 383), and riding a horse (322, 539). The meanings coalesce once we regard the acts of composing, receiving, and carrying the letters as stages in a single process: "reading" as a social economy. The word is one of the richest homonyms in the Middle English lexicon, its variants spanning more than seventeen pages in the *Middle English Dictionary*.

main agent of interpretation points up the extent to which his adventure becomes a kind of literary production.

The messenger's agency involves two crucial functions: his intermediary narrative role in transporting and promulgating the letters, and his extra-textual readerly role in shaping the key interpretive moments that complicate the main line of the romance. The first ultimately gives way to the latter, a theatrical responsibility for directing the reading. While the initial locus of interpretive authority may be the letters that the messenger is charged merely to "fonge" [bear] (299), the performative license he appropriates from the senders and recipients confers a power superior even to the king's (given the capricious, misguided, and nearly disastrous decisions that the other Athelston makes from early on).

Colorful as it may be, however, the messenger's aggrandizement comes to have a number of disquieting implications for the relationship between speech and literary transmission in the poem. Even as his quests naturalize the narrative, the social contingencies surrounding the letters ultimately imperil their success and threaten to undermine the epistolary economy itself. The messenger's journeys dilate not through conventional romance motifs—the advent of opposing forces or the hero's internal growth—but through the intrusion of his own self-concern. His own talk proves both self-serving and disingenuous, as when he cajoles money and dinner from the queen before departing with her letter to Alryke, rambling on about his hardship (315–32); and when he cons Wymound into lending him a horse, fully aware that the trip back to court will ensure Wymound's death (715–34).

As problematic as the messenger's self-interest proves, the most vexing aspect of his enterprises is the duplicitous nature of the goods he carries. The first set of letters is a tissue of lies, provoked by Wymound's envious slander that Egeland is a traitor to the throne and then calibrated by the king to lure Egeland's family to Westminster with the false promise about the sons, so that Egeland can be arraigned. Although in the narrower view we might construe the king's lie as felicitous, given his belief in Wymound's accusation (169–74) and the letters' successful execution of their intent, the broader narrative context eventually proves Wymound's slander to be an utter failure. The elaborate dramatization of Wymound's speech acts locates them at the very center of the poet's and the readers' concerns. The intimate scene in which Wymound presses home his lie, ushering Athelston into the royal bed chamber and spinning the yarn with portentous aplomb (121–68), adroitly balances the domestic vignette in which Egeland and his wife receive the letter and credit its hollow promise (202–34). Likewise, the maternal devotion with which Egeland's pregnant wife responds to the news (229–30) presages the queen's empathy shortly after, when she invokes her own pregnancy while beseeching the king to release the family from prison (259–66). Athelston's furious rebuff of his wife culminates with the most shocking incident in the entire romance, the king kicking her womb and killing their unborn child (282–96).[27]

These spectacles, centered so uncomfortably on the throttling of feminine constancy and so antipathetic in tone, diagnose the narrative's masculine agency as malignant, but with an interesting twist.[28] The narrator's comment following the stillbirth, "Thus may a traytour baret rayse [raise strife], / And make manye men ful evele at ayse [ill at ease]" (294–95), subtly displaces blame from the king and even from Wymound as a character. Prime responsibility for the calamities seems to rest, rather, with an allegorized principle of falsehood, the antithesis of typical romance virtues such as honor, courage, and loyalty. This vice is embodied in the figure of Wymound, clearly, but at crucial junctures, marking the beginning and end of the messenger's two disingenuous journeys, the text reifies it into an almost material entity. In the first instance, the "false lesynges" that reverberate in Wymound's mind before he approaches the king (83) attain mature shape as he presses his slander home: "And whenne that they were the chaumbyr withinne, / False lesyngys he gan begynne / On hys weddyd brother dere" (130–32).

In the second instance, the lies gain a kind of retrospective solidity as the messenger completes the third epistolary foray, bearing the bait that Wymound will inherit the earldom, with Egeland and his sons purportedly slain (711–64). The episode involves a series of trade-offs, from Wymound's offer to pay the messenger in coin; to the horse-loaning incident mentioned above; to the coup de grâce, Wymound's eventual delivery to the hands of baronial justice in Westminster Hall. Standing at the head of this sequence of exchanges—initiating the economy, as it were—is Wymound's silent reaction to the archbishop's letter: "Thanne that eerl made hym glade, / And thankyd God that lesyng was made: / 'It hath gete me this eerldome'" (723–25). Figuring the lie as a divinely wrought gift allows Wymound to evade responsibility for a time, but it also heightens the irony of his entrapment, since Alryke's letter is also mendacious, shaped, if more felicitously, to expose and exorcise the evil brother's culpability.

27. Trounce downplays this event by adducing a number of literary and historical analogues to imply that "the poet's mind is running on the routine punishments for peccant wives" (*Athelston,* 109). Maybe so, but the painfully detailed aftermath suggests an intense imagination of the scene, on both the poet's and audience's parts. The stanza following the assault places us voyeuristically inside the queen's chamber, alongside her maidens, where, shrouded in "dool inowgh," we are forced to watch the birth of "[a] knave-chyld . . . / As bryght as blosme on bowgh. / He was bothe whyt and red; / Off that dynt was he ded" (289–92).

28. On the story's feminine dynamic, read in relation to monarchical issues, see Elizabeth A. Rowe, "The Female Body Politic and the Miscarriage of Justice in *Athelston,*" *Studies in the Age of Chaucer* 17 (1995): 79–98.

The closing scene of the poem, staged before an assembly of the common parliament in Westminster Hall, sustains this irony by drawing attention to both the artifactual nature of Wymound's lie and his bodily incorporation of it. The king's accusation that the slaying of his unborn child owes to "'[Wymound's] falsenesse and thy lesyng'" (762) prompts Wymound's public denial that "he made nevere that lesyng" (766), a figure of speech Egeland's sons turn back when they implore the traitor to tell "'why thou that lesyng made'" (794). This penchant for materializing the root of the psychological and moral conflict sets the stage for the romance's final movement, where the two-edged moral pursuit of the perpetrator's confession and of justice more broadly is transformed into the lurid spectacle of Wymound's quartering and hanging—a perverse parallel, of sorts, to the portrait of Tryamour at the end of *Sir Launfal*. The narrator's rejoinder to the punishment, in the poem's final lines, goes beyond confirming Wymound's accountability and the triumph of a retributive judicial system: "This hadde he for hys lye. / Now Iesu, that is hevene-kyng, / Leve [allow] nevere traytour [to] have betere endyng, / But swych dome [judgment] for to dye. / Explicit" (809–13). This editorial speech act hones the poem's earlier anxiety about falsehood, borne out ambivalently through the messenger's complicity in the fraudulent news he bears. Here, more concretely, we have offered up for public consumption the punishment of "lesyng" incarnate: the lie made flesh, tortured, and condemned in prayer. However arresting the spectacle, the elaborate narrative cartography that brings us to this final embodiment of falsehood underscores its thorough conventionality within the poem—echoing Austin, once again, "a wrong thing [to say], in these circumstances, to this audience, for these purposes and with these intentions."[29]

The theatricality with which the romance displays Wymound's fate at the close draws attention to additional mechanisms that resolve the poem's meditation on the social consequences of bad *fama*. The resolution develops less through the characters, whether speakers or messengers, than through the social context surrounding them. In the second epistolary drama, after being rebuked by the king in pleading for a legal solution to Egeland's imprisonment and being forced to lay down the tokens of his archbishopric, Alryke recruits support among the town lords, outside the court. His own heroic quest, an itinerant journey that "must have been paralleled a hundred times in actual life,"[30] takes him clear out of the romance world, straight into the "uncouthe lond" of Fleet Street (498) and the yards around Saint Paul's, marked by "the Brokene-Cros off ston" (546). As

29. Austin, *How to Do Things*, 145. Daniel Pigg assesses the signifying power of Wymound's lies for feudal institutions, another aspect of their conventionality, in "The Implications of Realist Poetics in the Middle English *Athelston*," *English Language Notes* 32 (1994): 1–8.
30. Trounce, *Athelston*, 36.

Trounce notes, this cross was an important and conspicuous landmark from at least 1350 until its removal in 1390; standing just outside the north gate of Saint Paul's yard, it served as a locus of popular assembly and general opposition to the crown. On one level, then, Fleet Street and the cross stake out the geographical boundaries between Westminster and London that substantiate the romance's conflict between state and church.[31]

Alryke's excursion into this evocative space procures the help he seeks, yet it fulfills an even more important contextual function as well, bearing on the narrative preoccupation with epistolary production and transmission. The local references defining Alryke's journey map out quite precisely the site of London's fledgling manuscript-book enterprise, as it developed from the middle to the end of the fourteenth century. The main line of this trade, a short span of Paternoster Row, lay barely one hundred and fifty feet from the cathedral and the cross itself. In addition to assorted barons, the archbishop would also have encountered a loose-knit confederation of independent literary craftsmen: scribes, limners, and artisans. Indeed, London records suggest that by 1379 members of the Stationers Guild controlled shops in the immediate vicinity of the broken cross and moved the short distance to Paternoster Row upon its removal in 1390.[32]

Whatever political implications can be drawn from Alryke's venture, it seems fitting that the area in which he re-consolidates his authority was the hub of literary business as well as civic activism. The precision of the London geography allows us to imagine late-fourteenth-century bookmakers and readers as co-participants in the drama, since the archbishop's excursion clearly re-draws conventional social boundaries. When the barons kneel before Alryke, his formulaic utterance, "He nykkyd hem with nay" (503), severs traditional hierarchical relations. In turn, the imagery with which the barons commit to the fight against Athelston envisions a leveling of the vertical structures that govern the earlier half of the poem: "We

---

31. Trounce associates the lords in this respect with the baronial foes of King John, whose excesses provoked a tumultuous English interdict (*Athelston*, 33–34; references above from 37–38, 123). The lords also resemble the baronial class of readers this type of romance likely presumed, following Susan Crane, *Insular Romance: Politics, Faith, and Culture in Anglo-Norman and Middle English Romance* (Berkeley: University of California Press, 1986).

32. On the geography of the London book trade around the turn of the century, see C. Paul Christianson, "A Community of Book Artisans in Chaucer's London," *Viator* 20 (1989): 207–18; and "Evidence for the Study of London's Late-Medieval Manuscript-Book Trade," in *Book Production and Publishing in Britain, 1375–1475*, ed. Jeremy Griffiths and Derek Pearsall (Cambridge: Cambridge University Press, 1989), 87–108. Christianson's descriptions are supplemented by A. I. Doyle and M. B. Parkes, "The Production of Copies of the *Canterbury Tales* and the *Confessio Amantis* in the Early Fifteenth Century," in *Medieval Scribes, Manuscripts, and Libraries: Essays Presented to N. R. Ker*, ed. M. B. Parkes and Andrew G. Watson (London: Scolar, 1978), 163–67, 199–200. On the Stationers Guild, see H. T. Riley, *Memorials of London and London Life in the Thirteenth, Fourteenth, and Fifteenth Centuries* (London: Longmans, Green, 1868), 435.

schole drawe doun bothe halle and boures [chambers]; / Bothe hys cas-
telles and hys toures, / They schole lygge [lie] lowe and holewe" (525–27).
By means such as these, imaginative details engaging historical and political contexts, the exchanges between the king, archbishop, and barons help
realign the social geometry of the poem. Most particularly, their discourse
anticipates *Athelston*'s final image, punctuating the institutional contain-
ment of dangerous speech with the spectacle of Wymound's prone body
dragged through town and then hoisted up "ful hyghe" on a tree for all to
see (806).

We reach this point, though, only after the romance has played out its
moral climax on a spot that mirrors the region outside Saint Paul's. Upon
returning with the messenger, Wymound enters the "wyde halle" of Westminster (770), to be tried before his peers. Westminster Hall was not only
the seat of royal power but also, by 1345, the residence of the Chancery,
the administrative office whose duties included preparing and distribut-
ing correspondence throughout the realm.[33] That the poem repeatedly
engineers key developments through real locales charged with this type
of significance seems hardly coincidental. On one level, Westminster
Hall may betoken the accommodation of royal, ecclesiastical, and popular authority, resolving the friction symbolized by the broken cross and
the stripping of the archbishop's accoutrements. On another level, the
mixed associations shared by Westminster Hall and the broken cross
forge a relationship, however inchoate, between political and textual
power. To the extent that the narrative increasingly questions and even
undermines King Athelston's authority, his administration of the ordeal-
by-fire that seals Wymound's fate (774–79) is a rather hollow gesture.
Real power, by this point, lies elsewhere, with the agents of social exchange and renewal: the messenger, the barony, the peers who carry out
the punishment and leave the pusillanimous king and even the archbishop behind.

In the poem's final calculus, it is the economy of textual production that
enables these middling figures to challenge and perhaps even supplant
royal and ecclesiastical prerogative, to become themselves the arbiters of
social justice. Their appropriation of power, in other words, subsists in
their own conventionality: their participation in a cultural matrix that
identifies and confronts abuses of authority. Chief among these abuses,
Athelston dramatizes, are speech acts that frustrate the compacts on which
an increasingly fluid late-fourteenth-century society depends. This romance's anxiety about slander and lies, like *Sir Launfal*'s, diagnoses the socially destructive consequences of placing self-interest over the common

33. John H. Fisher, Malcolm Richardson, and Jane L. Fisher, eds., *An Anthology of Chancery English* (Knoxville: University of Tennessee Press, 1984), xiv.

good. The logic of such a reading seems as clear by the lies that prove felicitous in both romances, from a speech-act perspective, as by the slander
and accusations that imperil individual characters and threaten the body
politic. *Athelston* goes further than *Sir Launfal,* however, in acknowledging
that bad *fama* travels beyond the court, where its consequences can grow
more serious, indeed painful.

IV

Given medieval romance's pervasive concern with the circumstances of
its own production, a legacy of the earliest Continental courtly romances
(to say nothing of the *Roman de la Rose*), it is inevitable that the thematiza-
tion of *fama* in these two romances reflects back on authorial speech. In
celebrating the potential of the textualized image to break the circuit of
bad *fama, Sir Launfal's* solution is static and somewhat self-assured. The
transformative authority of writing, in the end, salvages both Launfal and
his mistress, the former from his passive introversion and faulty tongue,
the latter from her nearly disastrous brand of private patronage. Only
when their relationship gains a public face, when the poet seizes upon its
iconographic potential and reifies them into hero and heroine, do they become successful to anyone but themselves. Only then, by similar logic, does
the romance's author gain a name, if not a face.

Athelston remains more tentative about the codification of *fama,* and its
implications for authorial speech are likewise ambivalent. For all his heroic
potential, the authorial figure of the messenger remains bound to duplicity throughout the poem, whether from treacherous slander or the lies intended to repair it; his association with duplicity seems to suit him well. As
successful as the messenger's letters are in eventually rooting out the romance's most dangerous falsehood, the letters are unable to identify the
falsehood. Like all texts, Athelston's letters prove capable of embodying,
disguising, and advancing disingenuous intentions. Consistent with the
premises of speech-act theory, the diagnosis of infelicity, or linguistic failure, depends on the contexts and conventions the letters engage. Indeed,
that the conclusions to both *Athelston* and *Sir Launfal* are suffused with legal discourse underscores the fundamentally provisional nature of literary
mimesis, as a species of speech.[34] While readers have long valued *Athelston's* social verisimilitude, the acuity of its "English material," it beckons
us to understand that socially contingent *fama*—slander, defamation, lies,
even well-minded duplicity—can thwart the quest for literary representation altogether. In the face of such hazards, this romance seems to intuit,

---

34. On conjunctions between medieval legal and literary discourse, see R. Howard Bloch,
Medieval French Literature and Law (Berkeley: University of California Press, 1977).

even the most basic exchange of writing remains fraught with the misadventures of speech. With that cognizance *Athelston* may appear to move beyond romance, closer to Chaucer's more urbane idiom perhaps. If so, *Athelston*'s ambivalence about the codification of *fama* shapes up as a wholly honest utterance.

CHAPTER NINE

Fama *and Pastoral Constraints on Rebuking* Sinners: *The Book of Margery Kempe*

EDWIN D. CRAUN

Through all of the life narrated in *The Book of Margery Kempe,*[1] Margery is subject to correction, to blame imposed in the name of communal norms, by males in positions of religious and secular authority. Priests from her native Lynn to Canterbury to Jerusalem reprove her for socially disruptive acts of piety, especially weeping noisily in church and wearing white

In the final stages of research, I was assisted by the resourceful Jennifer Fisher under a Glenn Grant from Washington and Lee University; in the early stages, by Kelley Joy, a Robert E. Lee Scholar. My debts to Jan Ziolkowski for an erudite formal response to my paper at Fordham University and to Dan Smail for penetrating questions appear in several footnotes but extend far beyond them.

1. The extent to which Margery Kempe of Lynn authored the *Book* and the extent to which her two scribes, the first lay and the second clerical, did is still unsettled. In 1975, John Hirsh argued confidently from internal evidence that the second was closely involved in composition, a position which, although not widely accepted, has not been wholly refuted. If accepted, this collaborative authorship would open the way for seeing the cleric's learning and concerns as shaping the text somewhat, though "The *Book*'s insistence that Margery acquired gifts of scriptural exposition and devotional insight which repeatedly confounded clerics . . . makes it unsafe to attribute passages to the priest simply on the grounds that they are priestly in manner and matter" (Anthony Goodman, "The Piety of John Brunham's Daughter of Lynn," in *Medieval Women: Essays Dedicated and Presented to Professor Rosalind M. T. Hill,* ed. Derek Baker [Oxford: Blackwell, 1978], 347–58). Adding more uncertainty, even the traditional position on the roles of the two scribes—that the first wrote all of book I while the second revised I and wrote II—is not securely founded. The question of the scribes' role in authorship has been taken into new territory by Lynn Staley, who, distinguishing between an author (Kempe) and a screen/persona (Margery), regards the scribes as a trope employed by Kempe to lend authority to the *Book,* in the manner of established writing about holy women mediated by scribes (*Margery Kempe's Dissenting Fictions* [State College: Pennsylvania State University Press, 1994], 1–38). Given these profoundly unsettled issues, I have adopted the agnostic's dodge, simply referring to "the *Book*" and taking no position on authorship, a stance appropriate, I believe, to a chapter that explores the speech of a holy woman and her

clothes as a married woman.[2] Before he imprisoned her, the mayor of
Leicester "had long chedyn [chided] hir & seyd many euyl & horybyl
wordys on-to hir," calling her "a fals strumpet, a fals loller [Lollard, vagrant,
zealot], & a fals deceyuer of þe pepyl".[3] The *Book*'s Margery, in turn, rebukes the sins of others, often males in authority over her. Among them,
most notoriously, is Archbishop Thomas Arundel of Canterbury. A formidable man, as recent scholarship has emphasized, Arundel was the son of
the great Anglo-Norman earl Richard FitzAlan, a graduate of Oxford, a
bishop by the age of twenty-two, a leader of the rebellion against Richard
II, a judge of Lollards.[4] While she is waiting in Lambeth's great hall to petition him to grant her the right to take communion weekly and the freedom to name her own confessor, Margery overhears his retinue—priests
as well as men at arms—swearing "gret oþis." Margery's response is to rebuke boldly the archbishop's men, claiming that they will be damned unless they forsake the practice of swearing. Then, when she meets the
archbishop in his garden, she "boldly spak to hym for þe correccyon of his
meny [retinue, household]," accusing him of abusing his office by main-
taining traitors to God and proclaiming his responsibility for their sins ("3e
schal answer for hem les þan [unless] 3e correctyn hem." His response:
"Ful benyngly & mekely he suffred hir to sey hir entente & 3af a fayr answer").[5] This forthright rebuke of the highest ecclesiastical authority in England is a far cry from the images of women in the German law books
interpreted by Madeline Caviness and Charles Nelson in this volume:
women whose speech is silenced or sharply limited in the presence of secular judges, in part because of women's legendary verbal aggressiveness.[6]
And it comes in a period when local secular officials were vigorously pros-
ecuting disruptive speakers as scolds—often when they had impugned
those in power—as Sandy Bardsley's study of manorial and borough court
rolls demonstrates.[7]

---

adversaries as it is constructed for readers/listeners. As I argue here, the *Book*'s Margery is
presented as so thoroughly shaped by pastoral discourse on sin that it would be well nigh impossible to accomplish what criticism of the Christian Gospels often attempts: convincingly
sifting out the words of the holy person from the writers' (in this case, scribes') "overlay."

2. *The Book of Margery Kempe*, ed. Sanford Meech and Hope Emily Allen, Early English Text
Society, o.s., 217 (London: Oxford University Press, 1940), 27, 69, 154–57.

3. The verbs *rebuke*, *reprove* (or *repreve*), and *undyrnem* (and their related nouns) are used
interchangeably in the *Book* whenever anyone speaks of another's supposed sin, whether vir-
tuously or viciously, while the verb *slandyr* always signifies doing so viciously and *chid* usually
does so. *Correct* and *correction*, however, convey charitable speech about another's sin, as discussed below. Other verbs, like *flet* or *challenge*, are also part of this large semantic field, but
they are used less frequently and are usually paired with the more common terms.

4. Nigel Saul, *Richard II* (New Haven: Yale University Press, 1997).

5. *Book*, 37.

6. Caviness and Nelson, "Silent Witnesses."

7. Bardsley, "Sin, Speech, and Scolding," in this volume.

What, then, according to the *Book,* authorizes a layperson, someone subject to correction by clerics (a *subditus* in clerical terms), to rebuke her clerical superior, a *praelatus?* And what speech practices does Margery Kempe—not known for her indirection—observe that enable her to negotiate a dangerous situation so adeptly that he submissively accepts her rebuke? Correcting the sins of others, acting to reconstruct the lives of others by imposing blame and guilt, was always a potentially explosive act in the late medieval church. It was particularly charged in the early fifteenth century because Lollards were known for boldly denouncing the sins of groups and individuals, especially clerics (friars, for example, or confessors). And the danger was particularly acute for the *Book*'s Margery at Lambeth. There the power differential was at its greatest. Moreover, she had earlier been accused of Lollardy by the monks at the archbishop's own cathedral, and Lollards were often identified by two practices: rebuking those who swore great oaths, and allowing women to instruct men.[8]

In rebuking both the archbishop and his retinue, Margery, as the *Book* carefully registers, was practicing fraternal correction ("for þe coreccyon of hys meny"). In *confessionalia,* sermons, treatises on the vices and virtues, and *distinctiones,* pastoral writers took care to distinguish this speech practice, open to all Christians, from the correction practiced by priests, judges, abbesses, and other *praelati* or *superiores* charged with the care of souls (*cura animarum*) and the governance or direction (*regimen*) of others.[9] (Under the latter phrase often came parents' control of their children or householders' of domestics.)

The *Book*'s contemporary, the pastoral encyclopedist of sin Alexander Carpenter, defines correction assigned to superiors as an act of justice, directed toward the common good, which may involve not only admonition but punishment in order to restrain people from wrongdoing: "actus iusticie per quem intenditur bonum commune non solum per simplicem fratris ammonitionem sed etiam aliquando per punitionem."[10] Fraternal correction, in contrast, is presented as an act of charity that, while it also

8. On Margery's closeness to Lollard rhetoric at Lambeth, see Ruth Shklar, "Cobham's Daughter: *The Book of Margery Kempe and the Power of Heterodox Thinking,*" *Modern Language Quarterly* 56 (1995): 290–91. On the Lollard practices, see Anne Hudson, *The Premature Reformation* (Oxford: Clarendon, 1988), 371; and Margaret Aston, *Lollards and Reformers: Images and Literacy in Late Medieval Religion* (London: Hambledon, 1984), 47–52.

9. All pastoral texts cited below survive in British libraries in manuscripts roughly datable to Margery Kempe's lifetime (ca. 1373–after 1438) or earlier in the fourteenth century. Most critics agree that the *Book* was written in several stages late in Margery's life.

10. Alexander Carpenter, *Destructorium viciorum* (Paris, 1516), fol. Kii recto; also John Bromyard, *Summa praedicantium* (Nuremberg, 1485), A.21.7; and Bartolomeo di San Concordio, *Summa de casibus,* Bodleian Library Oxford MS Laud misc. 604, fol. 24v; from Thomas Aquinas, *Summa theologiae,* vol. 34, ed. Thomas Gilby (New York: McGraw Hill, 1975), 2.2.33.3.

intends to amend the conduct of the errant, uses only admonition: "est actus caritatis tendens ad emendationem fratris delinquentis per simplicem ammonitionem."[11] The sinning *frater* to be corrected specifically includes social superiors: "nomine fratris intelligitur omnis homo peccator siue inferior siue par siue superior."[12] The practice of fraternal correction is open to all Christians having charity, *subditi* as well as *praelati*, those appointed to rule others ("ad regendum alios constitutus"). To constitute this normative act of speech licensed by the church, correction/rebuke must be governed by a proper will (charitable) and intention (reformation of sin).[13]

In addition to authorizing correction of sin by the laity,[14] the late medieval church pressed fraternal correction as an obligation. Pastoral texts—and the preaching, hearing confessions, teaching, and general catechesis that were shaped by them—presented fraternal correction as a matter of precept, Jesus' words in Matt. 18:15 being reckoned as "lex evangelica": "Si autem peccaverit in te frater tuus, vade, and corripe eum."[15] It was thus an obligation for all Christians. Dismissing those who think that the institutional church alone should correct because it has the keeping of souls ("habet animas custodire"), the fourteenth-century English compiler of preaching materials John Bromyard insists—in his entry on friendship, interestingly—that everyone is bound by the law of charity to come to the aid of his neighbor ("quia quilibet tenetur proximo lege charitatis subuenire").[16] Later, in his general entry on "correctio" (fraternal and prelatical), he argues for its necessity by comparing it to a medicine for the sick

11. Carpenter, *Summa*, fol. Ki verso; Astesano da Asti, *Summa de casibus conscientiae*, Bodleian Library Oxford MS Canon misc. 208, fol. 121v.

12. Astesano, *Summa*, fol. 121v.

13. On what distinguishes normative from deviant speech in pastoral writing, see Edwin Craun, *Lies, Slander, and Obscenity in Medieval English Literature: Pastoral Rhetoric and the Deviant Speaker* (Cambridge: Cambridge University Press, 1997), 25–47.

14. To license *subditi* to correct *praelati* was also, of course, to permit clerics subordinate to any clerical superiors to correct their sins (monks, their abbots; parish priests, their bishops; any cleric, his confessor).

15. Astesano, *Summa*, fol. 122r–v; "Pro quo sciendum quod opera misericordie sunt sex," Bodleian Library MS Hamilton 30, fol. 155v.

16. Bromyard, *Summa*, A.21.7. Jan Ziolkowski has astutely suggested to me that Bromyard's treatment of fraternal correction in part under *amicitia* indicates monastic origin for the practice. This may very well be. Ailred of Rievaulx's *De spirituali amicitia* and his thirty-first sermon, both of which I consulted several years ago on CD-ROM, admonish monastics against anger and excessive zeal when they correct their brothers. See Ailred of Rievaulx, *De spirituali amicitia*, ed. Anselm Hoste, Corpus Christianorum Continuatio Mediaevalis 1 (Turnhout, Belgium: Brepols, 1971); digitized edition in CETEDOC Library of Early Christian Latin Texts, CD no. 1 (Turnhout, Belgium: Brepols, 1991), 3.84; Ailred of Rievaulx, *Sermones* I–XLVI, ed. Gaetano Raciti, Corpus Christianorum Continuatio Mediaevalis 2A (Turnhout, Belgium: Brepols, 1989), CETEDOC, CD no. 1, line 91. In *De spirituali amicitia* (2.253), Ailred also defines correction as the opposite of flattery. Both topoi are common in post-Lateran-IV pastoral texts. I plan to follow up this suggestion when researching further a book-length study of fraternal correction.

or wounded, a chain for the madman.[17] Often fraternal correction was listed, in both Latin and vernacular *pastoralia,* as one of the obligatory seven works of spiritual mercy.[18] To keep silent when seeing a brother sin was a sin, akin to hiding a homicide, and confessional works specify that neglecting correction, like neglecting the other deeds of spiritual mercy, had to be divulged in auricular confession.[19] Given that the *Book* presents Margery Kempe as desiring to be guided by spiritual directors and as aspiring to live out the imperatives of divine charity in the world, she would be bound to practice fraternal correction whenever she encounters manifest sin: the swearing of Cistercian monks at the shrine of the Holy Blood at Hailes; the extravagant dress of the retinue of Thomas Peveral, bishop of Worcester; her own son's lechery, somatized in venereal disease; swearing and telling falsehoods in the streets of London.[20]

For the late medieval clergy to insist that all Christians were bound to correct the sins of their fellows, to let the will and intention of speakers (known only to God and, perhaps, if they were sufficiently self-aware, to themselves) license specific acts of reproof was to risk abuse, as the clergy was well aware. Under the guise of clerically sanctioned speech, speakers could engage in clerically proscribed deviant speech, committing some of the several dozen Sins of the Tongue constructed by pastoral writing after the Fourth Lateran Council (1215) and then promulgated regularly in English parishes through preaching, confessional interrogations, and private admonition.[21] Thus, they could damage a person's *fama,* so valued in the largely oral culture of English mercantile cities.[22] To protect *fama,* the clergy also inculcated a set of constraints governing reprovers' speech: the intention of its speaker, its subject, its manner and wording, and the spaces in which it should be uttered.

Like fraternal correction, its three deviant sisters—improper reproof/rebuke, slander, and chiding—become a major strand in *The Book of Margery Kempe,* announced in its first preface: "Sche was so vsyd to be slawndred &

17. Bromyard, *Summa,* C.16.1.

18. "Pro quo," fols. 153v–154v; þe *Clensing of Manes Sawle,* Bodleian Library Oxford MS Bodl. 923, fol. 71r; Guillaume Peyraut, *Summa virtutum* (Lyons, 1668), 378; *Speculum Christiani,* ed. Gustaf Holmstedt, Early English Text Society, o.s., 182 (London: Oxford University Press, 1933), 44.

19. Nicholas Biard, *Distinctiones theologicae,* Bodleian Library Oxford MS Bodl. 563, fol. 29r; *Clensing,* fol. 71r–v; "Confessor venientem ad confessionem benigne," British Library MS Addit. 15237, fol. 92r; "In the begynyng it is necessarie unto a prest," British Library MS Cotton Vespasian A.xxv, fol. 153v.

20. *Book,* 109, 222–23, 245.

21. Craun, *Lies,* 1–72; Carla Casagrande and Silvana Vecchio, *I peccati della lingua: Disciplina ed etica della parola nella cultura medievale* (Rome: Instituto della Enciclopedia Italiana, 1987).

22. Barbara Hanawalt, *"Of Good and Ill Repute": Gender and Social Control in Medieval England* (New York: Oxford University Press, 1998), ix and throughout.

repreued, to be cheden & rebuked of þe world."[23] Margery suffers them down to the penultimate incident recounted in her "life." The *Book* sites slander and improper reproof initially in her hometown of Lynn, as her neighbors respond to her new and very public practice of ascetic and affective piety. They then dog her as she practices her way of life on pilgrimages throughout her life and whenever she returns to Lynn. Moreover, as she begins to assume the role of itinerant religious teacher, the deviant speakers become clerics (and other *praelati,* like the mayor of Leicester) as well as laics, men disturbed by her public mastery of scriptural argument and the pastoral rhetoric of sin, who assault her verbally with another Sin of the Tongue, chiding. Throughout, the *Book* discredits these "wicked tongues" because they violate the basic constraints established by the clergy to police social criticism.

In contrast to these deviant speakers, Margery, as the *Book*'s holy woman, observes clerical constraints whenever she rebukes sin. Scholars of mysticism and women's social history have been drawn to Margery's authoritative social criticism for several decades now. They have variously—and convincingly, in each case—attributed it to "the mixed life of contemplation-in-action" (Lagorio), to the mystic's voicing of a divine utterance that answers her desire (Lochrie), to a culturally constructed female disruptiveness (Wilson), and to the influences of Continental holy women (Lagorio; Dickman). Recently, scholars have sought the genesis of her social criticism in early fifteenth-century social conflicts: in the dissenting strategies of Lollards and other reformist groups (Shklar; Wilson) and in the conflict between clerical codes and those of bourgeois life (Staley).[24] Like Lynn Staley's finely historicized *Dissenting Fictions,* this essay argues that clerical codes directed Margery's social criticism, but it focuses not so much on what she says as on the ethical constraints she observes—that is, on the norms of her speech. These norms stamp her social criticism as clerically sanctioned fraternal correction; her critics violate these norms, reducing their speech to deviant assaults on her *fama.*

The *Book* constructs Margery Kempe initially as a bourgeois wife whose identity and self is defined by the "worship"—that is, the esteem, the good

23. *Book,* 2.
24. Valerie Lagorio, *"Defensorium contra oblectratores:* A 'Discerning' Assessment of Margery Kempe," in *Mysticism: Medieval and Modern,* ed. idem (Salzburg: Institut für Anglistik und Amerikanistik, 1986), 29–48; Karma Lochrie, *Margery Kempe and the Translations of the Flesh* (Philadelphia: University of Pennsylvania Press, 1997); Janet Wilson, "Margery and Alison: Women on Top," in *Margery Kempe: A Book of Essays,* ed. Sandra McEntire (New York: Garland, 1992), 223–37; Shklar, "Cobham's Daughter," 277–304; Janet Wilson, "Communities of Dissent: The Secular and Ecclesiastical Communities of Margery Kempe's *Book,*" in *Medieval Women in Their Communities,* ed. Diane Watt (Toronto: University of Toronto Press, 1997), 155–85; Susan Dickman, "Margery Kempe and the Continental Tradition of the Pious Woman," in *The Medieval Mystical Tradition in England,* ed. Marion Glasscoe (Cambridge: D. S. Brewer, 1984), 150–68; Staley, *Dissenting Fictions.*

name, the social worth—that others confer on her in response to her standing in a mercantile community focused on material profit. "Worship" in the *Book* is Janus-faced, as Derek Brewer finds "honour" in Chaucer to be. However, whereas honor in Chaucer looks inward toward goodness and outward toward marks of external reputation,[25] bourgeois worship is more openly communally constructed in its doubleness. One of its two faces is the person's status as determined both by lineage and by achievement within communal parameters; its other, the response from others which that deserves (adapted from *OED* I.1a and b). In signifying both reputation and its basis in personal worth, *worship* and *honour* are more complex than the other Middle English words related to *fama,* such as *fame, name, los, renoun,* which convey only reputation itself (apart, of course, from other senses like rumor or gossip and from phrases like "of good name"). In the second chapter, just as she emerges from the madness provoked by her confessor's sharp reproof, the *Book*'s Margery is driven to reassert her claims to "worship." The social marker of this struggle to reassert her "condition of worth" is her clothes. Once she regains her wits and resumes her duties in the household, she returns to wearing elaborate headdresses with gold piping, hoods ornamented by points and incisions, multicolored cloaks "that it schuld be þe mor staryng to mennys sygth [conspicuous in people's eyes] and hir-self þe mor ben worsheped [be thought of the more highly]"—a "very visible and aggressively competitive display" that maintains "social and class differentiations."[26] In response to her husband's criticism of her dress, she degrades him socially, claiming that he, a mere burgess, was an unlikely husband for someone of such "worthy kendred," whose father had been mayor of Lynn and an alderman of its most powerful and prestigious parish fraternity. To bring in more money so that she can outdress her prosperous neighbors and achieve standing on their terms, she sets herself up first as "on of the grettest brewers" and then as a miller.

When Margery's domestic industries inexplicably fail, with the barm of her ale falling repeatedly, horses refusing to draw in her mill, and her superstitious servants fleeing her house, the *Book* presents her for the first time as the object of gossip, which, unlike the bourgeois "worship" conferred on her in response to a clearly marked status, reads these events as deficiencies in her inner life:

A-noon as it was noysed a-bowt þe town of N. þat þer wold neyþyr man ne best don seruyse [serve] to þe seyd creatur, þan summe seyden sche was a-cursyd; sum seyden God toke opyn veniawns [open vengeance] up-on hir; sum seyden

25. Derek Brewer, *Tradition and Innovation in Chaucer* (London: Macmillan, 1982), 70.
26. *Book,* 9; David Aers, *Community, Gender, and Individual Identity: English Writing, 1350–1430* (London: Routledge, 1988), 76.

o [one] thyng; & sum seyd an-oþer. And sum wyse men, whos mend was mor
growndyd in þe lofe of owyr Lord, seyd it was þe hey mercy of our Lord Ihesu
Cryst clepyd & kallyd hir fro þe pride and vanyte of þe wretthyd [wretched]
world.[27]

The repeated "sum seyden" constructs gossip as it appears throughout
the *Book:* as variable and usually unreliable responses to the same event that
are determined by the speakers' wills and their resultant habits of thought.
Those whose thinking springs more from a charitable will read her adver-
sities as a God-given call to conversion from a worldly life; others read them
as manifest punishment, divine or unknowable, for something culpable in
her. Central to the "wondyrful [to be wondered at] chaungyng" of her life,
then, is the replacement of her fellow citizens' "worship" with the harsh
judgments of their uncharitable gossip: "Þei þat be-forn had worsheped
her sythen [afterwords] ful scharply repreuyd her."[28] Margery's neighbors' talk remains simple gossip in Chris Wickham's definition, "talking
about other people behind their backs,"[29] until it turns to her new ascetic
and affective practices: daily confession (even twice or thrice a day), "to
gret fastyng & to gret wakyng," and public tears of contrition—practices
which, as Lynn Staley writes of fasting, could not be assimilated into her
communities.[30] Then the *Book* labels their talk slander and improper as
uncharitable reproof, speech that moves from active fault-finding to as-
saulting her reputation maliciously.

The pastoral tradition openly confronts the kinship between slander
and fraternal correction as types of social blame: both involve speakers im-
puting evil to others and sometimes exposing their "hidden evils." Slander
deviates from correction when the speakers intend to blacken the *fama* of
others, to cause their hearers to have a bad opinion of them. So they speak
outside the hearing of their victims, attempting to persuade others of the
truth of what they say. By contrast, fraternal correction intends amendment of sin—and, of course, it is spoken directly to the sinner.[31] In fact,
this distinction between detraction and fraternal correction is sometimes
presented as a test case for the general pastoral principle that verbal sins
ought to be appraised according to the intention of the speaker ("peccata
verborum maxime sunt ex intentione dicentis iudicanda").[32] Pastoral writ-

27. *Book*, 10–11.
28. Ibid., 2.
29. Chris Wickham, "Gossip and Resistance among the Medieval Peasantry," *Past and Present* 160 (1998): 11.
30. Staley, *Dissenting Fictions*, 51.
31. The popular late-fourteenth-century catechetical manual *Speculum Christiani* treats
slander under correction, saying it is its perversion, the converting of a virtue into a vice; see
Speculum Christiani, ed. Holmstedt, 234.
32. Astesano, *Summa*, fol. 83r.

ers commonly identify six ways in which speakers can depreciate another's reputation, two of which Margery suffers in the *Book:* attributing something false to her and ascribing her good actions to an evil intention.[33]

The outright falsehood is a form of slander, used as reproof, that Margery confronts in the penultimate incident in the *Book.* In London, after she returns from accompanying her daughter-in-law to Germany, she is reproved mockingly in the streets by "sum dissolute personys" with words falsely attributed to her: "'A, þu fals flesch, þu xalt [shall] no good mete etyn.'" The *Book* traces back to a tale contrived by her fellow citizens in response to her earliest ascetic practices, some forty years before. In their story, Margery was dining, on a fast day, with a prosperous man who served his guests a plate of red herring and one of fine pike. Margery set aside the herring, loudly proclaiming "A, þu fals flesch, þu woldist now etyn reed heryng, but þu xult not han þi wille." Then she feasted on the excellent pike.[34]

The *Book* brands this story of hypocritical asceticism used to gratify a very particular fleshly desire as a diabolical falsehood not once but four times, attributing its staying power to those envious of "hir vertuows leuyng," "not of powyr to hyndryn hir but þorw [only having power to hinder her through] her fals tongys." (Envy is the root vice of slander in the pastoral tradition dating back to Gregory the Great.)[35] By such a network of gossip the words were transmitted over forty years or so in "many a plece wher sche was neuyr kid ne knowyn" to the point that they became "a maner of proverbe a-ȝen hir," used to give her "gret repref" in many places. So words generated and transmitted as slander, as words spoken out of her hearing to expose her "hidden evil" of hypocrisy and so damage her reputation for rigorous asceticism, are uttered publicly and to her face to cause her pain, not even with the pretense of correcting socially deviant behavior. In the process, these words become unjust and uncharitable reproof/rebuke (*convicium*), a Sin of the Tongue akin to slander in the pastoral tradition because it divulges blamable failing (*defectus culpae*)[36] but different from it because it aims to assault a person openly, not covertly, and because it aims to rob her of her *honor,* not denigrate her *fama.*[37] Although the *Book* men-

33. Carpenter, *Destructorium,* fol. Dvii verso; Bromyard, *Summa,* D.6.2; *Expositio libri de electionibus,* University College Oxford MS 71, fol. 72r; *Omne bonum* 1, British Library MS Royal G.E.6, part 2, fol. 498r.

34. *Book,* 243–44.

35. Craun, *Lies,* 13.

36. John Gower's satiric *Mirour de l'omme,* for example, presents Reproef as one of the two servants of Malebouche (slander), at one with his master in aiming to manifest others' evil in order to grieve them, not to move them to amend. John Gower, *Mirour de l'omme,* in *The Complete Works of John Gower,* vol. 1 (Oxford: Clarendon, 1899), line 2992.

37. Carpenter, *Destructorium,* fol. Dvii verso; Astesano, fol. 82r; Bartolomeo, *Summa,* fol. 23v; *Speculum conscientiae,* in *S. Bonaventurae Opera Omnia,* vol. 8, ed. Collegium S. Bonaventurae (Quaracchi, Italy: Ex Typographia Collegii S. Bonaventurae, 1898). This distinction be-

tions slanderous falsehoods at least one other time, the staple of Margery's reprovers is the fourth kind of slander: "quando [detractor] illud quod est bonum de se dicit mala intentione factum"[38] (when the detractor claims that something good in itself was done out of an evil intention). That intention is the "hidden evil" he exposes. Usually, Margery's slanderers attribute to a worldly will and worldly intentions the affective practices that she sees as the "grace and virtu wyth whech sche was endued throw þe strength of þe Holy Gost." That is, they accuse her of hypocrisy, as in the first instance of such slander that followed her tears of contrition:

> Hir wepyng was so plentyuows and so contwnyng þat mech pepul wend [thought] þat sche mygth wepyn & leuyn whan sche wold [leave off weeping when she wanted to], and þerfor many men / seyd sche was a fals ypocryte & wept for þe world for socowr & for worldly good.

Against their construal the *Book* sets where her will and mind are directed when she weeps:

> Sche bethowt hir fro hir chyldhod for hir vnkyndnes as ower Lord wold put it in hir mende ful many a tyme. And þan, sche beheldyng hir owyn wykkednes, sche mygth but sorwyn [could only sorrow] and wepyn & euyr preyn for mercy & forȝeuenes.[39]

Whereas the *Book* grounds Margery's early "worship" in communally valued externals like lineage, clothing, and economic success, its slandered Margery has no way to manifest publicly her internal experience before and during her extraordinary public acts of affective piety, and she has no way to validate their divine cause. As a result, battles over intentions and causes follow these acts wherever she goes. In the *Book*'s account of her conversations with the saintly Richard Caister, she explains that when mystical conversation with the saints and the Trinity is so sweet that it causes her to fall down, to wrest her body about, and to weep, others slander her, claiming a natural or diabolical ("sum euyl spyryt vexid hir") cause for her conduct. The bouts of passionate weeping that began with her envisioning the Passion and Crucifixion in Jerusalem are attributed to these causes, plus drunkenness, "and so ich man as hym thowte," a phrase that recalls the

tween *honor* and *fama,* traceable to Thomas Aquinas (*Summa* 2.2.72.1) but not observed by all writers on *convicium,* suggests that those who rebuke others improperly intend to rob them of the public repute others pay them in response to their virtue, while slanderers blacken a reputation that may be favorable or not (or, of course, mixed). Anne Grondeux demonstrates that this ancient sense of *fama* persists in the Middle Ages. "Le vocabulaire latin de la renommée au Moyen Âge," *Médiévales* 24 (1993): 15–16.

38. Bromyard, *Summa,* D.6.2.
39. *Book,* 2 and 13.

variable, speaker-generated gossip that followed her commercial failures. Like slanderous lies, this gossip about Margery's supposed evil intentions becomes the matter of public reproof. In contrast to these slanderers and reprovers, there are always those, like Caister, Julian of Norwich, and "gostly men" in Jerusalem, who discern that "þer was no disseyte [deceit] in hir maner of leuyng" because Margery discloses to them her affective and visionary life, especially her contrition for her sins and "compassyon wyth holy meditacyon & hy contemplacyon, & ful many holy spechys & dalyanwns [intimate conversation] þat owyr Lord spak to hir sowle."[40]

The *Book* can justly label the speech of Margery's critics as slander, exposing their evil propensity to envy her and their evil intention to denigrate her *fama* as a devout woman, precisely because they speak about her will, her intentions, and the other causes of her actions while lacking the direct, intimate knowledge of her that her spiritual advisers have:

> Oþer whech had no knowlach of hir maner of gouernawns, saue only be sygth owtforth er ellys be jangelyng [idle talk, gossip] of oþer personys, peruertyng þe dom of trewth [truthful judgment], seyd ful euyl of hir & causyd hir to haue mech enmyte & meche dysese [anxiety], mor þan sche xuld haue ellys had, had her euyl langage ne ben.[41]

The phrase "dom of trewth" invokes the basic semantics promulgated by pastoral writers on speech, both deviant and normative. Following scholastic theology, they argue that truth in perception consists of matching the knower's mind to the thing perceived (*adaequatio* or *aequatio* or *similitudo*) and that speaking the truth then involves the further matching of mind to the conventionally appropriate linguistic sign. This labor of achieving mental and verbal correspondence is an act of will and thus inherently ethical.[42] But the mental work of ascertaining what is true cannot discern Margery's will and intentions nor the causes of her extraordinary public displays of piety without knowing their vast affective and visionary foundation. To attempt such a reading is proof of an evil disposition of will and then, when the reading is spoken, of an evil intention. As a preacher says to the people who murmur against Margery's outcries during his sermon,[43] they are bound to avoid mortal sins of speech by judging ("demyn," the verbal form of "dom") such morally ambiguous conduct as good.[44] Moreover, "dom of trewth" indicates that Margery's slanderers choose to usurp God's role as judge when they pass on her a "dom"—a judgment, a

---

40. Ibid., 40, 69, 32–33, 42 (see also 69, 74, 83–84).
41. Ibid., 43.
42. Craun, *Lies*, 122–23.
43. On murmur as undeserved obloquy, see Craun, *Lies*, 77–112.
44. *Book*, 165.

sentence, a verdict (*Middle English Dictionary* 2)—a usurpation that slanderers always commit, insists Guillaume Peyraut in his widely read *Summa de vitiis*.[45] For these reasons the *Book* can label the secularizing, naturalizing, and demonizing of Margery's conduct as slander without itself slandering the speakers: their words are manifestly deviant in will and intention, just as they are false in what they signify about her inner life.

Like pastoral discourse on *detractio,* the *Book* is concerned to trace the destructive consequences of slander: the loss of *fama* itself and what that entails. While the set pastoral definition of *detractio* as "denigratio aliene fame"[46] may convey only the blackening of a reputation, pastoral writers usually develop the topos with a standard figure that clearly signifies loss of good name or good repute, the *bona fama* examined by Thomas Kuehn, F. R. P. Akehurst, and Jeffrey Bowman in this volume.[47] The slanderer, the treatises reason, sins more grievously than a thief because when he takes away a person's *fama* he steals a greater good than temporal riches—in fact, the greatest of earthly goods.[48] While goods may be restored, good name can never be: people will believe the falsehood of one loose speaker rather than the contrary protestations of twenty.[49] Thus, *fama* is commodified by the pastoral tradition, made an object valuable in personal relations—a point to be developed when we look at the constraints placed on fraternal correction. With her good name as a holy woman lost, Margery loses the trust of others who aspire to holiness, much as a man of ill repute loses the trust of court officials.[50] As a result, she is abandoned by former confreres, whom she needs, while on her many journeys/pilgrimages, for food, for spiritual conversation, and for protection from rape, robbery, and hostile officials. Moreover, the loss of good name—and surely the denigrating of her reputation that leads up to it—also inflicts pain in itself. When she worries that virgins will dance more merrily in heaven than she will, the voice of Christ renews a promise that she "xuldyst noon oþer Purgatory han þan slawndyr & spech of þe world." Although a woman with sex-

45. Guillaume Peyraut, *Summa de vitiis* (Cologne, 1479), fol. H1 recto.

46. Carpenter, *Destructorium,* fol. Dvii recto; *Expositio,* fol. 72r; Astesano, *Summa,* fol. 83r.

47. Kuehn, "*Fama* as a Legal Status"; Akehurst, "Good Name"; Bowman, "Infamy and Proof."

48. Peyraut, *Summa de vitiis,* fol. G10 recto; Bromyard, *Summa,* D.6.4.

49. Carpenter, *Destructorium,* fol. Dvii verso. The analogy of fame and temporal goods is developed in a typical way by the vernacular commentary on the Decalogue *Dives et Pauper* (1405–10), where slander is treated as a violation of "Thou shalt not steal": "A good name is betere þan many richesses and good grace and good loue pasith gold and syluer, Prouer. xxii [Proverbs 22:1]. For þe beste iowel and mest richesse þat man or woman may han upon erde is to had a good name and loue and grace among his neyзeborys and in þe contre. And þerfor bacbyterys, lesyngmongerys and wyckid spekerys þat robbyn man or woman of her goode name and bryngyn hem in wyckyd fame, þey ben þe warsete þeuys upon erde." *Dives et Pauper,* ed. Priscilla H. Barnum, vol. 1, part 2, Early English Text Society, o.s., 280 (Oxford: Oxford University Press, 1980), 131–32.

50. Bowman, "Infamy and Proof"; Kuehn, "*Fama* as a Legal Status," in this volume.

ual experience, she will be elevated to the status of a virgin because of how much pain slander inflicts.[51] Throughout the *Book*, Margery embraces slander as redemptive, even meritorious, suffering.[52]

Like slander, the other Sin of the Tongue that the *Book* couples with uncharitable reproof, chiding (*contentio*), accuses another person of sin, but it does so directly in the course of a dispute and in anger, not out of the victim's hearing and in envy.[53] Though Margery's enemies are not often labeled as chiders, the *Book*'s incidents of chiding are pivotal in Margery's life because they bring her into conflict with males of beyond-the-ordinary authority and power, not the laypeople (usually), friars, and parish priests who tend to slander her. These chiders react against her assumption of religious authority as religious teacher, expounder of Scripture, and corrector of sin. In the pastoral tradition, chiding/contention often involves dispute over what is true.[54] Thus, like reproof, it can be either vicious or virtuous: vicious if it struggles against the truth or maintains what is false (a sin of *significatio*) and virtuous if it argues for the truth and attacks what is false. It also may become vicious if those arguing for the truth do so with unsuitable harshness, transgressing rhetorical bounds.[55] In the most notorious conflict over what is true early in Margery's life of wandering, when she is visiting English monastic houses for her spiritual benefit, the *Book* identifies as her chiders none other than the monks and priests of Christ Church, Canterbury, who sin against her in both ways.

Although it is Margery's weeping in the cathedral, according to the *Book*, that sparks an initial rebuke from the monks and priests, the verbal conflict of *contentio* begins when an old monk who had been the rich and much-feared treasurer of a queen (probably John Kynton, chancellor of Queen Joanna, wife of Henry IV)[56] draws Margery into speaking about God:

> "What kanst þow seyn of God?" "Ser," sche seyth, "I wyl boþe speke of hym & heryn of hym," rehersyng þe monk a story of Scriptur. The munke seyde, "I wold þow wer closyd in an hows of ston þat þer schuld no man speke wyth þe."[57]

51. *Book*, 33, 119, 51.
52. E.g., ibid., 57.
53. In his pastoral exposition of the Sins of the Tongue, Chaucer's Parson also couples chiding and uncharitable reproof. Akin in their open and boorish assault on others, both inflict pain and threaten social cohesion. *The Riverside Chaucer*, ed. Larry Benson et al., 3rd ed. (Boston: Houghton Mifflin, 1987), X.621–34.
54. *The Book of Vices and Virtues*, ed. W. Nelson Francis, Early English Text Society, o.s., 217 (London: Oxford University Press, 1942), 63; *Jacob's Well*, ed. Arthur Brandeis, Early English Text Society, o.s., 115 (London: Kegan Paul, Tench, Trübner, 1900), 154; Astesano, *Summa*, fol. 119v.
55. Bartolomeo, *Summa*, fol. 23r; Astesano, *Summa*, fol. 119v.
56. *Book*, 270.
57. Ibid., 27.

EDWIN D. CRAUN

Thanks to several decades of scholarship on women and clerics, the social dynamic of this exchange needs little gloss: the unlettered bourgeois wife whose mastery of Scripture leads a powerful and lordly man, most likely a cleric, to desire to isolate and so silence her—whether the house of stone be a prison or an anchorage (perhaps, too, a community of nuns).[58] Margery's response in the *Book* is a direct, spirited, and public act of fraternal correction, designed to amend his error: "'A, ser,' sche seyd, '3e shuld meynteyn Goddys seruawntys, & 3e arn þe fyrst þat helden a-3ens hem. Ouyr Lord amend 3ow.'" This further assumption of religious authority provokes a young monk to claim that she speaks Scriptures either by agency of the Holy Ghost or of a devil because as a woman she could not have it "of þiself." Margery responds with an exemplum, a basic instrument of religious instruction, which all too clearly glosses their speech as the sin of chiding, as a contentious verbal assault rooted in contempt. It also establishes her religious superiority as someone who can even use chiding and reproof for her spiritual benefit (as she does with slander). In the exemplum, Margery directly parallels her situation with that of a man whose confessor enjoined him, as a penance, to hire men to chide him and also to reprove him for his sins but who, when he is mocked "a-mong many gret men as now ben hir," responded that he was getting his penance without expending any silver. Then, Margery thanks her chiders for providing her with the "schame, skorne, & despyte" that enable her to atone for her sins. The monks' response is to call her a "fals lollare" and threaten to burn her as a heretic.[59] In the telling of the exemplum, as Cynthia Ho argues, the *Book*'s Margery converts herself into an exemplary figure.[60]

At the beginning of the next chapter, looking back on the whole incident, the *Book* retrospectively reads the monks' chiding as their response to Margery's practicing fraternal correction and her speaking about Scripture: "Than thys creatur þowt it was ful mery to be reprevyd for Goddys lofe; it was to hir gret solas and cowmfort whan sche was chedyn & fletyn [rebuked, quarrelled with noisily] for þe lofe of Ihesu for repreuyng of synne, for spekyng of vertu, for comownyng in Scriptur whech sche lerynd in sermownys & be comownyng wyth clerkys."[61] So, the *Book* securely identifies her contested speech with the Canterbury clerics as clerically sanc-

<hr/>

58. Ibid., 270.
59. Ibid., 28. Here, as clearly elsewhere in the *Book,* the term *lollare* may carry the sense developed by Anne Middleton: "practicing religion out of place." In her copious weeping, her practice of fraternal correction, and her exemplum, Margery has, to invoke Middleton's words, "violated or revised the boundaries, the conventional and wholly unstated social 'rules.'" "Acts of Vagrancy: The C Version 'Autobiography' and the Statute of 1388," in *Written Work: Langland, Labor, and Authorship,* ed. Steven Justice and Katherine Kirby-Fulton (Philadelphia: University of Pennsylvania Press, 1997), 284.
60. Cynthia Ho, "Margery Reads Exempla," *Medieval Perspectives* 8 (1993): 149.
61. *Book,* 24.

tioned, even clerically enjoined, and she deftly attributes her contested knowledge of Scripture to what the post-Lateran IV clergy provided for lay education: preaching and catechesis. By doing so, the *Book* also firmly grounds its labeling of their speech as chiding: their speech resists the truth about Margery's own speech, her obedience to pastoral injunctions, and her orthodoxy; it also does so immoderately. Moreover, as falsehood spoken openly, it also takes on the nature of unjust reproof, intended to take away Margery's honor.

This early dispute raises acutely in the *Book* the vexed question of how to distinguish fraternal correction or charitable reproof from chiding and uncharitable reproof (no doubt the Canterbury monks would have labeled their own speech "correction" and Margery's "chiding"), just as the incident in London near the close of the *Book* raises the question of how to distinguish it from slander and uncharitable reproof. (The latter incident ends with Margery charitably correcting dinner guests who slanderously repeat the herring-and-pike anecdote she has just endured in the streets.) Pastoral texts on the Sins of the Tongue readily acknowledge that some speakers mask the deviant with the supposedly normative. Abusive and insulting reproof, Guillaume Peyraut argues at length, is often deceptively mingled with correction of sin in order to insult others, while public exposure of hidden sin under the guise of correction is commonly forbidden as treacherous slander.[62] On the other hand, pastoral texts concede that if a harsh reprover intends to correct sin and not to destroy honor, *convicium* is a venial, not a mortal, sin—or no sin at all.[63] And, as we shall see, certain circumstances justify public exposure of sin during correction. But such distinctions turn on the speaker's disposition of will and intention, not only because that defines a deviant act of speech but also because fraternal correction springs from the charitable will and the intention to prompt others to amend their lives. Since such inner desire and inner-directedness cannot be directly known by others, how can the *Book*'s Margery practice fraternal correction without being accused of the slander, chiding, and unjust and uncharitable reproof of which the *Book* accuses her adversarial townsmen or her fellow pilgrims or the monks at Christ Church, Canterbury?

In the *Book of Margery Kempe*, as we have seen, Margery's safety, indeed her life, depends upon manifesting unswervingly that it is indeed clerically sanctioned fraternal correction she is practicing when she rebukes Arch-

---

62. Peyraut, *Summa de vitiis*, fol. H6 recto; *Speculum Christiani*, 234; "frende ne sybbe who so byholdeth his lothely lokys," British Library MS Add. 30944, fol. 152r–v; "Seynt Iohon þe euangelist in his boke of pryvytes," British Library MS Harl. 6571, fol. 64v.

63. Heinrich, *Summa*, fol. 121r–v; Bartolomeo, *Summa*, fol. 23v–24r; John Acton, *Septuplum*, Caius College Cambridge MS 282, 3.6.

EDWIN D. CRAUN

bishop Arundel. Such is the case later, in a more extended encounter with
Archbishop Henry Bowet of York. In these and other incidents where the
Book presents Margery correcting sin in those who are *praelati,* as indeed
when she rebukes sin in laypeople of her own social standing,[64] she makes
a proper will and intention manifest by scrupulously adhering to the constraints that the pastoral tradition firmly established to govern fraternal
correction in general, but especially the correction of a *praelatus* by a *subditus.*[65] In this, the literalness that Nancy Partner finds characteristic of
Margery[66] stands her in good stead as someone who aspires to a life of active charity in a time and often in places where relations between the clergy
and the laity were fraught with danger. The impeccable reproofs that she
offers not only protect her from retaliation by clerical superiors but also
allow her to fulfill her pastorally dictated obligation of charity: offering correction to fellow Christians while preserving their *fama,* recognized as a
major and cherished human good in the pastoral tradition.

The most fundamental pastoral constraint on speech which imposes
blame on another is that a clerically designated sin must be its object.
About this the *Book* leaves no doubt when it recounts Margery's and her
husband's arrival at Lambeth Palace:

> And, as þei comyn in-to þe halle at aftyr-noon, ther wer many of þe Erche-
> bysshoppys clerkys & oþer rekles men boþ swyers [squires] & ȝemen [yeomen]
> whech sworyn many gret oþis & spokyn many rekles wordys, & þis creatur
> boldly vndyrname [rebuked] hem & seyd þe schuld been dampnyd but [un-
> less] þei left her [their] sweryng & oþer synnes þat þei vsyd.[67]

To speak such oaths, like Chaucer's Pardoner's "'By Goddes precious
herte,' and 'By his nayles' / And 'By the blood of Crist that is in Hayles,'"
is to treat God contemptuously, to reduce him to human level, to deny him

64. *Book,* 244–45.
65. Jan Ziolkowski and Dan Smail have suggested to me that Margery Kempe might simply be negotiating this situation by following her society's basic principles of social interac-
tion rather than consciously hewing to pastoral guidelines. That might indeed have been true
of the (or an) historical Margery Kempe. However, the *Book* quite specifically types her speech
in the most taxing of situations as correction of sin: "'ȝe schal answer for hem les þan ȝe correctyn hem'" (to Arundel [37]); "desiryng thorw þe spirit of charite her correccyon" (of her
response to the London dinner guests who repeat the old slander about her using fasting to
lay claim to the more desirable fish [245]); "hauyng trust of hys a-mendyng . . . wyth sharp
wordys of correpcyon" (of her speech to her wayward son [223]). Especially when the *Book's*
references link her words of correction to charity and her desire for sinners' amendment, it
is surely constructing her as someone who reads her own social encounters with sinners in
pastoral terms. And surely, as Dan Smail has also suggested, the pastoral rules were formulated out of late medieval society's social ground rules: the pastoral writers were reading
(Smail's language) their own culture.
66. Nancy F. Partner, "Reading the Book of Margery Kempe," *Exemplaria* 3 (1991): 66.
67. *Book,* 36; see also 110, 120, 124.

transcendence, to blaspheme.[68] It is also to violate the second commandment, as Margery sometimes points out. So grave a sin was such swearing that John Bromyard illustrates the obligation of all people to correct sinners by the example of swearers, citing the decretal attributed to Gratian, which states that if anyone does not publicly denounce swearers, he or she also becomes subject to God's condemnation.[69] No doubt as the result of such an extensive and harsh clerical campaign, Margery's correction of swearing throughout the *Book*, though it elicits various responses, is never rejected as unfounded. Indeed, choosing such a widely condemned act also saves her from the very accusations of misjudging others that the *Book* directs at her slanderers, who speculate about the cause and intent behind ambiguous signs, like her public weeping.

Although this canon, disseminated in pastoral materials, may license Margery's correction of the retinue in the *Book*, what of her correction of Arundel himself? The same decretal, and Bromyard's version of it, specifically license correcting a bishop if he neglects to amend such swearing: "si episcopus ista emendare neglexerit, acerrime corripiatur" and "Et episcopus qui negligit eos [iurantes] emendare a crimine corripiatur." Moreover, a bishop, as the head of a *familia*, was particularly bound to correct the sins of his *familiares*, those belonging to his household. According to Bromyard, the *familiares* of great prelates tend to sin quite freely because they believe that bearing a prelate's livery protects them from correction like a shield or a letter of safe conduct. Yet precisely because they are servants of a great prelate, Bromyard argues, others are likely to imitate their dissoluteness in clothing, words, and character, exactly what Margery rebukes in episcopal servants: extravagant clothing in the bishop of Worcester's hall, oaths at Archbishop Bowet's chapel at Cawood, and, of course, at Lambeth Palace.[70] Prelates who neglect to correct their *familiares* become subject to God's punishments: temporal suffering, *infamia*, and eternal damnation.[71] While John Bromyard's arguments are extended and firmly grounded in the canons, even the most rudimentary pastoral texts insist on the prelate's special responsibility to correct his retinue.[72] Thus, Margery's correction of Arundel in the *Book* is as authorized by canon law and pastoral writing as her correction of his swearing *familiares*, while her stress on prelatical responsibility, even accountability, before God is that of *auctoritates*:

68. Chaucer, *Canterbury Tales*, VI.651–62; Edwin Craun, "'Inordinata Locutio': Blasphemy in Pastoral Literature, 1200–1500," *Traditio* 39 (1983): 149–52.

69. Bromyard, *Summa*, C.16.2; *Corpus iuris canonici*, ed. A. Friedberg, vol. 1 (Leipzig: Tauchnitz, 1879), 22.1.10, p. 863.

70. *Book*, 109, 123, 36.

71. Bromyard, *Summa*, C.16.3.

72. *Book of Vices*, 200; *Speculum vitae*, ed. J. W. Smeltz (Ph.D. diss., Duquesne University, 1977).

"My Lord, owyr alderes Lord [Lord of all] al-myty God hath not ȝon [given] ȝow ȝowyr benefys & gret goodys of þe world to maynten wyth hys tretowrys [maintain those who betray him] & hem þat slen hym euery day be gret othys sweryng. Ȝe schal answer for hem les þan [unless] ȝe correctyn hem or ellys put hem owt of ȝowr seruyse."[73]

So textualized is the *Book*'s life of Margery, so fully conformed to authoritative writing, that she follows pastoral constraints on fraternal correction in other key ways. Of course, she corrects only what she knows to be true, unlike her slanderers, and the sin she corrects is one that she does not practice herself, both key provisos.[74] Above all, the *Book* makes it clear that Margery seeks the amendment of the sinners, the end or purpose of fraternal correction, what makes it a virtuous act: "hoc est proprie fraterna correctio quae ordinatur ad emendationem delinquentis."[75] So, when Margery suggests two remedies for the archbishop's complicity in his retinue's sinful oaths, correcting his men successfully or dismissing them from his service, she is manifesting the intent to amend his—and their— sin, which clearly constitutes her speech as normative fraternal correction. The very same remedies for a sinning episcopal retinue appear in the *Liber Celestis* of Margery's beloved Saint Bridget: "For if [a bishop] knawe one of his meine sin dedeli [that one of his retinue has committed deadly sin], he suld stir him to amendment. And, if he will noght amend him, he suld put him awai fro him; for, if he hald him still for his bodeli comfort or profite, he sall not be blameless of his sin."[76] In this, as in her innocence of swearing, the *Book*'s Margery follows ordinary pastoral constraints, delivering an impeccable reproof to the peccable archbishop, one which obviates any sense that she might be trespassing in correcting the trespasses of her Christian brother.

In addition to these restraints, which ought to be observed in all cases of fraternal correction in the *Book*, Margery follows scrupulously the particular ones governing *subditi* who correct *praelati*. Such speech, pastoral writers insist, ought to be tempered to suit the difference in status: reverent and meek, not impudent ("non cum protervia et duritia. Sed cum mansuetudine et reverentia").[77] Accordingly, the *Book* takes pains to note that Margery addresses Archbishop Arundel in exactly that way: "seying wyth reuerens, 'My Lord.'" In fact, she tactfully waits until she has shown

73. *Book*, 37.
74. Bromyard, *Summa*, C.16.3; "Pro quo," fols. 153v–154r; Biard, *Distinctiones*, fols. 28v–29r; Robert Holcot, *Super sapientiam Salomonis* (Speyer, 1483), *lectio* 175; "Vani sunt omnes homines," British Library MS Landsdowne 385, fols. 79v–80r.
75. Astesano, *Summa*, fol. 121v; Carpenter, *Destructorium*, fol. Ki recto.
76. *The Liber Celestis of Bridget of Sweden*, ed. Roger Ellis, Early English Text Society, o.s., 291 (Oxford: Oxford University Press, 1987), 197.
77. Bartolomeo, *Summa*, fol. 24v; "Pro quo," fol. 154v; see *Omne bonum*, fol. 436r.

"þis worshepful lord hir maner of leuyng" and has appealed to him as the authority who can grant her two petitions.[78] Even more crucial was the normative practice of rebuking superiors in private, not in public. Whether fraternal correction was to be private or public was endlessly debated in pastoral literature, and various kinds of circumstances were to govern the speaker's decision.[79] This issue was particularly forced in the case of *praelati* by Paul's public rebuke of Peter, the prince of the apostles, when Peter broke his practice of eating with the Gentiles of Antioch because some Judaizers had come from Jerusalem (Gal. 2:11–14). Commentators engaged in fierce debate over the propriety of such public correction: most notoriously and influentially, Jerome, who argued that Peter had not erred and so Paul's speech was not truly a rebuke, and Augustine, who argued the opposite—a scorching exchange of letters.[80] In commentaries and glosses on Galatians from the *Glossa ordinaria* on, and then in pastoral texts, Augustine's reading is appropriated to argue that *minores* or *subditi* may rebuke publicly *majores* or *praelati*, but only if their sins are manifest and if they subvert the force of evangelical teaching.[81] Otherwise, a superior was to be rebuked privately and reverently ("in occulto monisset reverenter"). Arundel's toleration of swearing in his great hall might be construed as manifest sin that subverts evangelical teaching, but Margery tactfully chooses to rebuke him alone in his garden, a practice which saves her speech from any taint of the kind of slander that broadcast her supposed "hidden evil" of hypocrisy as far as London. Small wonder that the *Book* has him listening to her "ful benyngly & mekely," as pastoral texts insisted that the person being corrected should respond when correction was delivered properly.[82]

The *Book* presents Margery's correction of Archbishop Arundel's fellow archbishop and fellow zealous pursuer of Lollards, Henry Bowet of York, as far more difficult for her to negotiate. She has been slandered at York so egregiously that former spiritual confreres turn her away, and the slander has been authorized from the minister's pulpit. In reaction to this slander, and to accusations of Lollardy, she is being publicly examined by Bowet on the orthodoxy of her beliefs and practice. She has risked conviction by rebuking the archbishop's retinue for swearing great oaths at the very moment when its members call her a Lollard. So, Margery fears for her life. Then, Bowet, quite unlike Arundel, sets up an adversarial exchange of words by speaking sharply to her:

78. *Book,* 36.

79. Astesano, *Summa,* fols. 123v–125v; Carpenter, *Destructorium,* fol. Kii verso.

80. Augustine, Bishop of Hippo, *S. Aureli Augustini Hipponiensis episcopi Epistulae,* ed. A. Goldbacher, Corpus Scriptorum Ecclesiasticorum Latinorum 34 (Vienna: F. Tempsky, 1895), 40, 75, 82.

81. Edwin Craun, "'3e by Peter and Poul!': Lewte and the Practice of Fraternal Correction," *The Yearbook of Langland Studies* 15 (2001): 15–25.

82. Astesano, *Summa,* fol. 123r–v; Bromyard, *Summa,* C.16.5; Biard, *Distinctiones* fol. 28v.

EDWIN D. CRAUN

At þe last þe seyd Erchebischop cam in-to þe Chapel wyth hys clerkys, & scharply / he seyde to hir, "Why gost þu in white? Art þu a mayden?" Sche, kne-lyng on hir knes be-for hym, seyd, "Nay ser, I am no mayden; I am a wife." He comawndyd hys mene to fettyn [fetch] a peyr of feterys & seyd sche xuld & ben feteryd, for sche was a fals heretyke.

After Bowet examines Margery on the Articles of Faith, to which she gives impeccably orthodox replies, his reference to the slander of her pro-vokes her to a rebuke that verges on the problematical:

"I am euyl enformyd of þe; I her seyn þu art a ryth wikked woman." And sche seyd a-geyn, "Ser, so I her seyn þat ʒe arn a wikkyd man. And, ʒyf ʒe ben as wykkyd as men seyn, ʒe xal neuyr come in Heuyn les þan [unless] ʒe amende ʒow whil ʒe ben her." Than seyd he ful boistowsly, "Why, þow, what sey men of me." Sche answeryd, "Oþer men, syr, can telle ʒow wel a-now [enough]."[83]

In contrast to her correction of Arundel earlier in the *Book*, this is pub-lic; it relies on hearsay, not direct knowledge; it seems retaliatory, often the purpose of feigned correction; and it seems to violate the pastoral prohi-bition of insult while correcting (except when light, moderated insults are necessary and do not threaten the *honor* or *fama* of the sinner).[84] Yet the *Book* has Margery manage to identify her speech as fraternal correction of a superior (*praelatus*) by addressing Bowet as "Ser" and by indicating that she intends his amendment. Moreover, she deftly avoids accepting the hearsay in this tit-for-tat exchange. Even more important, her refusal to name a specific sin satisfies the primary requirement of public rebuke of anyone: that it not divulge a secret sin, unless (it is sometimes argued) that sin immediately endangers others.[85] Thus, in the *Book*'s second major in-stance of correcting a high *praelatus,* as in the private correction of Arun-del, she avoids deftly any counteraccusation of slander, which in this case might endanger her, casting her as undermining a clerical authority that seeks to fulfill its pastoral responsibility of correcting her as a public de-viant.

During her examination in the *Book*, Margery mentions the specific sins of her priestly interrogators only once, and she does so with an approved pastoral practice: an exemplum. John Bromyard exemplifies the prudence necessary for any kind of correction with the prophet Nathan's use of a *cautum exemplum* when he confronts King David with arranging Uriah's death:

---

83. *Book,* 124–25.
84. Acton, *Septuplum,* 3.6; Heinrich, *Summa,* fol. 121r–v.
85. Bartolomeo, *Summa,* fols. 24v–25r; Astesano, *Summa,* fol. 124r–v; *Omne bonum,* fol. 463v; Simon of Boraston, *Distinctiones theologicae,* Bodleian Library MS Bodleian 216, fol. 32r.

206

quando voluit regem david de adulterio et homicidio corripere:caute propo-
suit exemplum de diuite qui habebat oues plurimas:et de paupere qui non
habuit nisi unum:quam diues pro peregrino sibi adueniente occidit.Ait ergo
regi.Responde mihi iudicium:qui respondit.Viuit dominus quoniam filius
mortis est vir qui fecit hoc.Cui propheta.Tu est ille vir. . . . Quia vero pulcro
exemplo et quasi ex iudicio proprio concludit.gratanter et salubriter repre-
hensionem admisit:dicens.peccaui domino. Huiusmodi igitur exemplo caute
et qaestione precendente in talium correctione seu admonitione est proce-
dendum:ut ipsi se iudicent quasi in alieno negocio:et contra arguentem non
irascantur.[86]

[When he desired to correct King David for adultery and murder, warily he
related an exemplum about a rich man who had many sheep and a poor man
who had only one, which the rich man killed for a stranger who was just ar-
riving. Therefore, he said to the king: "Reply with a judgment." The king answered: "As the Lord lives, the man who has done this is a child of death." The
prophet said to him: "You are that man." . . . Indeed, because Nathan argued
by means of a fine exemplum and as if from the king's own judgment, the king
joyfully and savingly admitted his own fault, saying "I have sinned against the
Lord." Therefore, correction or admonition of such people ought to be carried out by a careful exemplum of this kind and an antecedent question so
that they judge themselves, as if in an affair which does not pertain to them,
and are not angry with their reprover.]

The "talium" suggests that the threateningly powerful, especially, ought
to be corrected by means of such an exemplum, which elicits self-con-
demnation by the guilty, saving the corrector from imposing explicit
blame. When Margery is accused of telling vile tales about priests and commanded by Bowet to present one, the *Book* has her speak generally of a
priest. Observing a bear pull down a lovely pear tree, devour its blossoms,
and then defecate, the priest is told by a pilgrim that he, as a priest, is the
pear tree, and that he, as a sinner, is the bear. In the exemplum, Margery
has the pilgrim accuse the priest of the whole range of sins that she usually
attributes to worldly prelates: buying and selling, gluttony, lechery and "un-
clennesse" [which may mean masturbation], slander, swearing, and lying.[87] The three verbal sins, of course, have just been committed against
her by the Archbishop's "clerkes." Not surprisingly, the *Book* reports that
her chief inquisitor tells the archbishop, "þis tale smytyth me to þe hert";
he later comes privately to Margery to beg forgiveness for opposing her.
As in her rebuke of Archbishop Bowet, her strict hewing to pastoral prac-

---

86. Bromyard, *Summa*, C.16.3. Also *Distinctiones pro sermonibus*, Bodleian Library Oxford
MS Rawl. C.899, fol. 144r; *Distinctiones exemplorum*, Bodleian Library Oxford MS Canon
Script. Ecc. 118, fol. 11v.
 87. *Book*, 126–27.

tices, here using the exemplum to move a powerful person to rebuke himself, enables her to escape any accusation of committing a verbal sin while she successfully brings the inquisitor to repentance for his sins, including those against her.

Behind this exemplum (a pastoral practice the *Book* had earlier presented Margery as using in rebuking the monks of Canterbury) and behind all the pastoral constraints she observes so expertly in the *Book* lies the pastoral tradition's explicit acknowledgement that correction should not damage the sinner's *fama*. As Nicholas of Lyra glosses Matt. 18:15, the precept authorizing fraternal correction:

> debet tentare si possit fratrem emendare absque detrimento sue fame:quia fama computatur inter maiora bona hominis circa virtutes:et ideo corrigens fratrem debet quantum potest conseruare eius famam.[88]

> [One ought to attempt, if he can, to amend his brother without damage to his good name because good name is reckoned among the more important goods of men (together with the virtues); and therefore he who corrects his brother ought to preserve his fame as far as he can.]

A good name, pastoral writers recognize, is valuable (*utilis*) in temporal affairs, and its loss brings many other temporal losses, both to the sinner and to others associated with him or her.[89] (No doubt they are assuming the legal and commercial uses of *bona fama* developed by Kuehn, Akehurst, and Hanawalt.) Rebuking a superior publicly when it is not justified involves defaming him, taking away his good name. To do so is to be deviant in will and intention and to be responsible for the evil consequences, all three characteristics of sinful speech. If Margery is to correct sinners throughout the *Book* without incurring the sin of slander or chiding, she must speak to sinners in private if possible; address only what the clergy identifies as sin and what she knows to be true; be reverent, especially to *praelati*, and avoid harsh insults; resort to exempla where the official power differential is great; and avoid divulging hidden sins, especially those of her superiors. Only then can her speech have the authority vested in fraternal correction by the clergy.

The Book of Margery Kempe constructs its Margery as an exemplary figure, making a case for her as a holy woman, perhaps even (a minority position, to be sure) a saint who should be officially recognized.[90] Pastoral cate-

88. Nicholas of Lyra, *Postilla super totum Biblicum*, vol. 4 (1492; reprint, Frankfurt am Main: Minerva, 1971), fol. cvii recto.

89. *Omne bonum*, fol. 436v; Astesano, *Summa*, fol. 83r.

90. Wilson, "Communities," 159–64; Kathleen Ashley, "Historicizing Margery: *The Book of Margery Kempe*," *Journal of Medieval and Early Modern Studies* 28 (1998): 371; Susan Dickman, "A Showing of God's Grace: *The Book of Margery Kempe*," in *Mysticism and Spirituality in Medieval*

chesis on deviant speech and on fraternal correction frequently directs this rhetorical shaping during Margery's encounters with the less rigorous. The *Book* invokes clerical norms designed to regulate public speech in order to refute slanderous lies; restore the will, intention, and causes behind her public acts of affective piety; and retrieve her unjustly blackened reputation and her stolen good name as a holy woman. It may do so belatedly and outside the oral networks that constituted good or ill repute in fifteenth-century England, but it does so with the authority and permanence that writing possessed in mercantile and ecclesiastical culture. Thus, like Christine de Pizan's *Livre des fais et bonnes meurs du roi Charles V le Sage,* in Lori Walters's argument, the *Book* shapes gossip to its own ends, containing it, much as *Lanval* contains threatening talk in Richard Horvath's reading.[91] Margery observes the pastoral constraints on correcting sin with her characteristic literal-mindedness, retentiveness, desire for clerical approval, and aspirations to live charitably. While negotiating impeccably her encounters with the sinning archbishops certainly is exemplary, Margery is also depicted as manifesting active charity simply by correcting others' sins, by participating in what André Vauchez calls "the church's exaltation of apostolic action." Starting in the early thirteenth century, fraternal correction was a key clerical instrument for involving the laity in the pastoral movement's goals: "to inspire correct belief and correct behavior."[92] At crucial moments in the *Book*'s life of a holy woman, when she exposes vice in her social equals and *praelati,* clerical catechesis on fraternal correction authorizes her speech in the very process of imposing constraints on it, constraints that the *Book*'s discredited *malebouches* (slanderers), clerical as well as lay, fail to observe.

England, ed. William F. Pollard and Robert Boenig (Cambridge: D. S. Brewer, 1997), 176. For some of the *Book*'s other rhetorical strategies for validating Margery's exemplarity, see Goodman, "Piety," 348–49; and Wilson, "Communities," 159–64.

91. Lori J. Walters, "Constructing Reputations"; Richard Horvath, "Romancing the Word," both in this volume.

92. André Vauchez, *The Laity in the Middle Ages: Religious Beliefs and Devotional Practices,* trans. Margery Schneider and ed. Daniel Bornstein (Notre Dame, Ind.: University of Notre Dame Press, 2000), 99 and 104.

Conclusion

Thelma Fenster and Daniel Lord Smail

The essays in this volume have illustrated not only that talk played a crucial role in determining status and reputation in medieval society but that there was a good deal of talk about talk. Was there more such talk in medieval societies than in others? The answer is of course that talk adjusts status and conveys perceived information in all human societies, but not all societies acknowledge talk officially as a barometer of moral and legal standing, and not all do so with the kind of foregrounding that distinguishes the medieval evidence. Over a period of centuries, medieval people grappled with talk: they speculated about it, used it, disciplined and regulated it, and left a record of the results. Legal treatises, manuals detailing appropriate and inappropriate speech, literary works and images in the visual and plastic arts—all these easily make up an encyclopedic summa of medieval practice. It is that record and the interplay among its parts, the subject of these chapters, that makes the medieval period so valuable for study.

Stated or implied by nearly all essays in this volume is the understanding that the first element of the *fama* nexus was performance, from which the act of observing was of course inextricable. In the legal sphere, observed actions had practical, real-world consequences, for they created in viewers' minds certain presumptions regarding status and ownership. The usefulness of such knowledge was evident to one of Chris Wickham's twelfth-century Tuscans, who, in the course of efforts to itemize land pledges, remarked, "I have discovered more about them by the teaching of *fama* than by the inspection of documents."[1] There is little doubt that

---

1. Wickham, "*Fama* and the Law."

individuals who tilled land or performed similar tasks knew that their behavior would generate talk and hence presumptions of ownership.

If *fama* had distinct uses in property disputes, it was even more useful in
other situations, because many essential facts were not yet deposited in
state archives or other official repositories and often could be known only
through *fama* or notoriety. Thomas Kuehn has shown how one such essential fact, namely parenthood—something that we may regard as pas-
sively biological—had in fact to be performed. In the eyes of the law, it
mattered little whether Claude was Giovanni's biological father, because
that much biology could not be known in sixteenth-century Europe. What
mattered was that Claude acted in all respects as Giovanni's father, that observers witnessed his behavior, and that they drew the appropriate conclusions. As the authors of the relevant *consilium* remarked, "It cannot be
said that it is an empty rumor or voice, as it arose among honest persons
and is what they truly know." Though initially wary of attributing too much
weight to *fama,* the authors concluded that in this case "there is no doubt
that *fama* yields a full proof."

Medieval jurists resisted giving *fama* a role in making legal facts generally, and they drew a distinction between mere common knowledge and
the truly well known or "notorious." But when they turned their attention
to personal reputation, the role of *fama* was entirely different. One of the
most salient facts known to medieval legal jurisprudence was the fact of infamy, as both Jeffrey Bowman and Ron Akehurst have shown in their contributions. "*Infamia,*" according to Bowman, "was a condition the law
imposed on certain people that entailed legal and social disabilities." The
difficulty arose when it became necessary to prove a person's *infamia,* for
the condition was, in some respects, even less obviously knowable, at least
to the modern observer, than was Claude's status as father. Whole categories of legal infamy were developed in Iberian legislation to make the
process easier for judges: murderers, thieves, poisoners, and those who
consulted sorcerers, for example, were routinely denounced as infamous
by the Visigothic Code. Such infamy was then broadcast through talk. Errors or abuse could creep in at this stage: a passage from the thirteenth-
century *Siete Partidas* notes that "after the tongues of men have placed a
bad name on someone, he never loses it, although he may not deserve it."
In northern France, as Akehurst has noted, the status of being *mal renommé*
also entailed severe legal disabilities. To evaluate a person's reputation, of
course, a judge had to conduct an inquest into what others said or thought
about the person in question—an inquest, in effect, into *fama.*

If Roman canon-law jurists sought to "discipline" powerful *fama,* to use
Kuehn's apt expression, they were not alone. The juridical regulation of
speech, which seems to have developed in tandem with the growth of the
state across the later Middle Ages, was accompanied by Christian moralists'

condemnation of unrestricted talk; to them many kinds of speech could lead only to sin. The very theme of monastic silence may indeed suggest how deeply ingrained was the Christian disapproval of unsupervised tongues. At the same time, a category of idle talk was beginning to be defined as what women did. Female talkers were being turned into scolds, as Sandy Bardsley has shown. Idle talk and "woman"—both fluid and discursively constructable categories—became tautologous: idle, inconsequential talk was what women did, and women had the loose and lascivious tongues that led to idle talk. The moral condemnation and legal regulation of talk, as Bardsley has suggested, typically served to control the speech of women and other social subordinates and inferiors. Such regulation, not a natural feature of human societies, should probably be interpreted as historically constructed and linked to state-building and to encroaching patriarchy.

It is not surprising, then, that women as a category were ritually maligned in emerging law codes. Madeline Caviness and Charles Nelson have brought to light, in their study of the *Sachsenspiegel,* that illustrations accompanying the text put forward a program of negative *fama* for women as a class. Even though the text granted certain freedoms to women (or at least did not explicitly curtail them), the illustrations told a different story, portraying female figures in a consistently negative fashion. The dress and body language of participants in court proceedings were pictured as conforming to types that could be easily recognized and judged just as easily, a practice that shows how opinion could be shaped and good or bad reputation easily conveyed. In that way, the fourteenth-century pictorial record undid the benignity of the thirteenth-century text, repeating a *fama* that had been naturalized: woman's inferiority and untrustworthiness were "true" from nature because they could be found as such in the Bible, and were therefore "what everyone knew." In a sense, too, the conflict between text and image suggests that, as in Kuehn's essay, two versions of *fama* were being promulgated.

Women were not expected to speak with any kind of authority, moreover, as Edwin Craun has shown. Strictures against women's speech, based in good part on the debasement of women, necessarily inform our understanding of the paradox in Margery Kempe's act when she spoke up to Archbishop Thomas Arundel, a "formidable man" and the "highest ecclesiastical authority in England," in Craun's words. Margery rebuked the archbishop's men for swearing and the archbishop for allowing it. Craun has made clear how Margery subtly elevated her own speech above the archbishop's, reversing expected proportions. Affixing blame publicly— in our terms, making *fama*—was a dangerous act, yet Margery was able to do it with impunity. She fashioned herself through her *Book* as an "exemplary" Christian (thus writing her own *fama*), and in so doing she seized privileges that belonged to an elite class of men: control of the moral sphere and moralized knowledge, and the display of learning.

Another type of medieval *fama,* arising not spontaneously but by artful design, was associated with the personalities of authors. Over the period from at least the twelfth century to the fifteenth, a literature that had begun as oral and "of the public" (and therefore anonymous) became more and more the property of the authors who wrote it and signed their names. That process coincided, in certain types of medieval literature, with increasing attention to the author's own personality and reputation. Some texts, as Richard Horvath has observed, nervously negotiated the passage from "speech into text"; the romance form, in particular, displayed a "self-reflexive authorial theatrics" from its earliest days. Horvath has set his readings of the Middle English *Sir Launfal* and *Athelston* against the "self-conscious discourse of late medieval authorship at large." Noting the deployment of language as "speech act," Horvath has demonstrated that, as distinct from theorizing about language, this later medieval literature contextualized its ruminations on speech, seeing it as a thing-in-the-world, an event.

Perhaps the zenith of authorial self-consciousness, as Horvath describes it, are the authors who consciously sought to eradicate any distinction between the fame of their texts and their own personal fame. The Italian writers Petrarch and Dante leap to mind. Theirs was the Roman idea of *fama* as worldly glory, which Dante in particular tried to reconcile with the self-effacement that Christianity demanded.[2] A similar concern for the text as an alternate embodiment of the author, and of more besides, has come out of Lori Walters's analysis of two works by Christine de Pizan, the *Fais et bonnes meurs du sage roi Charles V,* a biography, and the *Advision Cristine,* Christine's autobiography. In *Charles V* especially, Christine invoked the values propounded by the king, an astute promoter of French cultural identity, and she conflated herself and her text with Charles and with France. Her richly imbricated text, as Walters's analysis shows, united the biographer and her subject in preserving the good memory of France as well as Christine's own. And if nineteenth-century evidence can be invoked, it worked. By then, Christine's large and varied oeuvre in poetry and prose was largely overlooked, except for two things: her alleged "feminine" example of devotion to her father and to her children, and her biography of Charles V.[3]

---

2. See Leo Braudy, *The Frenzy of Renown: Fame and Its History* (New York: Oxford University Press, 1986), 226–38.

3. Thelma Fenster and Christine Reno, "*Demoiselle* Christine and Héloïse *La Grande Amoureuse:* Reading Christine de Pizan and Héloïse in the Nineteenth-Century Feminine Press," in "*Riens ne m'est seur que la chose incertaine*": Études sur l'art d'écrire au Moyen Âge offertes à Eric Hicks par ses élèves, collègues, amies, et amis, ed. Jean-Claude Mühlethaler and Denis Billotte (Geneva: Slatkine, 2001): 195–207.

We have suggested that during the Middle Ages socially constructive and valuable talk was becoming increasingly circumscribed with moral and legal restrictions imposed by a centralizing society. As a public sphere became delineated and perceivably separable from a private one, a tendency emerged to "put talk in its place." Publicly, trust in even regulated talk gradually gave way to a suspicion about its reliability. This points not only to a fear of the sort of disembodied talk that could take on a life of its own but also, no doubt, to a change in the ways human beings perceived one another, at least for the public record. Greater social complexity and increasing institutionalization, which accompanied the growth of the state, probably made for greater mediation in relations between people, along with an official guardedness about speech. Today, talk still seems to operate influentially and more or less without challenge in everyday life, mirroring somewhat the earlier medieval situation. In the larger public or political sphere, however, talk is officially denigrated. Thanks to the essays here, we can hope to trace the beginnings of that suppression and re-channeling of talk as it coincided with the refashioning of Western societies and with new conceptions of the individual self.

Selected Bibliography

Amodio, Mark C., ed. *Orality in Middle English Poetry*. New York: Garland, 1994.

Bailey, F. G. *Gifts and Poison: The Politics of Reputation*. Oxford: Blackwell, 1971.

Bardsley, Sandy. "Scolding Women: Cultural Knowledge and the Criminalization of Speech in Late Medieval England, 1300–1500." Ph.D. diss., University of North Carolina at Chapel Hill, 1999.

Bergmann, Jörg R. *Discreet Indiscretions: The Social Organization of Gossip*. Trans. John Bednarz Jr. New York: Aldine de Gruyter, 1993.

Boitani, Piero. *Chaucer and the Imaginary World of Fame*. Totowa, N.J.: Barnes and Noble, 1984.

Boose, Lynda E. "Scolding Brides and Bridling Scolds: Taming the Woman's Unruly Member." *Shakespeare Quarterly* 42 (1991): 179–213.

Braudy, Leo. *The Frenzy of Renown: Fame and Its History*. New York: Oxford University Press, 1986.

Brison, Karen. *Just Talk: Gossip, Meetings, and Power in a Papua New Guinea Village*. Berkeley: University of California Press, 1992.

Casagrande, Carla, and Silvana Vecchio. *I peccati della lingua: Disciplina ed etica della parola nella cultura medievale*. Rome: Instituto della Enciclopedia Italiana, 1987. Translated as *Les péchés de la langue: Discipline et éthique de la parole dans la culture médiévale*, trans. Philippe Baillet. Paris: Cerf, 1991.

La circulation des nouvelles au Moyen Âge: XXIVe Congrès de la Société des historiens médiévistes de l'enseignement supérieur public. Rome: École française de Rome, 1994.

Collins, Gail. *Scorpion Tongues: Gossip, Celebrity, and American Politics*. New York: William Morrow, 1998.

Coss, Peter, ed. *The Moral World of the Law*. Cambridge: Cambridge University Press, 2000.

Courtemanche, Andrée. "La rumeur de Manosque: Femmes et honneur au XIVe siècle." In *Normes et pouvoir à la fin du Moyen Âge. Actes du colloque "La recherche en études médiévales au Québec et en Ontario," 16–17 mai 1989*, edited by Marie-Claude Déprez-Masson. Montreal: Édition CERES, 1989.

Craun, Edwin. "'Inordinata Locutio': Blasphemy in Pastoral Literature, 1200–1500." *Traditio* 39 (1983): 137–62.

——. *Lies, Slander, and Obscenity in Medieval English Literature: Pastoral Rhetoric and the Deviant Speaker.* Cambridge: Cambridge University Press, 1997.

Dunbar, Robin. *Grooming, Gossip, and the Evolution of Language.* Cambridge: Harvard University Press, 1996.

Edgerton, Samuel Y., Jr. *Pictures and Punishment: Art and Criminal Prosecution during the Florentine Renaissance.* Ithaca: Cornell University Press, 1985.

Fenster, Thelma. "Christine at Carnant: Reading Christine de Pizan Reading Chrétien de Troyes' *Erec et Enide.*" In *Christine 2000: Essays in Honor of Angus J. Kennedy,* edited by John Campbell and Nadia Margolis, 135–51. Amsterdam: Rodopi, 2000.

——. "*Fama,* la femme, et la Dame de la Tour: Christine de Pizan et la médisance." In *Au champ des escriptures: IIIe colloque international sur Christine de Pizan, Lausanne (18–22 juillet, 1998),* edited by Eric Hicks, 461–77. Études Christiniennes 6. Paris: Honoré Champion, 2000.

Fentress, James, and Chris Wickham. *Social Memory.* Oxford: Blackwell, 1992.

Foote, David. "How the Past Becomes a Rumor: The Notarialization of Historical Consciousness in Medieval Orvieto." *Speculum* 75 (2000): 794–815.

Fraher, Richard M. "Conviction according to Conscience: The Medieval Jurists' Debate concerning Judicial Discretion and the Law of Proof." *Law and History Review* 7 (1989): 23–88.

Gauvard, Claude. *"De grace especial": Crime, état et société en France à la fin du Moyen Âge.* 2 vols. Paris: Publications de la Sorbonne, 1991.

Gluckman, Max. "Gossip and Scandal." *Current Anthropology* 4 (1963): 307–16.

Goodman, Robert F., and Aaron Ben-Ze'ev, eds. *Good Gossip.* Lawrence: University Press of Kansas, 1994.

Gordon, Jan B. *Gossip and Subversion in Nineteenth-Century British Fiction: Echo's Economies.* New York: St. Martin's, 1996.

Gowing, Laura. *Domestic Dangers: Women, Words, and Sex in Early Modern London.* Oxford: Clarendon, 1996.

Greenidge, A. H. J. *Infamia: Its Place in Roman Public and Private Law.* Oxford: Clarendon, 1894.

Hanawalt, Barbara. *"Of Good and Ill Repute": Gender and Social Control in Medieval England.* New York: Oxford University Press, 1998.

Haviland, John Beard. *Gossip, Reputation, and Knowledge in Zinacantan.* Chicago: University of Chicago Press, 1977.

Helmholz, R. H. "Crime and Compurgation and the Courts of the Medieval Church." *Law and History Review* 1 (1983): 1–26.

——, ed., *Select Cases on Defamation to 1600,* Publications of the Selden Society 101. London: Selden Society, 1985.

Ingram, Martin. "'Scolding Women Cucked or Washed': A Crisis in Gender Relations in Early Modern England?" In *Women, Crime, and the Courts in Early Modern England,* edited by Jenny Kermode and Garthine Walker, 48–80. Chapel Hill: University of North Carolina Press, 1994.

Jones, Karen, and Michael Zell. "Bad Conversation? Gender and Social Control in a Kentish Borough, c. 1450–c. 1570." *Continuity and Change* 13 (1998): 11–31.

Kamensky, Jane. *Governing the Tongue: The Politics of Speech in Early New England.* New York: Oxford University Press, 1997.

Koonce, B. G. *Chaucer and the Tradition of Fame: Symbolism in* The House of Fame. Princeton: Princeton University Press, 1966.

Kuehn, Thomas. *Law, Family, and Women: Toward a Legal Anthropology of Renaissance Italy.* Chicago: University of Chicago Press, 1991.

Lawton, David. *Blasphemy*. Philadelphia: University of Pennsylvania Press, 1993.

Lesnick, Daniel. "Insults and Threats in Medieval Todi." *Journal of Medieval History* 17 (1991): 71–89.

Lévy, Jean-Philippe. "Le problème de la preuve dans les droits savants du Moyen âge." In *La preuve*, 2 vols., 2:137–67. Recueils de la Société Jean Bodin pour l'histoire comparative des institutions 17. Brussels: Editions de la Librairie encyclopédique, 1965.

Livingston, John Morgan. "Infamia in the Decretists from Rufinus to Johannes Teutonicus." Ph.D. diss., University of Wisconsin, Madison, 1962.

Lochrie, Karma. *Covert Operations: The Medieval Uses of Secrecy*. Philadelphia: University of Pennsylvania Press, 1999.

Malkiel, Maria Rosa Lida de. *La idea de la fama en la edad media castellana*. Mexico: Fondo de Cultura Económica, 1952. Translated as *L'idée de la gloire dans la tradition occidentale: Antiquité, Moyen Âge occidental, Castille* by Sylvia Roubaud. Paris: Klincksieck, 1968.

Marchal, Guy P. "Memoria, fama, mos maiorum." In *Vergangenheit in mündlicher Überlieferung*, edited by Jürgen von Ungern-Sternberg and Hansjörg Reinau, Colloquium Rauricum, vol. 1, 289–320. Stuttgart: B. G. Teubner, 1988.

Merry, Sally Engle. "Rethinking Gossip and Scandal." In *Toward a General Theory of Social Control*, edited by Donald J. Black, 2 vols., 1:271–302. New York: Academic Press, 1984.

Migliorino, Francesco. *Fama e infamia: Problemi della società medievale nel pensiero giuridico nei secoli XII e XIII*. Catania: Giannotta, 1985.

Neubauer, Hans-Joachim. *The Rumour: A Cultural History*. Trans. Christian Braun. London: Free Association Books, 1999.

Parker, Patricia. "On the Tongue: Cross Gendering, Effeminacy, and the Art of Words." *Style* 23 (1989): 445–65.

Peters, Edward. "Wounded Names: The Medieval Doctrine of Infamy." In *Law in Medieval Life and Thought*, edited by Edward B. King and Susan J. Ridyard, 43–89. Sewanee, Tenn.: Press of the University of the South, 1990.

Poos, L. R. "Sex, Lies, and the Church Courts of Pre-Reformation England." *Journal of Interdisciplinary History* 25 (1995): 585–607.

La renommée. Special number of *Médiévales: Langue, Textes, Histoire* 24 (1993).

Robreau, Yvonne. *L'honneur et la honte: Leur expression dans les romans en prose du Lancelot-Graal (XIIe–XIIIe siècles)*. Publications romanes et françaises. Geneva: Droz, 1981.

Rodimer, Frank J. *The Canonical Effects of Infamy of Fact: A Historical Synopsis and Commentary*. Washington, D.C.: Catholic University of America Press, 1954.

Rosnow, Ralph L. *Rumor and Gossip: The Social Psychology of Hearsay*. New York: Elsevier, 1976.

Schofield, Phillip R. "Peasants and the Manor Court: Gossip and Litigation in a Suffolk Village at the Close of the Thirteenth Century." *Past and Present* 159 (1998): 3–42.

Serra Ruiz, Rafael. *Honor, honra, e injuria en el derecho medieval español*. Murcia: Sucesores de Nogués, 1969.

Sharpe, James A. *Defamation and Sexual Slander in Early Modern England: The Church Courts at York*. Heslington, York: University of York, Borthwick Institute of Historical Research, 1980.

Smail, Daniel Lord. "Los archivos de conocimiento y la cultura legal de la publicidad en la Marsella medieval." *Hispania: Revista española de historia* 57 (1997): 1049–77.

Spacks, Patricia. *Gossip*. Chicago: University of Chicago Press, 1986.

Spender, Dale. *Man Made Language*. New York: New York University Press, 1980.

Stern, Laura Ikins. "Public Fame in the Fifteenth Century." *American Journal of Legal History* (forthcoming).

Stewart, Frank Henderson. *Honor*. Chicago: University of Chicago Press, 1994.

Tatarczuk, Vincent. *Infamy of Law: A Historical Synopsis and a Commentary*. Washington D.C.: Catholic University of America Press, 1954.

Tebbutt, Melanie. *Women's Talk? A Social History of "Gossip" in Working-Class Neighbour-hoods, 1880–1960.* Aldershot, England: Scolar Press, 1995.

Underdown, David. "The Taming of the Scold: The Enforcement of Patriarchal Authority in Early Modern England." In *Order and Disorder in Early Modern England,* edited by Anthony Fletcher and John Stevenson, 116–36. Cambridge: Cambridge University Press, 1985.

Veenstra, Jan R. *Magic and Divination at the Courts of Burgundy and France: Text and Context of Laurens Pignon's* Contre Les Devineurs *(1411).* Leiden: Brill, 1997.

White, Luise. *Speaking with Vampires: Rumor and History in Colonial Africa.* Berkeley: University of California Press, 2000.

Wickham, Chris. "Gossip and Resistance among the Medieval Peasantry." *Past and Present* 160 (1998): 3–24.

Ziolkowski, Jan, ed. *Obscenity: Social Control and Artistic Creation in the European Middle Ages.* Leiden: Brill, 1998.

Contributors

In addition to his numerous articles on medieval French and Occitan language, literature, and law, F. R. P. AKEHURST, Ph.D., J.D., Professor of French at the University of Minnesota, has edited (with Judith M. Davis) a *Handbook of the Troubadours* (1995) and is the translator of *The* Coutumes de Beauvaisis *of Philippe de Beaumanoir* (1992) and *The* Etablissements de Saint Louis: *Thirteenth-Century Law Texts from Tours, Orléans, and Paris* (1996). His translation of *Le conseil de Pierre de Fontaines* and an edition and translation of the *Costuma d'Agen* are being prepared for publication.

SANDY BARDSLEY completed her Ph.D. at the University of North Carolina at Chapel Hill in 1999 and is now Assistant Professor of History at Emory and Henry College. The subject of her dissertation was speech, scolding, and gender in late medieval England, and she has published an article on women's wages.

JEFFREY A. BOWMAN, Assistant Professor of History at Kenyon College, completed his Ph.D. at Yale University in 1997 and is the author of several published and forthcoming articles on Christian Spain and Mediterranean Francia in the High Middle Ages. One of his articles was awarded the Van Cortlandt Elliot prize of the Medieval Academy of America.

Fellow and past president of the Medieval Academy of America and the recipient of numerous awards and distinctions, MADELINE H. CAVINESS is Mary Richardson Professor and Professor of Art History at Tufts University. She is the author of eight books and more than fifty articles on medieval art history and gender. Her most recent books include *Visualizing Women in the Middle Ages: Sight, Spectacle, and Scopic Economy* (2001) and *Reframing Medieval Art: Difference, Margins, Boundaries,* an on-line publication of Tufts University.

EDWIN D. CRAUN is Henry S. Fox Jr. Professor of English at Washington and Lee University. He has published extensively on late medieval moral literature, including an important article on speech that appeared in *Traditio* in 1983. His most recent book is *Lies, Slander, and Obscenity in Medieval English Literature: Pastoral Rhetoric and the Deviant Speaker* (1997).

THELMA FENSTER, Professor of French, Fordham University, has published editions and translations of works by Christine de Pizan, such as the *Livre du duc des vrais amans* (1995; *Book of the Duke of True Lovers,* 1991). Two recent articles relate to the subject of this volume: "*Fama,* la femme et la Dame de la Tour: Christine de Pizan et la médisance," and "Reading Christine de Pizan Reading Chrétien de Troyes' *Erec et Enide.*"

RICHARD HORVATH is Visiting Assistant Professor of English at Marist College. He has published articles on Chaucer and Old English literature and is currently working on two projects: an edition of Thomas Hoccleve's holograph poetry, and a study of epistolary poetics and the development of authorship in late medieval England.

One of the leading authorities on law and society in Renaissance Italy, THOMAS KUEHN, Professor of History at Clemson University, is the author of three books, including *Law, Family, and Women: Toward a Legal Anthropology of Renaissance Italy* (1991). His most recent book is *Illegitimacy in Renaissance Florence* (2002).

CHARLES G. NELSON is Professor of German (Emeritus) at Tufts University where he also served as Dean of the Graduate School of Arts and Sciences. He is the author of a number of articles and papers on women, gender, and law in medieval German literature, including studies of Hrotsvit von Gandersheim and the Nibelunglied. With Madeline H. Caviness, he is working on a study of the four illustrated manuscripts of the *Sachsenspiegel,* which they hope to publish shortly as *Social Hierarchies and Gender under the Law: Word and Image in Medieval German Law Books.*

DANIEL LORD SMAIL, Associate Professor of History, Fordham University, has published numerous articles on society and law in late medieval Marseille, including an article on knowledge and *fama* that appeared in *Hispania.* He is the author of *Imaginary Cartographies: Possession and Identity in Late Medieval Marseille* (1999), which received the Herbert Baxter Adams Prize of the American Historical Association in 2000.

LORI J. WALTERS, Professor of French, Florida State University, has published many articles on French medieval literature, including Arthurian subjects and Christine de Pizan. She collaborated on an edition of the *Manuscrits de Chrétien de Troyes* (1993) and edited *Lancelot and Guenevere: A Casebook* (1996). She is serving a three-year term as co-president of the International Christine de Pizan Society.

CHRIS WICKHAM is Professor of Early Medieval History at the University of Birmingham. He has worked on the history of Italy in the early and central Middle Ages, specializing on social and landscape history, and has written a general survey, *Early Medieval Italy: Central Power and Local Society, 400–1000* (1981), five regional or microhistorical monographs, and "Gossip and Resistance among the Medieval Peasantry," one of the first articles to discuss gossip and talk in a medieval context. His most recent book is *Legge, pratiche e conflitti* (2000), and he is working on a book on post-Roman Europe and the Mediterranean. He is an editor of *Past and Present*.

Index

Page numbers for illustrations are in italics.

Index

Livre des fais et bonnes meurs du roi Charles V le Sage (*continued*)
213; as eyewitness testimony, 134–36; as mirror for princes, 119–20, 138
Lollard (Lollardy), 163, 188–89, 192, 205
los, 10, 77–78, 193
Lucretia, 127–30

mala fama. See fama and reputation: *mala fama*
maldit, 77
mal renommé(s), 77, 80–81, 211. *See also* exclusion; *fama* and reputation: *mala fama; infamy; renommée*
mauvaise renommée, 82
memory: and *fama*, 2, 3, 118; as images, 57–58; as process, 6; in works of Christine de Pizan, 118–20, 125–26, 130–31, 134–36; and written law, 92
Migliorino, Francesco (*Fama e infamia*), 3n, 29–30, 35
Miller, William Ian, 34, 38
mirror for princes, 119–20, 138
Morgengabe (morning gift), 62–64, *64*
mouth: and aggressiveness in women, 58–59; as site of sin, 147–48. *See also* "Sins of the Tongue"

Neubauer, Hans-Joachim, 2–3
Nora, Pierre, 120
notoire, 3, 77, 82–85, 92. *See also* common knowledge
notoriety, 75–76, 84, 95, 211. *See also* exclusion; infamy
notorium, 30, 85, 93

oath-taking: depicted, 51–52, 60–62, *60, 62, 65,* 67, 71–72; and gender, 47, 60–64, 66–67, 71–72; and perjury, 91
opinion, 3, 30; and *fama*, 45; personified by Christine de Pizan, 121–23
orality: and law, 51, 75, 83, 88; and romance tradition, 78, 167–68. *See also* speech acts
ordeal, 91, 95–96

pastoral tradition: in *Book of Margery Kempe*, 191–92, 194–208; on correction, 189–92, 194–95, 201, 203, 205, 208; and *fama*, 202; and speech, 190–91, 194–98, 201, 208. *See also* "Sins of the Tongue"
performance, 1–4, 168, 210. *See also* public acts
perjury, 81, *82,* 90–91, 99–100. *See also* falsehood; infamy; testimony; witnesses
Philippe de Beaumanoir, 64, 66, 76, 79–92. *See also Coutumes de Beauvaisis*
pitture infamanti (portraits of shame), 36–37

plague. *See* Black Death
pris, 77–78. *See also* reputation
proof, legal: in customary law, 84, 93; guidelines for assessing, 95–96; in *Visigothic Code,* 109–113
public acts, 3–4, 19–20, 38, 79; and role of biographer, 133; and Siena–Arezzo dispute, 23–25; speech acts as, 168, 182–84. *See also* public space
public space, 19, 24–25, 214; punishment carried out in, 79–81, *82,* 89, 99–101, 154, 182–84; and rebuke, 205–6; and shame, 36–37, 79–80, 89, 195

rape, 47, 67–68, *69,* 88–89, 127–30
rebuke, 188n, 189, 191–92, 195, 199–208. *See also* correction
renommée, 3, 10, 77–78; *bonne renommée,* 79–82; *Commune Renommée,* 7–8; *mal renommé,* 77, 80–81, 211. *See also fama* and reputation: *bona fama, mala fama;* renown; reputation
renown, 2–3, 78, 95, 122, 124, 193. *See also* common knowledge; *fama* and reputation; *renommée;* reputation
reputation: concept of, in Christine de Pizan, 118, 123–26, 131–35; and *fama,* 2–11, 16, 77, 103, 165–66, 211; and gender, in *Sachsenspiegel,* 72; and honor, 33–34; versus infamy, 103–7; legal, 94–97; and rebuke, 195; and *renommée,* 77, 79–82; in shame culture, 77–79; of state (Florence), 37; of state (France), 78, 124–26; and status, 26, 33–34, 66, 129. *See also* defamation; *fama* and reputation: *bona fama;* worship
romance tradition: and audience expectations, 168–69, 172; orality in, 78, 167–68
rumor, 1–3, 8–11, 72, 147, 211; and common knowledge, 16, 29; as *privata fama,* 25–26. *See also* gossip; hearsay; talk

Sachsenspiegel (The Saxon Mirror): and gender, 47, 56, 60, 72; hand gestures in, 47, 50–53, *55,* 56–72, *57, 58-60, 62-65, 67-71;* history of, 47–49; manuscripts consulted, 48–50; and Saxon law, 60–72
Schmidt-Wiegand, Ruth, 52, 56–57
scolding, 146, 149, 154–61; legal terminology for, 159–61; relation to hue and cry, 155–57; rise of, after Black Death, 159–61; and women, 154. *See also* "Sins of the Tongue"; speech: evil
Scripture, 124, 129–31, 190
secrecy, 4, 20–21, 25, 32, 38
shame, 2, 5–6, 35–37; culture of, 77–79
Siete Partidas, 96; on infamy, 102–8, 115–17